Close Company

Dec. 1990

To Dell:

Hope you enjoy this
book. It reminded me of
you as you have such a
special relationship with your
mother and your daughter.
    Hope my most literate
of friends has a Happy Birthday!
        Love,
    Marcia

Close Company

Stories of Mothers and Daughters

Edited by CHRISTINE PARK
and CAROLINE HEATON

Ticknor & Fields

NEW YORK

First American edition 1989
Collection, Introduction, and Notes copyright © 1987
by Christine Park and Caroline Heaton

For information about permission to reproduce selections
from this book, write to Permissions, Ticknor & Fields,
52 Vanderbilt Avenue, New York, New York 10017.

Library of Congress Cataloging-in-Publication Data

Close company.

1. Mothers and daughters — Fiction.   2. Women — Fiction.
3. Short stories — Women authors.   I. Park, Christine, date.
II. Heaton, Caroline.
PN6120.95.M7C5   1989   808.83'1   89-4683
ISBN 0-89919-832-5
ISBN 0-89919-900-3 (pbk.)

Printed in the United States of America

P   10 9 8 7 6 5 4 3 2 1

For
James & Diane
and Nira

Contents

Acknowledgments

Acknowledgments are due to the following for permission to include the stories which appear in this book:
Ama Ata Aidoo and the Longman Group Ltd for 'The Late Bud' from *No Sweetness Here* (Longman, 1979), copyright © Ama Ata Aidoo 1970; Margaret Atwood and John Farquharson Ltd for 'Significant Moments in the Life of My Mother' from *Bluebeard's Egg* (Jonathan Cape, 1987), copyright © O. W. Toad Ltd 1983; Judith Chernaik for 'Honor Thy Father and Thy Mother' (originally published in the Yale Review, 1972), copyright © Judith Chernaik 1972; The Crossing Press for 'Children's Liberation' from *Mother, Sister, Daughter, Lover* by Jan Clausen (The Crossing Press, 1980), copyright © Jan Clausen 1980; Secker & Warburg Ltd for 'The Sempstress' by Colette from *My Mother's House*, translated by Una Vincenzo Troubridge and Ed McLeod, and *Sido*, translated by Ed McLeod (Secker & Warburg Ltd, 1953); 'Virgin Soil' by George Egerton from *Keynotes & Discords* (Virago Press Ltd, 1983), originally published in *Discords* (Elkin & Mathews & John Lane, 1894); Alison Fell and London Management for 'The Shining Mountain', broadcast on BBC Schools Radio 1986, copyright © Alison Fell 1986; Curtis Brown and Century Hutchinson Ltd for 'Swans' from *You Are Now Entering the Human Heart* by Janet Frame (Victoria University Press, 1983), copyright © Janet Frame 1983; David Higham Associates Ltd and Hamish Hamilton Ltd for 'The Pangs of Love' from *The Pangs of Love and Other Stories* by Jane Gardam (Hamish Hamilton Ltd, 1983), copyright © Jane Gardam 1981, 1982, 1983; 'The Unnatural Mother' by Charlotte Perkins Gilman from *The Forerunner* (November 1916 issue); China Books for 'Love Must Not Be Forgotten' by Zhang Jie, translated by Gladys Yang, from *Seven Contemporary Chinese Writers* (China Books in co-operation with Panda Books, Beijing, China, 1986), copyright © China Books 1986; Jamaica Kincaid and Pan Books

Introduction

The mother-daughter relationship has a particular quality for, as Simone de Beauvoir wrote in *The Second Sex*, 'the daughter is for the mother at once her double and another person'. In recent years, as women have begun to question the influences on their sense of self, the importance and vitality of the bond has been explored in new ways. We became aware, on turning to fiction, that this theme has an obvious fascination, even compulsion for women writers. Many fine and moving short stories centre on this relationship, offering a vivid picture of women from different cultures and periods. Through these stories the perennial drama of female conflicts and choices is depicted, sometimes in familiar, sometimes in startling forms.

It seemed to us no coincidence that some of the most powerful short stories by women deal with this topic. For a woman's sense of identity, as well as her view of her place in society, is likely to be largely shaped in response to her relationship with the woman who has served as her earliest model, be it mother, grandmother, or another woman. Yet the bond is often fraught with danger. And the short story form, with its immediacy and condensed imagery, appears perfectly to capture the complexity of this relationship.

In selecting stories for this collection we have looked for those that reflect the diverse elements of our theme. Each is a pleasure to read in its own right but also gains by being read in juxtaposition with its neighbours. In most, the relationship between mother and daughter is the essence of the story. In some, like Fay Weldon's 'Weekend' and Katherine Mansfield's 'Young Girl', it remains part of the subtext; and in still others, particularly Emily Prager's 'A Visit from the Footbinder', the relationship between mother and daughter, though not the obvious focus of the story, is still thematically crucial.

One striking aspect of the stories is the way in which, again and again, mothers and daughters provide a challenge for one another. The challenge is a two-way process, essentially life-giving, bringing necessary and inevitable change. Attention has so often been focused on the sparring between fathers and sons – whilst in the background the women are shown cosily passing on domestic secrets and maternal skills. These stories portray a richer and more complex female reality, potentially quite as explosive as the male, though, in the happier outcomes, as in the stories by Efua Sutherland and Dina Mehta, mother and daughter propel each other towards new growth, independence and a real friendship of equals.

But the journey towards this ideal state of affairs can involve a painful questioning of the previous generation's values and choices. It has been made all the more difficult by the social upheaval of the last twenty years in which there has been a tremendous reappraisal of woman's role. Private questioning is invested with a new urgency within this atmosphere of public challenge to old traditions. Just what a mother is to hand down to a daughter, and what a daughter has a right to expect of her mother, have become subjects for excited debate, to which these stories bear vivid witness.

Many of the stories where the daughter's viewpoint is paramount show the mother's world as apparently fixed and secure, the daughter's as fragmented and confusing. This is not surprising; we think of the world as more unstable now than ever before. Looking back, even to our own childhoods, let alone to our mothers', nostalgia creeps in. It is tempting to see earlier periods as altogether cosier, safer. Though based in historical reality, this perception has also to do with the persistence into adolescence of a child-like belief that mothers inhabit a remote, even fairy-tale world of certainties, the immutable country of the past. The growing daughter, by contrast, faced with all sorts of frightening and limitless choices, feels herself to belong to the uncertain world of the future.

Margaret Atwood's 'Significant Moments in the Life of My Mother' concerns itself with some of these issues. In the daughter's powerful evocation of her mother's childhood, the young woman reaches towards an understanding of how her own early life came to be shaped. With each new perception we recognise the distance the daughter has travelled in order to achieve her share of objectivity. The story of the relationship between mother and daughter is always in the subtext, never stated, understood only through the quality of the observations.

Sue Miller's 'Given Names' also deals in part with nostalgia and a remembered childhood world. Here the grandparents' holiday home provides a framework for repeated carefree summers, but in adolescence the girl develops deeper insights which cast shadows on the stability she has taken for granted.

The social and historical backgrounds against which mothers and daughters confront one another inform their individual relationships. And one of the great pleasures of these stories is the colourful and exact depiction of time and place, be it the Jewish heritage in Judith Chernaik's moving story of American immigrants, the very different treatment of this theme in Fay Zwicky's story of a Jewish mother and daughter in Australia, the bleakly evoked New York setting of Jan Clausen's story, the immaculately realised backwoods Canada of Alice Munro's 'Princess Ida', or the lyrical portrait of an African village in Efua Sutherland's 'New Life at Kyerefaso'.

In many of the stories mothers are portrayed in the traditional role, though very often what women have experienced for themselves is not at all what they want for their daughters. Whether these new aspirations coincide with a daughter's expectations is another matter. When confronted with her mother's ambitions, a daughter sometimes responds with a complete volte face, as is nicely illustrated in Dina Mehta's 'The Voice of Authority' and Dikken Zwilgmeyer's 'An Everyday Story'.

Some of the women in these stories feel powerless to help their daughters break from a mould they themselves have found constraining. In Emily Prager's 'A Visit from the Footbinder', Lady Guo Guo initially baulks at perpetuating a literally crippling tradition when it comes to her youngest daughter, but eventually bows beneath the weight of society's expectations. Pass seven centuries forward to Fay Weldon's 1970s Britain and we find the heroine, Martha, despite the trappings of 'liberation', education, career and affluence, internalising the old mythology of the perfect wife and mother.

Where a mother does manage to carve out a more emancipated and independent life for herself – or even wishes to – the daughter's response isn't always wholehearted approval. In Margaret Atwood's story, the mother's admission that she would like to have been an archaeologist elicits a very familiar reaction: 'I must have been thirty-five at the time, but it was still shocking and slightly offensive to me to learn that my mother might not have been totally contented fulfilling the role in which fate had cast her: that of being my mother.'

In 'Princess Ida', Alice Munro's portrayal of a mother who adopts an unusual career, refusing to conform to the narrow expectations of her small-town environment, is seen through the eyes of her daughter, with a blend of pride and embarrassment, irritation and affection. Michelene Wandor, in a very different way, takes up the point that mothers are as capable as daughters of shocking and challenging. A daughter's desire for a safe standard against which she can rebel and a secure figure to whom she can return, grumbling about motherly injunctions, is humorously observed – as is a mother's capacity for endless change and growth.

Katherine Mansfield's 'The Young Girl' explores what happens when a daughter lacks this kind of stable figure. The 'Young Girl' of the title has a weak mother – amiable, but absent-minded and irresponsible. The daughter responds by assuming too early an adult mantle: it is Katherine Mansfield's genius for subtle suggestion which allows us just a glimpse of the eager child beneath her unappealing exterior.

A daughter's urge to rebel, while still needing her mother's approval, is developed in both Ama Ata Aidoo's 'The Late Bud' and Sylvia Plath's 'The Day Mr Prescott Died'. The challenge generated by a daughter's rebellious behaviour is a theme that informs many of the stories. There can be a desire to subvert the status quo; but equally there can be a desire to infuse it with new energies. Alice Walker's 'Everyday Use' and Efua Sutherland's 'New Life at Kyerefaso' make a happy contrast in the way they draw out these different aspects. In 'Everyday

Use', Dee's arrogant assumption of the role of 'family curator' is juxtaposed with her mother and younger sister's quiet living out of a loved tradition. Efua Sutherland's 'New Life at Kyerefaso' also presents a matriarchal society, but this time the daughter's actions, whilst breaking with tradition, bring richness and renewal.

The robust mermaid in Jane Gardam's funny and affectionate retelling of Hans Andersen's story believes she has her own way of subverting the status quo. 'I don't understand this 'suffered for love', she says, referring to her sister's self-sacrifice. Once again a sense of a strong female line informs the story and provides the good-humoured ballast against which the young mermaid can try out her unconventional ideas.

Good humour also invests Colette's magnificent story, 'The Sempstress', but here the mother's response is more ambiguous. In this story Colette captures the moment in which a girl first begins to think for herself, whilst her mother is left wryly wondering how many questions will rebound on *her* when her own values come up for inspection.

One of the questions raised by these stories is what is it that a daughter requires of a mother? It is tempting to ask, as many mothers have – can a mother ever get it right? The stories suggest that certain qualities do have an overriding value. The daughters in these pages seem to be asking for stability. The little girls in the Janet Frame story want their mother to be omnipotent. The daughter in the Margaret Atwood story, and the wilful but appealing girl in Ama Ata Aidoo's 'The Late Bud', need to know that they are of paramount importance to their mothers. Others speak of the anguish of not being sure that their mothers are *there* for them, or that they take sufficient interest in their lives. Some daughters with inadequate mothers seek identification with a surrogate mother: in Sue Miller's story it is the young aunt who takes over this role: in Jan Clausen's 'Children's Liberation' it is the grandmother, tough as nails, and 'accustomed to driving hard bargains'. Through the character of the woman who comes to help on the mountain, Alison Fell, in her wonderful fable, creates the image of the good mother as gentle and nurturing. A model is being sought, even if it is one which must be discarded or 'remade' as the daughter matures.

This rejection of the early model is part of the process of growing up and developing one's own identity. For a young girl it means separation from the same-sex parent, with whom there may have been a very special harmony, a blissful sense of identification. Both Margaret Atwood and Alice Munro write of the daughter's growing awareness of herself as 'other'. This is also the theme of Jamaica Kincaid's strange and powerful fantasy, 'My Mother', in which the imagery echoes the daughter's confusion over the boundaries between herself and her mother: 'The shadow of my mother danced around the room to a tune that my own shadow sang . . .'

Other stories also chart the growing-away process: in Jeanette Winterson's 'Psalms', the daughter's gritty humour and her private fantasy life secure her a measure of independence in the face of her mother's overpowering religious obsessions. The daughter in Fay Zwicky's 'Hostages', on the contrary, moves from a repudiation of her mother and Jewish heritage to an anguished recognition of their 'shared fate'.

And that 'shared fate' is what all these stories are about: even where the relationship between mother and daughter is a troubled one, the female legacy remains powerful. Ultimately, whether through joy or pain, our stories celebrate womanhood across cultures and time. We hope their different visions will suggest the richness and variety of choices open to a woman, and even provide a bridge between the separate, yet connected, worlds of mothers and daughters.

Christine Park and Caroline Heaton, London 1987

Close Company

The Sempstress
Colette

'Do you mean to say your daughter is nine years old,' said a friend, 'and she doesn't know how to sew? She really must learn to sew. In bad weather sewing is a better occupation for a child of that age than reading story books.'

'Nine years old? And she can't sew?' said another friend. 'When she was eight, my daughter embroidered this tray cloth for me, look at it . . . Oh! I don't say it's fine needlework, but it's nicely done all the same. Nowadays my daughter cuts out her own underclothes. I can't bear anyone in my house to mend holes with pins!'

I meekly poured all this domestic wisdom over Bel-Gazou.

'You're nine years old and you don't know how to sew? You really must learn to sew . . .'

Flouting truth, I even added:

'When I was eight years old, I remember I embroidered a tray cloth . . . Oh! It wasn't fine needlework, I dare say . . . And then, in bad weather . . .'

She has therefore learned to sew. And although – with one bare sunburnt leg tucked beneath her, and her body at ease in its bathing suit – she looks more like a fisherboy mending a net than an industrious little girl, she seems to experience no boyish repugnance. Her hands, stained the colour of tobacco-juice by sun and sea, hem in a way that seems against nature; their version of the simple running stitch resembles the zigzag dotted lines of a road map, but she buttonholes and scallops with elegance and is severely critical of the embroidery of others.

She sews and kindly keeps me company if rain blurs the horizon of the sea. She also sews during the torrid hour when the spindle bushes gather their circles of shadow directly under them. Moreover, it sometimes happens that a quarter of an hour before dinner, black in her white dress – 'Bel-Gazou! your hands and frock are clean, and don't forget it!' – she sits solemnly down with a square of material between her fingers. Then my friends applaud: 'Just look at her! Isn't she good? That's right! Your mother must be pleased!'

Her mother says nothing – great joys must be controlled. But ought one to feign them? I shall speak the truth: I don't much like my daughter sewing.

When she reads, she returns all bewildered and with flaming cheeks, from the island where the chest full of precious stones is hidden, from the dismal castle where a fair-haired orphan child is persecuted. She is soaking up a tested and time-honoured poison, whose effects have long been familiar. If she draws, or colours pictures, a semi-articulate song issues from her, unceasing as the hum of bees round the privet. It is the same as the buzzing of flies as they work, the slow waltz of the house-painter, the refrain of the spinner at her wheel. But Bel-Gazou is silent when she sews, silent for hours on end, with her mouth firmly closed, concealing her large, new-cut incisors that bite into the moist heart of a fruit like little saw-edged blades. She is silent, and she – why not write down the word that frightens me – she is thinking.

A new evil? A torment that I had not foreseen? Sitting in a grassy dell, or half buried in hot sand and gazing out to sea, she is thinking, as well I know. She thinks rapidly when she is listening, with a well-bred pretence of discretion, to remarks imprudently exchanged above her head. But it would seem that with this needle-play she has discovered the perfect means of adventuring, stitch by stitch, point by point, along a road of risks and temptations. Silence . . . the hand armed with the steel dart moves back and forth. Nothing will stop the unchecked little explorer. At what moment must I utter the 'Halt!' that will brutally arrest her in full flight? Oh, for those young embroiderers of bygone days, sitting on a hard little stool in the shelter of their mother's ample skirts! Maternal authority kept them there for years and years, never rising except to change the skein of silk, or to elope with a stranger. Think of Philomène de Watteville and her canvas on which she embroidered the loss and the despair of Albert Savarus . . .

'What are you thinking about, Bel-Gazou?'

'Nothing, mother. I'm counting my stitches.'

Silence. The needle pierces the material. A coarse trail of chain-stitch follows very unevenly in its wake. Silence . . .

'Mother?'

'Darling?'

'Is it only when people are married that a man can put his arm round a lady's waist?'

'Yes . . . No . . . It depends. If they are very good friends and have known each other a long time, you understand . . . As I said before: it depends. Why do you want to know?'

'For no particular reason, mother.'

Two stitches, ten misshapen chain-stitches.

'Mother? Is Madame X married?'

'She has been. She is divorced.'

'I see. And Monsieur F, is he married?'

'Why, of course he is; you know that.'

'Oh! Yes . . . Then it's all right if one of the two is married?'

'What is all right?'

'To depend.'

'One doesn't say: "To depend."'

'But you said just now that it depended.'

'But what has it got to do with you? Is it any concern of yours?'

'No, mother.'

I let it drop. I feel inadequate, self-conscious, displeased with myself. I should have answered differently and I could not think what to say.

Bel-Gazou also drops the subject; she sews. But she pays little attention to her sewing, overlaying it with pictures, associations of names and people, all the results of patient observation. A little later will come other curiosities, other questions, and especially other silences. Would to God that Bel-Gazou were the bewildered and simple child who questions crudely, open-eyed! But she is too near the truth, and too natural not to know as a birthright, that all nature hesitates before that most majestic and most disturbing of instincts, and that it is wise to tremble, to be silent and to lie when one draws near to it.

Significant Moments in the Life of My Mother

Margaret Atwood

When my mother was very small, someone gave her a basket of baby chicks for Easter. They all died.

'I didn't know you weren't supposed to pick them up,' says my mother. 'Poor little things. I laid them out in a row on a board, with their little legs sticking out straight as pokers, and wept over them. I'd loved them to death.'

Possibly this story is meant by my mother to illustrate her own stupidity, and also her sentimentality. We are to understand she wouldn't do such a thing now.

Possibly it's a commentary on the nature of love; though, knowing my mother, this is unlikely.

My mother's father was a country doctor. In the days before cars he drove a team of horses and a buggy around his territory, and in the days before snow ploughs he drove a team and a sleigh, through blizzards and rainstorms and in the middle of the night, to arrive at houses lit with oil lamps where water would be boiling on the wood range and flannel sheets warming on the plate rack, to deliver babies who would subsequently be named after him. His office was in the house, and as a child my mother would witness people arriving at the office door, which was reached through the front porch, clutching parts of them-selves—thumbs, fingers, toes, ears, noses—which had accidentally been cut off, pressing these severed parts to the raw stumps of their bodies as if they could be stuck there like dough, in the mostly vain hope that my grandfather would be able to sew them back on, heal the gashes made in them by axes, saws, knives, and fate.

My mother and her younger sister would loiter near the closed office door until shooed away. From behind it would come groans, muffled screams, cries for help. For my mother, hospitals have never been glamorous places, and illness offers no respite or holiday. 'Never get sick,' she says, and means it. She hardly ever does.

Once, though, she almost died. It was when her appendix burst. My grandfather had to do the operation. He said later that he shouldn't have been the person to do it: his hands were shaking too much. This is one of the few admissions of weakness on his part that my mother has ever reported. Mostly he is portrayed as severe and in charge of things. 'We all respected him, though,' she says. 'He was widely respected.' (This is a word which has slipped a little in the scale since my mother's youth. It used to outrank *love*.)

It was someone else who told me the story of my grandfather's muskrat farm: how he and one of my mother's uncles fenced in the swamp at the back of their property and invested my mother's maiden aunt's savings in muskrats. The idea was that these muskrats would multiply and eventually be made into muskrat coats, but an adjoining apple farmer washed his spraying equipment upstream, and the muskrats were all killed by the poison, as dead as doornails. This was during the Depression, and it was no joke.

When they were young – this can cover almost anything these days, but I put it at seven or eight – my mother and her sister had a tree house, where they spent some of their time playing dolls' tea parties and so forth. One day they found a box of sweet little bottles outside my grandfather's dispensary. The bottles were being thrown out, and my mother (who has always hated waste) appropriated them for use in their dolls' house. The bottles were full of yellow liquid, which they left in because it looked so pretty. It turned out that these were urine samples.

'We got Hail Columbia for that,' says my mother. 'But what did we know?'

My mother's family lived in a large white house near an apple orchard, in Nova Scotia. There was a barn and a carriage-house;

in the kitchen there was a pantry. My mother can remember the days before commercial bakeries, when flour came in barrels and all the bread was made at home. She can remember the first radio broadcast she ever heard, which was a singing commercial about socks.

In this house there were many rooms. Although I have been there, although I have seen the house with my own eyes, I still don't know how many. Parts of it were closed off, or so it seemed; there were back staircases. Passages led elsewhere. Five children lived in it, two parents, a hired man and a hired girl, whose names and faces kept changing. The structure of the house was hierarchical, with my grandfather at the top, but its secret life – the life of pie crusts, clean sheets, the box of rags in the linen closet, the loaves in the oven – was female. The house, and all the objects in it, crackled with static electricity; undertows washed through it, the air was heavy with things that were known but not spoken. Like a hollow log, a drum, a church, it amplified, so that conversations whispered in it sixty years ago can be half-heard even today.

In this house you had to stay at the table until you had eaten everything on your plate. '"Think of the starving Armenians," mother used to say,' says my mother. 'I didn't see how eating my bread crusts was going to help them out one jot.'

It was in this house that I first saw a stalk of oats in a vase, each oat wrapped in the precious silver paper which had been carefully saved from a chocolate box. I thought it was the most wonderful thing I had ever seen, and began saving silver paper myself. But I never got around to wrapping the oats, and in any case I didn't know how. Like many other art forms of vanished civilisations, the techniques for this one have been lost and cannot quite be duplicated.

'We had oranges at Christmas,' says my mother. 'They came all the way from Florida; they were very expensive. That was the big treat: to find an orange in the toe of your stocking. It's funny to remember how good they tasted, now.'

When she was sixteen, my mother had hair so long she could sit on it. Women were bobbing their hair by then; it was getting to be the twenties. My mother's hair was giving her headaches, she says, but my grandfather, who was very strict, forbade her to cut it. She waited until one Saturday when she knew he had an appointment with the dentist.

'In those days there was no freezing,' says my mother. 'The drill was worked with a foot pedal, and it went *grind, grind, grind*. The dentist himself had brown teeth: he chewed tobacco, and he would spit the tobacco juice into a spittoon while he was working on your teeth.'

Here my mother, who is good mimic, imitates the sounds of the drill and the tobacco juice: '*Rrrrr! Rrrrr! Rrrrr! Phtt! Rrrrr! Rrrrr! Rrrrr! Phtt!* It was always sheer agony. It was a heaven-sent salvation when gas came in.'

My mother went into the dentist's office, where my grandfather was sitting in the chair, white with pain. She asked him if she could have her hair cut. He said she could do anything in tarnation as long as she would get out of there and stop pestering him.

'So I went out straight away and had it all chopped off,' says my mother jauntily. 'He was furious afterwards, but what could he do? He'd given his word.'

My own hair reposes in a cardboard box in a steamer trunk in my mother's cellar, where I picture it becoming duller and more brittle with each passing year, and possibly moth-eaten; by now it will look like the faded wreaths of hair in Victorian funeral jewellery. Or it may have developed a dry mildew; inside its tissue-paper wrappings it glows faintly, in the darkness of the trunk. I suspect my mother has forgotten it's in there. It was cut off, much to my relief, when I was twelve and my sister was born. Before that it was in long curls: 'Otherwise,' says my mother, 'it would have been just one big snarl.' My mother combed it by winding it around her index finger every morning, but when she was in the hospital my father couldn't cope. 'He couldn't get it around his stubby fingers,' says my mother. My father looks down at his fingers. They are indeed broad compared with my mother's long elegant ones, which she calls boney. He smiles a pussy-cat smile.

So it was that my hair was sheared off. I sat in the chair in my first beauty parlour and watched it falling, like handfuls of cobwebs, down over my shoulders. From within it my head began to emerge, smaller, denser, my face more angular. I aged five years in fifteen minutes. I knew I could go home now and try out lipstick.

'Your father was upset about it,' says my mother, with an air of collusion. She doesn't say this when my father is present. We smile, over the odd reactions of men to hair.

I used to think that my mother, in her earlier days, led a life of sustained hilarity and hair-raising adventure. (That was before I realised that she never put in the long stretches of uneventful time that must have made up much of her life: the stories were just the punctuation.) Horses ran away with her, men offered to, she was continually falling out of trees or off the ridgepoles of barns, or nearly being swept out to sea in rip-tides; or, in a more minor vein, suffering acute embarrassment in trying circumstances.

Churches were especially dangerous. 'There was a guest preacher one Sunday,' she says. 'Of course we had to go to church every Sunday. There he was, in full career, preaching hellfire and damnation' – she pounds an invisible pulpit – 'and his full set of false teeth shot out of his mouth – *phoop*! – just like that. Well, he didn't miss a stride. He stuck his hand up and caught them and popped them back into his mouth, and he kept right on, condemning us all to eternal torment. The pew was shaking! The tears were rolling down our faces, and the worst of it was, we were in the front pew, he was looking right at us. But of course we couldn't laugh out loud: father would have given us Hail Columbia.'

Other people's parlours were booby-trapped for her; so were any and all formal social occasions. Zippers sprang apart on her clothes in strategic places, hats were unreliable. The shortage of real elastic during the war demanded constant alertness: underpants then had buttons, and were more taboo and therefore more significant than they are now. 'There you would be,' she says, 'right on the street, and before you knew it they'd be down around your galoshes. The way to do was to step out of them with one foot, then kick them up with your other foot and whip them into your purse. I got quite good at it.'

This particular story is told only to a few, but other stories are for general consumption. When she tells them, my mother's face turns to rubber. She takes all the parts, adds the sound effects, waves her hands around in the air. Her eyes gleam, sometimes a little wickedly, for although my mother is sweet and old and a lady, she avoids being a sweet old lady. When people are in danger of mistaking her for one, she flings in something from left field; she refuses to be taken for granted.

But my mother cannot be duped into telling stories when she doesn't want to. If you prompt her, she becomes self-conscious and clams up. Or she will laugh and go out into the kitchen, and shortly after that you will hear the whir of the Mixmaster. Long ago I gave up attempting to make her do tricks at parties. In gatherings of unknown people, she merely listens intently, her head tilted a little, smiling a smile of glazed politeness. The secret is to wait and see what she will say afterwards.

At the age of seventeen my mother went to the Normal School in Truro. This name – 'Normal School' – once held a certain magic for me. I thought it had something to do with learning to be normal, which possibly it did, because really it was where you used to go to learn how to be a schoolteacher. Subsequently my mother taught in a one-room school house not far from her home. She rode her horse to and from the school house every day, and saved up the money she earned and sent herself to university with it. My grandfather wouldn't send her: he said she was too frivolous-minded. She liked ice-skating and dancing too much for his taste.

At Normal School my mother boarded with a family that contained several sons in more or less the same age group as the girl boarders. They all ate around a huge dining-room table (which I pictured as being of dark wood, with heavy carved legs; but covered always with a white linen tablecloth), with the mother and father presiding, one at each end. I saw them both as large and pink and beaming.

'The boys were great jokers,' says my mother. 'They were always up to something.' This was desirable in boys: to be great jokers, to be always up to something. My mother adds a key sentence: 'We had a lot of fun.'

Having fun has always been high on my mother's agenda. She has as much fun as possible, but what she means by this phrase cannot be understood without making an adjustment, an allowance for the great gulf across which this phrase must travel before it reaches us. It comes from another world, which, like the stars that originally sent out the light we see hesitating in the sky above us these nights, may be or is already gone. It is possible to reconstruct the facts of this world – the furniture, the clothing, the ornaments on the mantelpiece, the jugs and basins and even the chamber pots in the bedrooms, but not the emotions, not with the same exactness. So much that is now known and felt must be excluded.

This was a world in which guileless flirtation was possible, because there were many things that were simply not done by nice girls, and more girls were nice then. To fall from niceness was to fall not only from grace: sexual acts, by girls at any rate, had financial consequences. Life was more joyful and innocent then, and at the same time permeated with guilt and terror, or at least the occasions for them, on the most daily level. It was like the Japanese haiku: a limited form, rigid in its perimeters, within which an astonishing freedom was possible.

There are photographs of my mother at this time, taken with three or four other girls, linked arm in arm or with their arms thrown jestingly around each other's necks. Behind them, beyond the sea or the hills or whatever is in the background, is a world already hurtling towards ruin, unknown to them: the theory of relativity has been discovered, acid is accumulating at the roots of trees, the bull-frogs are doomed. But they smile with something that from this distance you could almost call gallantry, their right legs thrust forward in parody of a chorus line.

One of the great amusements for the girl boarders and the sons of the family was amateur theatre. Young people – they were called 'young people' – frequently performed in plays, which were put on in the church basement. My mother was a regular actor. (I have a stack of the scripts somewhere about the house, yellowing little booklets with my mother's parts checked in pencil. They are all comedies, and all impenetrable.) 'There was no television then,' says my mother. 'You made your own fun.'

For one of these plays a cat was required, and my mother and one of the sons borrowed the family cat. They put it into a canvas bag and drove to the rehearsal (there were cars by then), with my mother holding the cat on her lap. The cat, which must have been frightened, wet itself copiously, through the canvas bag and all over my mother's skirt. At the same time it made the most astonishingly bad smell.

'I was ready to sink through the floorboards,' says my mother. 'But what could I do? All I could do was sit there. In those days things like that' – she means cat pee, or pee of any sort – 'were not mentioned.' She means in mixed company.

I think of my mother driven through the night, skirts dripping, overcome with shame, the young man beside her staring straight ahead, pretending not to notice anything. They both feel that this act of unmentionable urination has been done, not by the cat, but by my mother. And so they continue, in a straight line that takes them over the Atlantic and past the curvature of the earth, out through the moon's orbit and into the dark reaches beyond.

Meanwhile, back on earth, my mother says: 'I had to throw the skirt out. It was a good skirt, too, but nothing could get rid of the smell.'

'I only heard your father swear once,' says my mother. My mother herself never swears. When she comes to a place in a story in which swearing is called for, she says 'dad-ratted' or 'blankety-blank.'

'It was when he mashed his thumb, when he was sinking the well, for the pump.' This story, I know, takes place before I was born, up north, where there is nothing underneath the trees and their sheddings but sand and bedrock. The well was for a hand pump, which in turn was for the first of the many cabins and houses my parents built together. But since I witnessed later wells being sunk and later hand pumps being installed, I know how it's done. There's a pipe with a point at one end. You pound it into the ground with a sledge hammer, and as it goes down you screw other lengths of pipe onto it, until you hit drinkable water. To keep from ruining the thread on the top end, you hold a block of wood between the sledge hammer and the pipe. Better, you get someone else to hold it for you. This is how my father mashed his thumb: he was doing both the holding and the hammering himself.

'It swelled up like a radish,' says my mother. 'He had to make a hole in the nail, with his toad-sticker, to ease the pressure. The blood spurted out like pips from a lemon. Later on the whole nail turned purple and black and dropped off. Luckily he grew another one. They say you only get two chances. When he did it though, he turned the air blue for yards around. I didn't even know he knew those words. I don't know where he picked them up.' She speaks as if these words are a minor contagious disease, like chicken pox.

Here my father looks modestly down at his plate. For him, there are two worlds: one containing ladies, in which you do not use certain expressions, and another one – consisting of logging camps and other haunts of his youth, and of gatherings of acceptable sorts of men – in which you do. To let the men's world slip over verbally into the ladies' would reveal you as a mannerless boor, but to carry the ladies' world over into the men's brands you a prig and maybe even a pansy. This is the word for it. All of this is well understood between them.

This story illustrates several things: that my father is no pansy, for one; and that my mother behaved properly by being suitably shocked. But my mother's eyes shine with delight while she tells this story. Secretly, she thinks it funny that my father got caught out, even if only once. The thumbnail that fell off is, in any significant way, long forgotten.

There are some stories which my mother does not tell when there are men present: never at dinner, never at parties. She tells them to women only, usually in the kitchen, when they or we are helping with the dishes or shelling peas, or taking the tops and tails off the string beans, or husking corn. She tells them in a lowered voice, without moving her hands around in the air, and they contain no sound effects. These are stories of romantic betrayals, unwanted pregnancies, illnesses of various horrible kinds, marital infidelities, mental breakdowns, tragic suicides, unpleasant lingering deaths. They are not rich in detail or embroidered with incident: they are stark and factual. The women, their own hands moving among the dirty dishes or the husks of vegetables, nod solemnly.

Some of these stories, it is understood, are not to be passed on to my father, because they would upset him. It is well known that women can deal with this sort of thing better than men can. Men are not to be told anything they might find too painful; the secret depths of human nature, the sordid physicalities, might overwhelm or damage them. For instance, men often faint at the sight of their own blood, to which they are not accustomed. For this reason you should never stand behind one in the line at the Red Cross donor clinic. Men, for some mysterious reason, find life more difficult than women do. (My mother believes this, despite the female bodies, trapped, diseased, disappearing, or abandoned, that litter her stories.) Men must be allowed to play in the sandbox of their choice, as happily as they can, without disturbance; otherwise they get cranky and won't eat their dinners. There are all kinds of things that men are simply not equipped to understand, so why expect it of them? Not everyone shares this belief about men; nevertheless, it has its uses.

'She dug up the shrubs from around the house,' says my mother. This story is about a shattered marriage: serious business. My mother's eyes widen. The other women lean forward. 'All she left him were the shower curtains.' There is a collective sigh, an expelling of breath. My father enters the kitchen, wondering when the tea will be ready, and the women close ranks, turning to him their deceptive blankly smiling faces. Soon afterwards, my mother emerges from the kitchen, carrying the tea pot, and sets it down on the table in its ritual place.

'I remember the time we almost died,' says my mother. Many of her stories begin this way. When she is in a certain mood, we are to understand that our lives have been preserved only by a series of amazing coincidences and strokes of luck; otherwise the entire family, individually or collectively, would be dead as doornails. These stories, in addition to producing adrenalin, serve to reinforce our sense of gratitude. There is the time we almost went over a waterfall, in a canoe, in a fog; the time we almost got caught in a forest fire; the time my father almost got squashed, before my mother's very eyes, by a ridgepole he was lifting into place; the time my brother almost got struck by a bolt of lightning, which went by him so close it knocked him down. 'You could hear it sizzle,' says my mother.

This is the story of the hay wagon. 'Your father was driving,' says my mother, 'at the speed he usually goes.' We read between the lines: *too fast.* 'You kids were in the back.' I can remember this day, so I can remember how old I was, how old my brother was. We were old enough to think it was funny to annoy my father by singing popular songs of a type he disliked, such as 'Mockingbird Hill'; or perhaps we were imitating bagpipe music by holding our noses and humming, while hitting our Adam's apples with the edges of our hands. When we became too irritating my father would say, 'Pipe down.' We weren't old enough to know that his irritation could be real: we thought it was part of the game.

'We were going down a steep hill,' my mother continues, 'when a hay wagon pulled out right across the road, at the bottom. Your father put on the brakes, but nothing happened. The brakes were gone! I thought our last moment had come.' Luckily the hay wagon continued across the road, and we shot past it, missing it by at least a foot. 'My heart was in my mouth,' says my mother.

'I didn't know until afterwards what had really happened. I was in the back seat, making bagpipe music, oblivious. The scenery was the same as it always was on car trips: my parents' heads, seen from behind, sticking up above the front seat. My father had his hat on, the one he wore to keep things from falling off the trees into his hair. My mother's hand was placed lightly on the back of his neck.

'You had such an acute sense of smell when you were younger,' says my mother.

Now we are on more dangerous ground: my mother's childhood is one thing, my own quite another. This is the moment at which I start rattling the silverware, or ask for another cup of tea. 'You used to march into houses that were strange to you, and you would say in a loud voice, "What's that funny smell?" If there are guests present, they shift a little away from me, conscious of their own emanations, trying not to look at my nose.

'I used to be so embarrassed,' says my mother absentmindedly. Then she shifts gears. 'You were such an easy child. You used to get up at six in the morning and play by yourself in the play room, singing away . . .' There is a pause. A distant voice, mine, high and silvery, drifts over the space between us. 'You used to talk a blue streak. Chatter, chatter, chatter, from morning to night.' My mother sighs imperceptibly, as if wondering why I have become so silent, and gets up to poke the fire.

Hoping to change the subject, I ask whether or not the crocuses have come up yet, but she is not to be diverted. 'I never had to spank you,' she says. 'A harsh word, and you would be completely reduced.' She looks at me sideways; she isn't sure what I have turned into, or how. 'There were just one or two times. Once, when I had to go out and I left your father in charge.' (This may be the real point of the story: the inability of men to second-guess small children.) 'I came back along the street, and there were you and your brother, throwing mud balls at an old man out of the upstairs window.'

We both know whose idea this was. For my mother, the proper construction to be put on this event is that my brother was a hell-raiser and I was his shadow, 'easily influenced,' as my mother puts it. 'You were just putty in his hands.'

'Of course, I had to punish both of you equally,' she says. Of course. I smile a forgiving smile. The real truth is that I was sneakier than my brother, and got caught less often. No front-line charges into enemy machine-gun nests for me, if they could be at all avoided. My own solitary acts of wickedness were devious and well concealed; it was only in partnership with my brother that I would throw caution to the winds.

'He could wind you around his little finger,' says my mother. 'Your father made each of you a toy box, and the rule was – ' (my mother is good at the devising of rules) '– the rule was that neither of you could take the toys out of the other one's toy box without permission. Otherwise he would have got all your toys away from you. But he got them anyway, mind you. He used to talk you into playing house, and he would pretend to be the baby. Then he would pretend to cry, and when you asked what he wanted, he'd demand whatever it was out of your toy box that he wanted to play with at the moment. You always gave it to him.'

I don't remember this, though I do remember staging World War Two on the living-room floor, with armies of stuffed bears and rabbits; but surely some primal patterns were laid down. Have these early toy-box experiences – and 'toy box' itself, as a concept, reeks with implications – have they made me suspicious of men who wish to be mothered, yet susceptible to them at the same time? Have I been conditioned to believe that if I am not solicitous, if I am not forthcoming, if I am not a never-ending cornucopia of entertaining delights, they will take their collections of milk-bottle tops and their mangy one-eared teddy bears and go away into the woods by themselves to play snipers? Probably. What my mother thinks was merely cute may have been lethal.

But this is not her only story about my suckiness and gullibility. She follows up with the *coup de grâce*, the tale of the bunny-rabbit cookies.

'It was in Ottawa. I was invited to a government tea,' says my mother, and this fact alone should signal an element of horror: my mother hated official functions, to which however she was obliged to go because she was the wife of a civil servant. 'I had to drag you kids along; we couldn't afford a lot of babysitters in those days.' The hostess had made a whole plateful of decorated cookies for whatever children might be present, and my mother proceeds to describe these: wonderful cookies shaped like bunny rabbits, with faces and clothes of coloured icing, little skirts for the little girl bunny rabbits, little pants for the little boy bunny rabbits.

'You chose one,' says my mother. 'You went off to a corner with it, by yourself. Mrs X noticed you and went over. "Aren't you going to eat your cookie?" she said. "Oh, no," you said. "I'll just sit here and talk to it." And there you sat, as happy as a clam. But someone had made the mistake of leaving the plate near your brother. When they looked again, there wasn't a single cookie left. He'd eaten every one. He was very sick that night, I can tell you.'

Some of my mother's stories defy analysis. What is the moral of this one? That I was a simp is clear enough, but on the other hand it was my brother who got the stomach ache. Is it better to eat your food, in a straightforward materialistic way, and as much of it as possible, or go off into the corner and talk to it? This used to be a favourite of my mother's before I was married, when I would bring what my father referred to as 'swains' home for dinner. Along with the dessert, out would come the bunny-rabbit cookie story, and I would cringe and twiddle my spoon while my mother forged blithely on with it. What were the swains supposed to make of it? Were my kindliness and essential femininity being trotted out for their inspection? Were they being told in a roundabout way that I was harmless, that they could expect to be talked to by me, but not devoured? Or was she, in some way, warning them off? Because there is something faintly crazed about my behaviour, some tinge of the kind of person who might be expected to leap up suddenly from the dinner table and shout, 'Don't eat that! It's alive!'

There is, however, a difference between symbolism and anecdote. Listening to my mother, I sometimes remember this.

'In my next incarnation,' my mother said once, 'I'm going to be an archaeologist and go around digging things up.' We were sitting on the bed that had once been my brother's, then mine, then my sister's; we were sorting out things from one of the trunks, deciding what could now be given away or thrown out. My mother believes that what you save from the past is mostly a matter of choice.

At that time something wasn't right in the family; someone wasn't happy. My mother was angry: her good cheer was not paying off.

This statement of hers startled me. It was the first time I'd ever heard my mother say that she might have wanted to be something other than what she was. I must have been thirty-five at the time, but it was still shocking and slightly offensive to me to learn that my mother might not have been totally contented fulfilling the role in which fate had cast her: that of being my mother. What thumbsuckers we all are, I thought, when it comes to mothers.

Shortly after this I became a mother myself, and this moment altered for me.

While she was combing my next-to-impossible hair, winding it around her long index finger, yanking out the snarls, my mother used to read me stories. Most of them are still in the house somewhere, but one has vanished. It may have been a library book. It was about a little girl who was so poor she had only one potato left for her supper, and while she was roasting it the potato got up and ran away. There was the usual chase, but I can't remember the ending: a significant lapse.

'That story was one of your favourites,' says my mother. She is probably still under the impression that I identified with the little girl, with her hunger and her sense of loss; whereas in reality I identified with the potato.

Early influences are important. It took that one a while to come out; probably until after I went to university and started wearing black stockings and pulling my hair back into a bun, and having pretensions. Gloom set in. Our next-door neighbour, who was interested in wardrobes, tackled my mother: '"If she would only *do* something about herself,"' my mother quotes, '"she could be *quite attractive*."'

'You always kept yourself busy,' my mother says charitably, referring to this time. 'You always had something cooking. Some project or other.'

It is part of my mother's mythology that I am as cheerful and productive as she is, though she admits that these qualities may be occasionally and temporarily concealed. I wasn't allowed much angst around the house. I had to indulge it in the cellar, where my mother wouldn't come upon me brooding and suggest I should go out for a walk, to improve my circulation. This was her answer to any sign, however slight, of creeping despondency. There wasn't a lot that a brisk sprint through dead leaves, howling winds, or sleet couldn't cure.

It was, I knew, the *zeitgeist* that was afflicting me, and against it such simple remedies were powerless. Like smog I wafted through her days, dankness spreading out from around me. I read modern poetry and histories of Nazi atrocities, and took to drinking coffee. Off in the distance, my mother vacuumed around my feet while I sat in chairs, studying, with car rugs tucked around me, for suddenly I was always cold.

My mother has few stories to tell about these times. What I remember from them is the odd look I would sometimes catch in her eyes. It struck me, for the first time in my life, that my mother might be afraid of me. I could not even reassure her, because I was only dimly aware of the nature of her distress, but there must have been something going on in me that was beyond her: at any time I might open my mouth and out would come a language she had never heard before. I had become a visitant from outer space, a time-traveller come back from the future, bearing news of a great disaster.

Psalms

Jeanette Winterson

If you've ever tried to get a job as a tea-taster you will know as intimately as I do the nature of the preliminary questionnaire. It has all the usual things: height, weight, sex, hobbies new and old, curious personal defects, debilitating operations, over-long periods spent in the wrong countries. Fluency, currency, contacts, school tie. Fill them in, don't blob the ink and, if in doubt, be imaginative.

Then, on the last page, before you sign your name in a hand that is firm enough to show spirit, but not enough to show waywardness, there is a large empty space and a brief but meaningful demand.

You are to write about the experience you consider to have been the most significant in the formation of your character. (You may interpret 'character' as 'philosophy' if such is your inclination.) This is very shocking, because what we really want to talk about is that time we saw our older sister compromised behind the tool shed, or the time we very deliberately spat in the communion wine.

When I was small, I had a tortoise called Psalms. It was bought for me and named for me by my mother in an effort to remind me continually to praise the Lord. My mother had a horror of graven images, including crucifixes, but she felt there could be no harm in a tortoise. It moved slowly, so I could fully contemplate the wonders of creation in a way that would have been impossible with a ferret. It wasn't cuddly, so that I wouldn't be distracted as I might with a dog, and it had very little visible personality, so there was no possibility of us forming an intimate relationship as I might with a parrot. All in all, it seemed to her to be a satisfactory pet. I had been agitating for a pet for some time. In my head I had a white rabbit called Ezra that bit people who ignored me. Ezra's pelt was as white as the soul in heaven but his heart was black . . .

My mother drew me a picture of a tortoise so that I would not be too disappointed or too ecstatic. She hated emotion. I hoped that they came in different colours, which was not unreasonable since most animals do, and, when they were all clearly brown, I felt cheated.

'You can paint their shells,' comforted the man in the shop. 'Some people paint scenes on them. One chap I know has 26 and if you line 'em end to end in the right order you got the Flying Scotsman pulling into Edinburgh station.'

I asked my mother if I could have another twelve so that I could do a tableau of the last supper, but she said it was too expensive and might be a sin against the Holy Ghost.

'Why?' I demanded as the man left us arguing in front of the gerbils. 'God made the Holy Ghost, and he made these tortoises, they must know about each other.'

'I don't want the Lord and his disciples running round the garden on the backs of your tortoises. It's not respectful.'

'Yes, but when sinners come into the garden they'll be taken aback. They'll think it's the Lord sending them a vision.' (I imagined the heathen being confronted by more and more tortoises; they weren't to know I had thirteen, they'd think it was a special God-sent tortoise that could multiply itself.)

'No,' said my mother firmly. 'It's Graven Images, that's what. If the Lord wanted to appear on the backs of tortoises he'd have done it already.'

'Well can I just have two more then? I could do The Three Musketeers.'

'Heathen child,' my mother slapped me round the ears. 'This pet is to help you think about our Saviour. How can you do that if you've got The Three Musketeers staring up at you?'

The man looked sympathetic, but he didn't want to get involved so we packed up the one tortoise in a box with holes and went to catch the bus home. I was excited. Adam had named the animals, now I could name mine. 'How about The Man in the

Iron Mask?' I suggested to my mother who was sitting in front of me reading her *Band of Hope Review*. She turned round sharply and gave a little screech.

'I've cricked my neck, what did you say?'

I said it again. 'We could call it Mim for short, but it looks like it's a prisoner doesn't it?'

'You are not calling that animal The Man in the Iron Mask, or anything for short, you can call it Psalms.'

'Why don't I call it Ebenezer?' (I was thinking that would match Ezra.)

'We're calling it Psalms because I want you to praise the Lord.'

'I can praise the Lord if it's called Ebenezer.'

'But you won't, will you? You'll say you forgot. What about the time I bought you that 3-D postcard of the garden of Gethsemane? You said that would help you think about the Lord and I caught you singing "On Ilkley Moor Baht 'at".'

'Alright then,' I sulked. 'We'll call it Psalms.'

So we did, and Psalms lived very quietly in a hutch at the bottom of the garden and every day I went and sat next to him and read him one of his namesakes out of the Bible. He was an attentive pet, never tried to run away or dig anything up, my mother spoke of his steadfastness with tears in her eyes. She felt convinced that Psalms was having a good effect on me. She enjoyed seeing us together. I never told her about Ezra the demon bunny, about his ears that filtered the sun on a warm day through a lattice of blood vessels reminiscent of orchids. Ezra the avenger didn't like Psalms and sometimes stole his lettuce.

When my mother decided it was time for us to go on holiday to Llandudno she was determined to take Psalms with us.

'I don't want you being distracted by Pleasure,' she explained. 'Not now that you're doing so well.'

I was doing well; I knew huge chunks of the Bible by heart and won all the competitions in Sunday School. Most importantly, for an evangelical, I was singing more, which you do, inevitably, when you're learning Psalms. On the train my mother supplied me with pen and paper and told me to make as many separate words as I could out of Jerusalem. My father was dispatched for coffee and she read out loud interesting snippets from her new paperback, *Portents of the Second Coming.*

I wasn't listening; practice enabled me to pour out the variations on Jerusalem without even thinking. Words slot into each other easily enough once sense ceases to be primary. Words become patterns and shapes. Tennyson, drunk on filthy sherry one evening, said he knew the value of every word in the language, except possibly 'scissors'. By value he meant resonance and fluidity, not sense. So while my mother warned me of the forthcoming apocalypse I stared out of the window and imagined that I was old enough to buy my own Rail Rover ticket and go off round the world with only a knapsack and a penknife and a white rabbit. A white rabbit? I jumped a little at this intrusion into my daydream. Ezra's pink eyes were gleaming down at me from the frayed luggage rack. Ezra wasn't invited on this trip, I had been determined to control him and make him stay behind. In the box next to me I felt Psalms fidgeting. My mother was oblivious.

'Just think,' she said enthusiastically. 'When the Lord comes back the lion will lie down with the lamb.'

But will the rabbit come to terms with the tortoise?

Like Psalms, I was feeling nervous, as one would when one's fantasy life gets out of control. Ezra's eyes bored into my soul and my own black heart. I felt transparent, the way I do now when I meet a radical feminist who can always tell that I shave my armpits and have a penchant for silk stockings.

'I'm trying to be good,' I hissed. 'Go away.'

'Yes,' continued my mother, all unknowing. 'We'll live naturally when the Lord comes back, there'll be no chemicals or aerosol deodorants. No fornicating or electric guitars.' She looked up sharply at my father. 'Did you put saccharine in this coffee? You know I can't drink it without.' My father smiled sheepishly and tried to placate her with a packet of Bourbons, which was a mistake because she hated anything that sounded foreign. I remembered how it had been when my auntie had come back from Italy and insisted on having us round for pasta. My mother was suspicious and kept turning it over with her fork and saying how much she liked hot pot and carrots. She didn't mind natives so much or people who lived in the jungle and other hot places because she felt they couldn't help it. Europe, though, was close enough to Britain to behave properly and, in not behaving properly, was clearly perverse and due to be rolled up when the Lord came back. (In the Eternal City there will be no pasta.)

I tried to distract myself from her gathering storm by concentrating on the notices in our carriage. I took in the exhortation to leave the train clean and tidy and felt suitably awed by the dire warnings against frivolously pulling the communication cord. Ezra began to chew it. Tired and emotional, though fondly imagining we shared a common ground other than the one we were standing on, we reached our boarding house at nightfall and spent the holiday in various ways. One morning my mother suggested we take Psalms with us to the beach.

'He'll enjoy a change of air.'

I hadn't seen Ezra for a couple of days otherwise I might have been more alive to the possibilities of catastrophe. We set off, found a patch that wasn't too windy, said a prayer and my father fell asleep. Psalms seemed comforted by the sand beneath his feet and very slowly dug a very small hole.

'Why don't you take him to that rock in the breakers?' My mother pointed. 'He won't have seen the sea before.' I nodded, and picked him up pretending I was Long John Silver making off with booty. As we sat on the rock sunning ourselves a group of boys came splashing through the waves, one of them holding a bow and arrow. Before my eyes he strung the bow and fired at Psalms. It was a direct hit in the centre of the shell. This was of no matter in itself because the arrow was rubber-tipped and made no impression on the shell. It did make an impression on Psalms, though, who became hysterical and standing on his back legs toppled over into the sea. I lunged down to pick him out but I couldn't distinguish between tortoise and rocks. If only my mother had let me make him into one of The Three Musketeers I could have saved him from a watery grave. He was lost. Dead. Drowned. I thought of Shelley.

'Psalms has been killed,' I told my mother flatly.

We spent all afternoon with a shrimping net trying to find his corpse, but we couldn't and at six o'clock my mother said she had to have some fish and chips. It was a gloomy funeral supper and all I could see was Ezra the demon bunny hopping up and down on the prom. If it had not been for my father's devotion and perseverance in whistling tunes from the war in a loud and lively manner we might never have recovered our spirits. As it was, my mother suddenly joined in with the words, patted me on the head and said it must have been the Lord's will. Psalms's time was up, which was surely a sign that I should move onto another book of the Bible.

'We could go straight onto Proverbs,' she said. 'What kind of pet would be proverbial?'

'What about a snake?'

'No,' she refused, shaking her head. 'Snakes are wily, not wise.'

'What about an owl?'

'I don't want an owl in my room. Owls are very demanding and besides when your Uncle Bert parachuted into the canal by mistake, it was an owl I saw just before I got the telegram.'

Death by water seemed to be a feature of our family, so why not have something that was perpetually drowned? 'Let's get some fish, they're proverbial, and they'll be quiet like Psalms was, and they'll remind us of the Flood and our own mortality.' My mother was very taken with this, especially since she had just eaten a fine piece of cod. She liked it when she could experience the Bible in different ways.

As for me, I was confronted with my own black heart. You can bury what you like but, if it's still alive when you bury it, don't look for a quiet life. Is this what the tea board wants to know about? Is it hoping to read of tortoises called Psalms?

I don't believe it. They must have an identikit picture of what constitutes a suitable forming experience, like playing quarterback in the school team and beating Wales, or saving a rare colony of worker bees from extinction.

My mother bought some brown ink in Llandudno and sketched Psalms on a few square inches of stiff card. She caught his expression very well, though I still feel the burden of being the only person who has ever seen what emotion a tortoise can express when about to drown. Such things are sobering and stretch down the years. I could have saved him, but I felt he limited my life. Sometimes I take out the sketch and stare at his mournful face. He was always mournful, though I think that was a characteristic of the breed because I have never met a jubilant tortoise. On the other hand, perhaps I never made him happy. Perhaps we were at emotional odds like Scarlett O'Hara and Rhett Butler. Perhaps a briny end was better than a gradual neglect. I ponder these things in my heart. My mother, always philosophical in her own way, enjoyed a steady stream of biblical pets: the Proverbial fish, Ecclesiast the hen who never laid an egg where we could find it, Solomon the Scotch terrier and, finally, Isaiah and Jeremiah, a pair of goats who lived to a great age and died peacefully in their pen.

'You can always depend on the prophets,' declared my mother whenever anyone marvelled at the longevity of her goats. The world was a looking glass for the Lord – she saw him in everything. Though I do warn her, from time to time, never to judge a bunny by its pelt . . .

Meet My Mother

Michelene Wandor

Once upon a time my mother was a mother just like any other mother. Once upon a time she couldn't bear not letting me know, on a regular basis, what she thought was wrong with the world, and in particular, wrong with me. What would make her happiest in the whole world, the happiest person in the whole wide world, is if I got married and settled down. Married and settled down. There's a sort of sticky inevitability about those words. Like marriage is a soufflé which has risen like a bird in the oven, and then as the cold air of settling down hits it, it sinks and sogs its way back down into the dish from which it has first risen, all the air and light knocked out of it. Not, I may say, that I could use such a brilliant image in front of my mother, once upon a time. Oh no. If I had, her eyes would have glazed over, and she would have asked me if I wanted another cup of tea. Once upon a time I couldn't talk to my mother.

Once upon a time my mother's biggest crusade was to see me married and settled. Her crusade. I know it's probably a word from the wrong tradition, but it describes her fervour like no other word could. For her it wasn't a crusade, it was as normal and expected as breathing. Once upon a time.

Her favourite way, once upon a time, was to exert emotional blackmail. Just for me, she would say. Just think of me. How can I die without having the pleasure of seeing you married, of having – Heaven keep the Evil Eye from me – a grandchild. Or two. Or maybe, if I'm very lucky, three.

When my sister got married, I didn't hear the beginning or the end of it. White. How lovely she looked in white. How lovely I would look in white, white was always my favourite colour, she says to me. In fact, I never liked wearing white. In fact I hate wearing white. In fact, I never wear white, and she could not have failed to notice the fact. So when she tells me that white is my favourite colour, I think, thank you very much, you wait till I'm in the middle of my twenties, and I have all my fashion tastes and worries sorted out, and then you spring it on me that white is my favourite colour. Well, forget it. That's what I think, once upon a time, but of course I don't say it, because once upon a time I don't even bother to talk to my mother.

Or she'd use the cultural blackmail. My cousins got bar-mitzvahed and bat-mitzvahed – they're twins, a boy and a girl, and their parents are good liberal Jews – so she came back from the service and the party, and she said, oh, it was such a lovely service, and they even had a lady minister, and her mouth is curling a little in disapproval, but she's still trying to draw me back into the fold, a reverend lady, and she spoke so clear you could understand every word she said, and afterwards there was a reception in a most beautiful hotel, and the food – oh, there were horses doovers and fish and meat and coffee and I even shamed myself, she said, and took liberties with the wine, and then she giggled and then perhaps it was the wine taking liberties with her, but she leaned towards me and said – and I just listened to the innocence in her voice, and she said, Look, darling, if ever you want to arrange a function, and she's saying it so sweet, butter wouldn't melt in her mouth, if you ever want to arrange a function, you could do worse than choose that hotel. So I decide to match her innocence. And what sort of function would you have in mind, I ask? Oh, she says airily, waving her hand vaguely in the air, any function – a party, a wedding, anything.

A funeral, I say? That offends her. It's meant to. Don't joke, she says, her eyes suddenly serious. She turns away from me, and mock spits three times in the air, to warn away any bad devils who might take any of our words literally. A wedding, she says, you could do worse than have a wedding. At least then you would sleep legal.

There's no law about sleeping, I say, deliberately misunderstanding her, taking her literally. This is a game we have played since I was very young, in which each of us only listens to a little bit of what the other is saying.

You know what it says in the Book of Isaiah, she says. No, I don't, I counter. I've never read the Book of Isaiah, how should I know what it says? Triumphant, she moves in for the kill: That's exactly the trouble with you, she says, you haven't read – I haven't read Proust, Mum, I say (I only call her Mum when I know I'm beaten). Feeble, I know. She is not impressed. I don't want to hear about your pagan habits, she yells, you should know what it is to be a Jew.

Once upon a time my mother used to talk like this. And each time, at a certain point, this is where we would end up. You should know what it is to be a Jew. Ever since I refused to go home for Pesach when I was eighteen – that was my first rebellion – and every time we have this row, we have to go through the *ganze megilla*, which always ends with her in tears and me getting angry and saying nasty and cold and hurtful things, just to stop myself from collapsing into her arms and blubbering how sorry I am to be such a disappointment to her. So this time I resort to the safe family tactic and suggest we should have a cup of tea. That always works. As long as she feels I am still prepared to do battle in principle, she lets me off for the time being. She doesn't know that I have an ulterior motive. Something up my sleeve.

So when the tea is made and we are sipping it, I decide now is the time to tell her.

'Mum,' I say. 'I've got something to tell you.'

'You're moving house again,' she suggests.

'No. Something more important than that.'

'You could come and live at home,' she says. 'I hoover your room every week. It's all ready for you. You just need clean sheets on the bed. I can do it for you in a minute.'

'Listen, Mother –' Now I'm getting serious and she knows it.

'I think I'm a lesbian,' I say.

'Pour me some more tea, dear,' she says. So I do. She adds milk, sugar, stirs it, slow as slow, while I watch her face and try to anticipate what will happen next. Silence. I try another tack.

'I've got a lover.'

'You should give up sugar,' she says, putting two spoons in her own cup. 'I read in *Woman's Own* it's bad for the heart.'

'It's a woman,' I say, determined now that she won't stop me.

'What is a woman?' she asks me, in a sort of mock-drunk, mock-philosophical tone, her eyelids heavy and portentous, as though she has just spoken after a silence of many years.

'My lover is a woman, Mummy.' Now I'm appealing to the time in her memory when I was the beautiful baby she likes to remember as perfect: clean, tidy, smiling, clever and precocious. 'My lover,' I say, just in case she hasn't quite got the point, 'is a lesbian.'

'Oh,' says my mother, enlightenment dawning in the upward inflection of her voice. 'What part of Lesbia is she from?'

I could kill her. I really could. Of all the mean, rotten, cheap jokes. And all the more rotten and mean and cheap because I give way and collapse into giggles.

'So whatever happened to the struggle with heterosexuality?' she adds, mocking, her eyes bright and alert.

'I have decided to give up heterosexuality. I have decided that, while the project of altering the balance of power within heterosexual relationships is still a valid one, it is no longer one I can espouse – so to speak. There is no revolutionary hope for the heterosexual, and I have therefore decided to love myself and become a lesbian.'

She sips her tea, looks up at me, and says, 'Just like that?'

'Almost,' I say, a little modest. What does she want, a blow by blow account?

She recovers her fire: 'You should have kept Brian on. He was a nice boy, and he was learning to cook nicely and he would have made a lovely father and helped you with the baby.'

I didn't know where to start. 'Brian? Father? Baby? What are you talking about? Brian was five years ago.'

'I liked him,' she says. 'He was almost like a son to me.'

'Yes, he used to bring his socks for you to darn,' I said, sarcastic.

'It's criminal the way people just throw things away nowadays. I believe in darning.' Her pronouncement for the day. I sighed. I knew this tack. She would go on to talk about the values of the olden days. 'In those days, we had a sense of values,' she says. 'The trouble with you young people is you have no sense of values.'

'That's what I've been trying to tell you,' I say. 'I value a relationship, and I'm trying to tell you about it.'

'You mean, you got a relationship?'

'Yes. I've been telling you.'

'I thought you just decided to be a lesbian.'

'It doesn't just happen like that,' I said.

'Oh. I thought you made a political decision,' she persists.

'Well, I did,' I say. 'But –'

And the rotten cow finishes my sentence for me. 'But you fancied someone,' she says, kind as anything.

'Yes,' I say, very lamely.

'Well,' she says, getting up from the table. I wonder what's coming next. 'Well, I shall just have to give you two scarves for Chanukah,' she says.

'She isn't Jewish, Mum,' I say. Well, that does it. She turns on me. 'You got to become a lesbian, you should at least have the decency to shack up with a nice Jewish girl. What would your father say if he was still alive?'

'Mum, how can I find a nice Jewish girl? *I'm* not a nice Jewish girl.'

'You're my daughter,' she says, still very angry, 'and you should know what upsets me. You should think about your mother.'

'I'm sorry, Mum.'

'You're sorry you're a lesbian, or you're sorry your girlfriend isn't Jewish?'

'I don't know. Yes. I do. I'm not sorry. That I'm a lesbian. I'm not at all sorry about that. I'm very pleased about that. And I'm not sorry Rowena's a – well, not Jewish.'

'Rowena.' She sniffs. 'What kind of a goyische name is that. Rowena.'

'Well, that's what I have to tell you, Mum.'

'And you're not sorry?'

'No.'

'Good. Then we know where we stand. You'll both come over for supper on Sunday night. I'll meet her.'

Well, I thought that was achievement enough. My mother hadn't collapsed into a heap, hadn't killed herself, had invited me and Rowena round for supper.

Let me describe Rowena to you.

You remember in the first bit of the seventies it was all army reject dungarees and those lovely, comfortable shoes, Kickers, they were called, and sort of tatty T-shirts and anything that didn't look positively dirty, but was somehow designed to give the effect of efficient, strong, functional female-ness. Sort of army surplus-type gear. Then there was the punk era, and that rubbed itself off – if you'll pardon the phrase – on feminists, and all the floppy and dull-coloured gear was out, and Rowena, who has always spent at least half an hour every morning worrying about what the hell to wear – anti-government demo, or relative's wedding, it doesn't matter which – Rowena has dyed her hair a sort of cerise, with a deep purple streak down the middle, and she's wearing straight, tight black satin stretch trousers, with little black sequins stuck on at random, the sort of tight shiny trousers that make every curve and contour show, and she is so sexy. Really. I couldn't bear it the first day she went out looking like that. I wanted her all to myself. Anyway, then she has these silver high-heeled sandals, and this is the gear she's wearing to meet my mother. Oh, and she has a sort of luminous green and pink floppy T-shirt, sort of belted up round her bum. She and I have a bit of a to-and-fro, with me trying to persuade her to look a bit drab and oppressed, because that way we'll stand a better chance with my mother. The way Rowena looks in all that gear, she'll just confirm every terrible prejudice my mother has about *shicksas*, that they're all tarts and terrible seductions to nice Jewish boys – or in this case the nice Jewish girl she would like me to be. Piss off, says Rowena, kissing me lightly, so her lipstick doesn't smudge. I'm going to seduce your Mum, she says.

And honestly, she did. Just as we were going up the front steps, she twisted one of her ankles in those silly shoes, and somehow managed to rip a bit of the seam on the inside leg of her black trousers. So she arrives with a bit of white thigh showing, and almost before she's said a polite hello, she's asked my mother for a needle and thread. Mum couldn't have wanted a better introduction. She rushes for her sewing basket and before you know where you are, the two of them are deep in discussion about the relative merits of pure sanforised cotton or acrylic sewing yarn, and which works better for the machine and for what fabric – and within five minutes I was the odd one out, and before I know where I am, I'm serving the food – chicken soup, and chicken with latkes (homemade, of course) and sweet and sour cabbage – oh, delicious stuff – I can taste it now – and of course when they've finished with the sewing, they go on to the food. Rowena is into cooking Chinese food, and you'd think they would never run out of recipes to exchange. I end up turning the television on and falling asleep in front of Melvyn Bragg on the South Bank Show, doing a programme about lost African cultures.

Next thing, my mother is going off to an older women's group, and then she gets involved in pension rights, and she can't finish a skirt she's making for me because she has to go on a demonstration. Then she forgets my birthday. And why? Because she's going on a day trip to Greenham. She spends the entire day before making sandwiches, and God knows what to take with her, and she's so busy, she forgets my birthday. Well, of course, I didn't say anything. How could I, I've spent my whole life pooh-poohing rituals and occasions like that, and I always have to be reminded of everyone's birthday, so who am I to fall into a heap because my mother, who kept the family's birthdays religiously, and always sent a card – stupid cards with baskets of flowers on them, that kind of thing, but still, a card; how can I complain?

Then, one evening, when I have a local tenants' meeting to go to, I notice Rowena is getting all her war paint on, and when

I ask her where she's going, she reminds me that it's the women's disco tonight, which I'd forgotten. So I chirp up, oh, I'll come on after the meeting, we can have a bop. And she's off-putting; I don't think I'll stay long enough, she says. Oh? You look as though you're dressed for a long siege, I say. And paranoia being my middle name, I ask her whether she's going with someone. Sort of, she says. Don't think I know her, I say, mock-contemplative. Sortov; no. She just arrived in this country, or something? In a manner of speaking, says Rowena. Actually – and she puts down her hair gel, the better to face me – I'm taking your mother. I promise you, I fell on to a chair with shock. My mother, at a women's disco, surrounded by – well, us. Rowena looks very apologetic; my mother, she says, was asking her about me, and my friends. And then my mother suggested having a quick look in at the women's disco. Rowena was quite adamant that the suggestion came from my mother.

The next thing, my mother goes punk. She dyed her hair green. Well, green highlights. Well, the first time I saw her, the way the light shone on her hair, it looked sort of bluey green. I suppose in the olden days it would have been what people called a blue rinse. All her friends think she's just had a blue rinse. But I know that really she's gone elderly punk.

Then she joins a Jewish feminist group, and after one meeting, she comes back all excited late at night and she phones me at midnight to harangue me for half an hour about how patriarchal the Judaeo-Christian heritage is, and have I really thought hard and long about the story of Eve in Genesis? Well, usually my reaction, when she asks me if I've read this or that book in the Old Testament, is to bridle and answer back, and this time is no different, and I come up with No, and I haven't read *War and Peace* either, and suddenly I hear myself, and I think, what am I saying, who am I talking to, so I pretend that my cocoa's boiling over and I hang up the phone and I sit there and have a little think.

Rowena's sitting up in bed reading a little light bedtime Foucault, and she can see I'm upset. She puts her book down and puts her arm round me, and I start talking.

'You must think I'm going round the twist. For years I've been complaining about my mother, how she doesn't understand me, how bigoted she is, how I can't talk to her, how she makes me feel guilty, why can't I have a mother I can talk to like a friend, share things with, have the perfect socialist-feminist mother –daughter relationship, instead of this fucked up bourgeois blackmail job. And now look at me. I'm upset when she forgets my birthday. I feel uncomfortable at the idea that she's going out and having a good time, I get stomach ache at the thought that she may go off cooking, I can't stand the way her house gets more and more untidy, because she's giving priority to other things. What on earth is the matter with me?'

Rowena pats me maternally on the shoulder. 'There are some,' she says, 'would say it was latent competition with your mother for your father that is making you unable to see your mother's actions as other than a direct threat.'

'Freudian garbage,' I say. Rowena shrugs, and indicates that she's a bit bored with the conversation and wants to get back to her book. I don't mind, really, because I don't want to talk any more. I want to think.

So I think. I sit there and I think. And I think, once upon a time I had a mother who was just what she should be. Manipulative, bigoted, a pain in the neck, didn't understand me, didn't want to understand me, wanted me to be all the things she thought I should be. Once upon a time I could dread going round to visit her on Sunday, I could be on my guard against her attacks, and secretly I could enjoy eating her home-made biscuits, made with butter, delicious and crumbly, and I could take material round for her to make clothes for me, and borrow a knitting pattern from her, and this was our exchange. Once upon a time I had a mother. Now she's gone. And I don't know what I'm going to do.

Perhaps I'll talk to Rowena again. In the morning.

The Voice of Authority

Dina Mehta

In the first days of her illness, when the fever was intermittent Uma thought of her mother-in-law, whom she hated. What she remembered most about her was her voice. When the fever raged, Uma heard that voice again, harsh and strident, barking commands, hurling reproaches at a bowed head draped with the faded end of a cotton sari. And always as background music to that voice was the sound of the little mill on the kitchen floor, at which, her hands encircling the peg in the flat stones, she had been made to sit and grind the rice and wheat and grams and jowar till her aching shoulders and arms cried out for respite. Every last pinch of the fine flour that flowed from between the two grinding stones had to be carefully gleaned, because the sight of anything going to waste filled her mother-in-law with a cold, consuming wrath. This may have been because in her village home as a young girl she had lived through two famines when the rains failed, but to Uma the craggy old woman had a natural kinship with stones and aridity . . .

Then Uma grew very ill. Dark, scalding shadows enfolded her, and she did not hear the voice or the mill any more. Their place was taken by other tyrants who peered and murmured at her out of a mist and pricked, tapped, thumped, doused, prodded and pummelled her. Needles jabbed, clothes were yanked off and on. She was made to go to sleep, she was rudely awakened from her drenched, weary slumbers. Ah, for some peace! If only she could double up and disappear under the rough fabric of the blanket, cower under its male embrace like some frightened animal burrowing into its hole! And why wasn't Suresh there to comfort her, Suresh who had braved his mother's wrath and exchanged looks with her across the room so heavy-laden with the promise of love, that her young bride's heart had fluttered with an ill-concealed delight, and made his mother twice as harsh with her? For the old woman had believed that it was beneath the sovereignty of man to love his wife so openly. A man's conduct must be lordly or he would offend the gods, he must keep his woman in her place or she would upset all norms and wear the lower end of her sari on her head! But where was Suresh? Why did his voice come to her from such a long distance when she needed him so? Suddenly Uma did not care any more. All she wanted was to hold on forever to the trickle of liquid silence which invaded her body as the hypodermic needle entered the thigh . . .

Then Uma was much better, but for a long period of enforced horizontality she lay on her back, helpless and obedient to the will of those who attended on her. It seemed to her that they subjected her to every form of incivility. Her privacy was invaded a hundred times a day; her modesty torn to shreds. All the earthly indignities that mortals must suffer in secret – just because they are mortals – were shamelessly exposed to the world. Her secret self stood ajar, and she did not like it. Her illness was discussed over her bed as if she were not lying on it, and that made her feel anonymous, cancelled out. An impotent anger stirred in her every time her presence was dismissed, her qualms ignored, her susceptibilities brushed aside. Nothing pleased her. The curiosity of visitors was offensive, but when she was left alone, she felt neglected, and took to brooding over all the negative, unkind things that happened to her. Streams of self-pity converged on her in random, undisciplined waves as she wilfully pondered on the kind of exit she would finally make – for all creatures must make this ultimate, decisive exit. Would she grow old and lose blitheness? Would she grow careworn and lose elegance? Would she grow lonely and lose love? So she lay there like a broken down and dethroned queen, now pitying herself that she had a worm's eye-view on life, now cross that she had no more authority than the worm.

Uma was feeling particularly resentful one sunny morning after Muni bhabhi, who always smelled of the kitchen and washing-up, had given her passive body a brisk rub-down with her rough, calloused hands and then thrown open the bedroom windows. (Suresh had, a month ago, tentatively suggested a nurse, but the relatives had been horrified and clamorous: so many females in the family, and a *paid* creature to walk into his home to take care of one of their own! Did he think their hands and feet were made of fragile glass or did he think they were lost to all sense of duty and shame?)

'Now I will do your hair,' said Muni bhabhi. Uma watched sullenly as with little fluttering gestures her husband's sister smoothed the bedcovers, her bangles setting up an agitated jingle. Muni had none of her mother's bony uprightness, her rigid perfection. In old age she would not be magnificently gnarled and tenacious and windswept. In no way would she be menacing, the source of strange rays. She sagged already. Her flesh had a looseness, a disorganised profusion that repelled Uma. Had Muni been a Western woman, she would have squeezed all that loose fat into a corset. As it was, her saris always had that baggy, clean pillowcase look, because she did not starch them into stiff white folds of efficiency – which was the way Uma liked to wear her cotton saris.

The whiff of garlic strengthened as her sister-in-law leaned over her and Uma said abruptly, 'I'll do my hair myself. Leave the mirror where it is.'

'It will tire you out.'

'No it won't. You better go home. It's late and you have to cook.'

'I have yet to bring your tea.'

'Jyoti can very well bring my tea.'

'Any little time Jyoti has at home, she spends with her nose in her books,' said Muni with an aggrieved sniff. Uma knew that in her mind higher education for a daughter was suspect, unnecessary, and even dangerous, so she turned away her head impatiently and maintained a discreet silence.

'Cutting up dead bodies is not a woman's proper work,' went on Muni bhabhi. 'We already have two doctors in the family: Vinoo's third son, and my husband's nephew. Jyoti is past twenty. Why do you keep her without a husband so long?'

Uma made a gesture of irritation, but maintained her silence.

She did not want this conversation. It always put her on the defensive.

'It is not good,' Muni bhabhi continued vaguely, austerely. She often took refuge in vagueness.

'Why is it not good?' Uma hitched herself up against the pillows. 'Is her chastity so perishable that Jyoti must be married off before she herself knows the difference between honour and shame?'

Muni's face almost expressed shock at the utter impropriety of voicing such a thought, but gave up the struggle and became vague again as she said, 'Why not have her horoscope read, at least?'

'What for? I have no intention of having her horoscope hawked from door to door — wherever a marriageable son can be found.'

'Not from door to door. But what is wrong with Jeevram's family? Never has there been a breath of scandal about that family. And anyone can see that the boy Harish is sweet on Jyoti.'

Uma sighed. *Harish.* It was not that she objected so much to his long hair and tight pants, his fleet of pointed shoes and transistors or his father's quickly-amassed millions, but the expression of complacent insolence on his face and something else there, something entirely self-contained, self-concerned, that baffled her. Yet according to Muni bhabhi Jyoti should have been betrothed to Harish years ago, as would have been proper to the fiction of their situation: had they not grown up together, had measles together, pulled each other's hair in the same park and read in the same class at school, and hadn't the two families lived as neighbours for two generations and did they not belong to the same caste? Muni would have been astonished to learn that in reality neither Jyoti nor Harish was prepared to give their hearts to the enactment of such a drama — and for that God be praised!

'. . . and such a *modern* family in every way,' Muni was saying.

'Listen!' Uma's voice was louder than she had intended. 'Suresh and I have discussed this many times . . .'

Muni bhabhi winced and almost clapped her hands to her ears. She wished Uma would not take her husband's name in so blatant a fashion. After all, there were limits to *how* modern one could be . . . She herself carefully guarded her tongue from ever speaking *her* husband's name aloud, for that would be inauspicious, and might bring harm to him from some jealous, malevolent spirits. So she deadened her ears to what Uma was saying, made her mind a complete blank and began to set the room to rights, her bare feet slapping on the tiled floor. When she finished, she said aloud, 'The sonar will be here in the evening, to pierce Jyoti's ears. Surely you should have had it done long ago?'

'It was done of course,' Uma interrupted herself to say irritably, 'but you know very well she had trouble with her ears, and the earrings had to be removed to allow them to heal. The skin closed up again with time.'

'Well, I have it all arranged,' Muni went on virtuously. 'I have seen the astrologer and the auspicious time is between four and five in the evening – or we will have to wait till next month.' She hesitated near the door. 'Well, I'm off. I'll be back in the evening to take Jyoti to the temple before the goldsmith arrives.' With that she made a quick exit as if to forestall a protest from Uma.

Uma scowled after her. Getting Jyoti's ears pierced, to her sister-in-law's way of thinking, was the first step towards getting the girl ready for marriage. Perhaps it *was* time . . . but what annoyed her was that Jyoti should have agreed so tamely to the sonar and the astrologer and the temple, when she could have had the whole thing done at the hospital where she worked without all this fuss. Ready for marriage, her Jyoti. Uma gave a pleased half-smile, then it was swallowed up in a heavy frown. She loved her daughter with fierce pride, without apology, but what was the matter with her? There was in Jyoti some dreadful lack of vigour, an absence of straightforward desires, of a shapely human will. It was as if she suffered from a marked, meaningless incapacity to do what she wanted, as if she were not framed for recognising, let alone seizing, her own felicity. Was it because the idea of doing what she *ought*, implanted early in the depths of her soul, and diligently cultivated over the years, had by now removed the possibility of pure, independent movement of the will?

Quickly Uma shied away from this perilous question. Her Jyoti was studying to become a doctor. She wanted her to be a *good* doctor, an *excellent* doctor, for India needed doctors. She wanted the study of science to cool, harden and fill the girl with a silent, forbearing strength, because women needed such strength; and because one day she would hold patients under her spell, and when sufferers too feeble to be laws unto themselves turned to her in their despair, her strength would be a shield unto them.

'But are you sure this is what Jyoti wants?' Suresh had asked, his brow puckered in thought.

'Of course I'm sure!' Uma had said.

She now settled down more comfortably among her pillows. Her Jyoti would lead a useful, purposeful life. She would retain a sense of human identity, the firm core of self, and not become a nameless, biological robot in a docile mass. Above all, she would not immolate herself in the kitchen, engage in work that was endless, trivial and deadening. Yes, yes, *she* at least must refuse to be clipped, caged, have her gifts destroyed or locked up forever within herself, just because she was born a woman . . .

And Uma's mind went back in time to the day when she had brought Jyoti home from the hospital. Her mother-in-law had looked at the baby with such a terrible silent confrontation that it had made Uma feel almost faint. The long, rather ascetic and very handsome face was not smiling, not embarrassed; it had gazed down on the sleeping child in a curious, dreadful way, with a kind of viperous, beady-eyed satisfaction. Trembling Uma had hardened her expression. She is only an old, dry object, she had told herself, like a stuffed crocodile, her insides filled with straw. I must not let her see the faintness, but only that I'm capable of fighting her. I must show her that this child of mine can be anything a son could have been, and more.

Suresh had said to his mother, his voice taut with anger. 'Well? Have you no words to say when you look into the face of my first-born?'

The brilliant, beady eyes had snapped with malice, the lips had narrowed slowly with iron. 'She has two eyes and a nose and a mouth.'

'She is lovely, *lovely* do you hear?'

'She is a female.' The verdict was final, unanswerable.

'I am proud of her!' shouted Suresh.

'Of a first-born who is a worthless girl-child.'

'Were you not a girl-child once? And without you, where would I and my brothers have been? Can you turn your heart to stone when you think that?'

Her expression had remained unencumbered by sympathy, the long thin nose had pointed like a dagger at the sleeping child. Each of her other three sons had begun their line with a fine, squalling boy, but Uma had disgraced her fourth and favourite son – for it was, of course, *her* fault that the child was a girl. But perhaps even this the old woman could have found it in her heart to forgive – the baby was *so* lovely – but that in some way she felt it was Suresh's fault also, because of the shameless way in which he loved his wife. Too openly, so that even strangers and servants could see. It was not seemly for a man to display so much weakness. *Her* husband had shown her little tenderness, even as a bride, though she had taken infinite pains to please him. He had always been a man with an inner anger, and had once beaten her mercilessly because she burnt the rice – though she had been three months' pregnant with her third child. But this was only as it should be. Sound beating comes from lust for your woman, and like a good wife she had cherished the old perverted sign of affection. But with Suresh it was different – this frail, soft creature had cast a spell over her son. And if such a reversal of the old order and such flouting of old values displeased *her*, how much more had it offended the gods? She would consult a priest to see what could be done to avert celestial wrath, before worse events (than girl children) rained about her.

Uma closed her eyes. She felt tired, suddenly. Her body was ticking at low pressure, concentrating within on the process of convalescence. It seemed to be taking sensible charge of itself, while it gave a curious freedom to her mind to roam at will . . .

In her country the old and the new touched each other at differing levels, she thought, and somehow in the midst of this dichotomy Jyoti had to find a stable place for herself, to grow to her full stature as a human being. Astrologers still crossed swords with scientists, medicine with mantras, fatalism with endeavour, fear with self-knowledge. And she did not want Jyoti to evade her growth by non-commitment or vicarious living, but to be acutely aware of contemporary realities and dilemmas . . .

Uma heard the rattle of a loaded tray safely landed, breathed in the aroma of tea, the smell of freshly-warmed milk, and opened her eyes. Jyoti stood quietly by her bed.

Uma looked at her daughter with new eyes, with a sense of being more clear-sighted than ever before. It was as if her body had become a kind of sensitive perceptor, marvellously attuned to what another may be feeling or thinking. So strong was this sensation that she felt quite dizzy with her prescience.

'Your tea, mother.' Jyoti gestured towards the tray on her bedside table. Had she always been so graceful? Her neck and shoulders were boneless, her arms were so long and smooth that one could almost tie knots with them. 'Let me pour it out for you. How are you today?'

Jyoti did not meet her mother's eyes as she picked up the teapot. She was far away somewhere, in a world of her own. It was as if a part of her was always *stored away* in some secret place, and for the first time this thought did not irritate Uma. What did Jyoti dream about, she wondered, every time she allowed a book to slip down on her lap, or when she stood at the window, gazing out at the sea? For always in her eyes and on her skin and hair there lingered a touch of dreams . . .

'I'm much better,' said Uma, 'except that the pain in my left side is still there.' And she noted with astonished distaste that she was bidding for sympathy.

Jyoti's response was quick. 'Oh, but that is just a reflex and it will go away, Dr Marfatia assured me last night.'

She sat down on the bed, cup in hand, and the concern in her eyes made Uma say quickly, 'It's nothing, really. It's almost not there today. Ah, how I look forward to the day when there will be a doctor in the house! How is your work getting on, dear?'

Jyoti's eyes had clouded over and there was a swift masking of pain as she dropped them quickly. 'All right,' she mumbled, averting her face. As the graceful head drooped, in a flash and with unaccustomed clarity Uma saw her daughter as she had stood humbly before her years ago, with bowed head, and a guilty confused face. And out of the past she heard her own voice saying:

'Have you learnt it, or have you not?'

'Yes, mother.'

'Don't mumble! Look up!' said the voice of authority.

'Yes, mother.' To a ten-year-old authority could only mean the equivocal rules, the incomprehensible tensions, the horrible, contingent power of grown-ups to approve or chastise, allow or forbid, give or withhold.

'Then why didn't you know it?'

Silence. As Jyoti stood there, lost, condemned, torn out of her lovely dream world, unworthy of love, feeling her inadequacy as if it were a desperate shame, a paper had fluttered out from between the pages of the *Elementary Physiology* Uma had been waving furiously at her. Jyoti had stooped to pick it up, but Uma had been quicker and pounced on the oblong sheet of paper. It was a water-colour of a bird in flight. The execution was crude, self-taught, but there was a power, a wild, palpitating grace in the outspread wings that Uma had failed to appreciate at that moment.

'So! This is what you've been doing all evening, have you, while you were supposed to learn the skeletal system for the test tomorrow? You cheat hours of school work every day to make stupid blotches on paper! Have you no sense of responsibility? Do I have to sit with you, evening after evening, going through your work? When I was your age, I had none of the opportunities we are affording you . . .'

The voice of authority had churned on and on, critical, damaging, deadly. It made itself dull by repetition. It was maddening. It scraped on the child's nerves like a sharp-toothed saw, but Uma could not stop herself because she felt black with the rage inside. Self-righteousness gave her a flow of power which screamed in her bowels and burnt in her limbs and lent a terrible accuracy of aim to her words. And she suffered victories of anger, victories of untrammelled autonomy as she gave her daughter a little shove towards the desk. It was not a hard shove, but it wounded the little girl. Jyoti had not looked up as she bent obediently over her books.

Why, I brought out the very worst in my lovely little daughter, thought Uma as she gazed at the troubled young woman who sat beside her. She appeared composed enough, but in the back of her mind was there a sense of foundering and confused flight? *I* caused her diffidence and her hesitations, thought Uma, stricken; *I* was behind the lack of assurance, the slowness, because I pushed her around. If today she is like a graceful sketch done by a very light pencil, it is *my* fault. If she confronts people not with joy but with *effort*, I am the cause of it. If she is a timid, conscientious and worrying Jyoti, it is due to *my* disorders, my huge involvement with a woman I had hated, who had triumphed over me because the only child I ever bore turned out to be a girl . . .

'Mother,' Jyoti said suddenly, 'I don't want to go to the hospital any more. I don't want to study medicine. That was your idea, not mine.' The last words she said with the quickness of breath of someone let out of a suffocating enclosure, of someone whose panic is suddenly past.

'Yes.' Uma lay back in bed and closed her eyes. Her reaction amazed her. She felt neither dismay nor anger. Suddenly she was so uninvolved. It was as if her body needed rest to heal itself, and none of its rationed fire could be spared to set light to emotions which would only burn her up. She felt herself relax, as in a warm, salt bath. Had it required days of pain and loneliness of spirit to achieve this liberation? When she opened her eyes again, Jyoti seemed to have changed in some undefinable but crucial way.

'Do you know what you want?' asked Uma gently.

'Yes,' came the unhesitating answer.

Uma felt a moment of real panic. She wants to marry that vain, brittle, self-centred Harish. She wants . . . with an effort she forced herself to say quietly, 'What is it you want?'

'I want to paint!'

Of course, thought Uma tiredly, she wants to paint, I should have known it for years. How could I have been so myopic? She stared at her daughter's face, which was very pale, but which revealed itself now as the finished product of her will, though she still appeared stunned by her own action, stunned partly by the fact of her having acted at all.

'I didn't mean to break it to you like this,' whispered Jyoti.

'Of course you didn't.' Uma raised a hand and let it fall back on the bed.

'Mother,' cried Jyoti in anguish, 'I'm sorry, so sorry to be such a disappointment to you! But this is what I want to do, this is what I must do!'

Uma shook her head and tried to smile, while an agonising, protective tenderness for her daughter welled up in her heart. Her thoughts were in a turmoil, and it seemed to her later that she had passed a vast time in reflection, but now she was exulting, that her daughter was no longer part of someone else's scheme, an expectation in someone else's mind. She wants to paint, shouted a voice in her head. She wants to contribute something of value, she *wants*! How to explain to Jyoti that though she had killed a cherished hope, the sensation was not entirely unsatisfactory? For Jyoti was herself the more increased. She existed more, she had grown vivid. Sitting beside her on the bed, she had quietly broken the whole unbearable situation across her knees. Her Jyoti was a giant.

Uma smiled upon her daughter as she held out her hand for the cup of tea.

A Visit from the Footbinder

Emily Prager

'I shall have the finest burial tomb in China if it's the last thing
I do,' Lady Guo Guo muttered triumphantly to herself. It was
mid-afternoon at the height of the summer, and the Pavilion of
Coolness was dark and still. She tottered over to the scrolls of
snow scenes which lined the walls and meditated on them for
a moment to relieve herself from the heat.

'Sixteen summers in the making, sixteen memorable summers
and finally ready for décor. Oh, how I've waited for this moment. I think blue for the burial chamber overall, or should it
be green? Ah, Pleasure Mouse, do you think blue for Mummy's
burial chamber or green?'

Pleasure Mouse, aged six, second and youngest daughter of
Lady Guo Guo, pondered this as she danced a series of jigs
around her mother. 'Blue would be lovely on you, Mummy,
especially in death. Green, a bit sad and unflattering, I
think.'

'You are so right, Pleasure Mouse. Green reeks of decay.
Such an unerring sense of taste in one so young – I see a fabulous
marriage in your future. In two or three seasons, after Tiger
Mouse has been wed,' Lady Guo Guo looked away. 'Revered
Mummy,' Pleasure Mouse was leaping up and down and tug-
ging at her mother's very long sleeves, 'at what hour will the
footbinder come tomorrow? How long does it take? Can I wear
the little shoes right away? Will I be all grown up then like
Tiger Mouse?'

Lady Guo Guo shuffled quickly toward the teakwood table
on which lay the blueprints of the pavilions erected to date.
Pleasure Mouse ran in front of her and darted and pounced at

her playfully like a performing mongoose at his colleague the performing snake.

As a result of this frolicking, Lady Guo Guo lost her balance and, grabbing on to the edge of the table to steady herself, she snapped angrily, 'No answers, Pleasure Mouse! Because of your immodest behaviour I will give no answers to your indelicate questions. Go now. I am very displeased.'

'Yes, Mummy, I am sorry, Mummy,' said Pleasure Mouse, much chastened, and, after a solemn but ladylike bow, she fled from the Pavilion of Coolness.

Pleasure Mouse raced across the white-hot courtyard, past the evaporating Felicitous Rebirth Fishpond, and into the Red Dust Pavilion, which contained the apartments of her thirteen-year-old sister, Tiger Mouse. Inside, all was light or shadow. There were no shades of grey. The pungent aroma of jasmine sachet hung on the hot, dry air like an insecure woman on the arm of her lover. As usual, Tiger Mouse was kneeling on the gaily tiled floor, dozens of open lacquer boxes spread around her, counting her shoes.

As Pleasure Mouse burst into the chamber, Tiger Mouse glanced up at her and said haughtily, 'I have one thousand pairs of tiny satin shoes. If you don't believe me, you can count them for yourself. Go ahead,' she said with a sweeping gesture, 'count them. Go on!' Wavering slightly, hair ornaments askew, she got to her feet. Then she went on: 'I have the tiniest feet in the prefecture, no longer than newborn kittens. Look. Look!'

Tiger Mouse toddled intently to a corner of the chamber in which stood the charcoal brazier used for heating in winter. Now, of course, it lay unused, iron-cold in the stifling heat. For a moment, she encircled it with her arms and rested her cheek and breast against the cool metal. Then she reached beneath it and amid a chorus of protesting squeaks brought out two newborn kittens, one in each hand, which she then placed beside each of her pointy little feet.

'Come,' she said. 'Look,' and she raised her skirt. Pleasure Mouse ran and squatted down before her. It was true. The newborn kittens, eyes glued shut, ears pasted to the sides of their heads, swam helplessly on the tiled floor, peeping piteously for milk. They were far more lively than Tiger Mouse's feet but certainly no bigger. Pleasure Mouse was terribly impressed.

'It is true what you say, Older Sister, and wonderful. No bigger than newborn kittens – '

'No *longer* than newborn kittens,' Tiger Mouse barked.

'Indeed,' Pleasure Mouse responded in a conciliatory tone and then, by way of a jest to lighten the moment, added, 'Take care the mother cat does not retrieve your feet.' Pleasure Mouse laughed sweetly and ran trippingly alongside Tiger Mouse as the latter, smiling faintly, wavered back to her many shoes and knelt before them.

'Tiger Mouse,' Pleasure Mouse twirled around in embarrassment as she spoke, unsure of the consequences her questions might elicit, 'the footbinder comes tomorrow to bind my feet. Will it hurt? What will they look like afterwards? Please tell me.'

'Toads.'

'What?'

'My feet are like the perfect Golden Lotus. But yours, horned toads. Big, fat ones.'

'Oh, Tiger Mouse –'

'And it didn't hurt me in the least. It only hurts if you're a liar and a cheat or a sorcerer. Unworthy. Spoiled. Discourteous. And don't think that you can try on my shoes after, because you can't. They are mine. All one thousand pairs.'

'Yes, Tiger Mouse.' Pleasure Mouse dashed behind her and snatched up one pair of the tiny shoes and concealed them in the long sleeve of her tunic. 'I must go for my music lesson now, Older Sister,' she said as she hurried toward the chamber door. She opened just short of exiting and turned and bowed. 'Please excuse me.'

'But perhaps,' said Tiger Mouse, ignoring her request, 'the pain is so great that one's sentiments are smashed like egg shells. Perhaps for many seasons, one cries out for death and cries unheeded, pines for it and yearns for it. Why should I tell you what no one told me?'

'Because I'd tell you?' answered Pleasure Mouse. But Tiger

Mouse went back to counting her shoes. The audience was over.

Pleasure Mouse scampered out of the Red Dust Pavilion, past the evaporating Felicitous Rebirth Fishpond, and through the gate into the recently completed Perfect Afterlife Garden. When she reached the Bridge of Piquant Memory, she stopped to catch her breath and watch as her mother's maids watered the ubiquitous jasmine with the liquid of fermented fish in hopes that this might make it last the summer. The stench was overpowering, threatening to sicken, and Pleasure Mouse sped away along the Stream of No Regrets, through the Heavenly Thicket and into the Meadow of One Hundred Orchids, where her friends, the One Hundred Orchid Painters, sat capturing the glory of the blossom for all time.

Aged Fen Wen, the master painter, looked up from his silken scroll and smiled. For sixteen years, he had laboured on Lady Guo Guo's burial tomb, at first in charge of screens and calligraphic scrolls, and now, since they were done, of wall hangings, paintings, window mats, and ivory sculpture. He had watched as Pleasure Mouse grew from a single brushstroke to an intricate design, and though he was but an artisan, he considered himself an uncle to her.

For her part, Pleasure Mouse adored Fen Wen. No matter where the old man was at work on the great estate, no matter how many leagues away, as soon as she awoke in the morning she would run and find him. During the winter when her family returned to the city, she missed him terribly, for although she loved her father, she rarely saw him. With Fen Wen there was no need to observe formalities.

Fen Wen was sitting, as was each of the ninety-nine other Orchid Painters, on an intricately carved three-legged stool before an ebony table on which lay a scroll and brushes. There were one hundred such tables, and in front of each grew a single tree, each one supporting an orchid vine, each vine bearing one perfect blossom. The trees grew in twenty rows of five across, and aged Fen Wen was giving leaf corrections at the southwestern corner of the meadow, where Pleasure Mouse now found him and, without further ado, leapt into his lap.

'Venerable Fen Wen,' she said, as she snuggled into his chest and looked deep into his eyes, 'guess what.'

Fen Wen wrinkled his Buddha-like brow and thought. 'The emperor has opened an acting school in his pear garden?' he said finally.

'No.'

'You have fallen in love with an imitator of animal noises?'

'No, no,' Pleasure Mouse giggled happily.

'I give up,' said Fen Wen, and Pleasure Mouse wiggled out of his lap and skipped in place as she related her news.

'The footbinder is coming tomorrow to bind my feet. And afterwards I shall wear tiny shoes just like these,' she produced the pair she had stolen from Tiger Mouse, waved them before Fen Wen, then concealed them again, 'and I will be all grown up –'

Pleasure Mouse halted abruptly. Fen Wen's great droopy eyes had filled with tears, and the Orchid Painters around him modestly looked away.

'Ah,' he sighed softly. 'Then we won't see you any more.'

'No. What do you mean? Why do you say that?' Pleasure Mouse grabbed on to Fen Wen's tunic and searched deeply into his eyes.

'At first, of course, you will not be able to walk at all, and then later when you have healed, you may make it as far as the front Moon Gate, but, alas, Pleasure Mouse, no farther. Never as far as this Meadow. Never as far. They won't want you to. Once your – '

'Won't be able to walk?' said Pleasure Mouse quizzically. 'What do you mean? Lady Guo Guo walks. Tiger Mouse walks . . .'

Now began a silence as aged Fen Wen and the ninety-nine other Orchid Painters turned glumly toward the east, leaving Pleasure Mouse, age six, second and youngest daughter of Lady Guo Guo, alone and possessed of her first conceptual thought. Past experience joined with present and decocted future. Nuggets of comprehension, like grains of rice in a high wind, swirled behind her eyes, knocked together and blew apart. Only this softly spoken phrase was heard on earth.

'They cannot run,' she said, 'but I can.' And she ran, through the Meadow of One Hundred Orchids, down the Path of Granted Wishes, and out of the Sun Gate into the surrounding countryside.

Just outside the market town of Catchow, a mile or so down the Dragon Way near the vast estate of the prefect Lord Guo Guo, lay situated the prosperous Five Enjoyments Tea House. On this spot one afternoon in the tenth century, three hundred years before the tea house was built and our story began, a Taoist priest and a Buddhist nun were strolling together and came upon a beggar. Filthy and poor, he lay by the side of the road and called out to them. 'Come over here. I am dying. I have only this legacy to leave.' The beggar was waving something and the Taoist priest and the Buddhist nun moved closer to see what it was.

'Look,' said the beggar, 'it is a piece of the very silk with which the emperor bade a dancing girl swaddle her feet that they might look like points of the moon sickle. She then danced in the centre of a six-foot lotus fashioned out of gold and decorated with jewels.' The beggar fell backward, exhausted by his tale, and gasped for breath. The Taoist priest and the Buddhist nun examined the dirty, bloody, ragged scrap of cloth and glanced at each other with great scepticism.

'Ah yes. It is an interesting way to step from Existence into Nonexistence, is it not?' said the Buddhist nun.

'Indeed,' replied the Taoist priest. 'So much easier to escape Desire and sidle closer to Immortality when one can follow only a very few paths. But alas, in time, this too will pass.'

There was a rattle in the beggar's throat then, and his eyes rolled upward and grasping the scrap of silk, he died.

The Taoist priest and the Buddhist nun murmured some words of prayer over the beggar's body, linked arms and con-tinued their travels. The ragged scrap of bloody cloth fluttered to the ground and was transformed by the Goddess of Resig-nation into a precious stone that lay at that very spot until the year 1266, when it was discovered and made into a ring by the famous courtesan Honey Tongue, star attraction of The Five

Enjoyments Tea House, which had been built nearby some years before.

Pleasure Mouse, taking extreme care not to be seen, scrambled up the back stairs of The Five Enjoyments Tea House and sneaked into the luxurious apartments of her father's good friend, the famous courtesan, Honey Tongue. She startled the beauteous lady as she sat before her mirror tinting her nails with pink balsam leaves crushed in alum. 'Oh!' exclaimed Honey Tongue. 'Why, it's Pleasure Mouse, isn't it? Sit down, little one, you're out of breath. What brings you here?'

Pleasure Mouse collapsed on a brocade cushion and burst into tears. The beauteous lady floated to her side and hugged her warmly to her perfumed breast. 'Oh dear,' crooned Honey Tongue, rocking back and forth, 'oh dear oh dear oh dear,' until finally Pleasure Mouse was able to speak: 'Tomorrow, the footbinder comes to bind my feet and – '

Honey Tongue brought her hands to her mouth and laughed behind them. She rose from Pleasure Mouse's cushion and, still laughing, wafted back to her seat before her mirror. She fiddled for a moment with her hair ornaments and began to apply the stark white Buddha adornment to her face and afterward the deep-rose blush.

As all this seemed to contain great meaning, Pleasure Mouse ceased speaking and ran to her side, watching in the mirror everything the lovely lady did. When she was done plucking her eyebrows and smoothing on the final drop of hair oil, she smiled the loveliest of sunny smiles and said, 'It's a bargain, Pleasure Mouse. The pain goes away after two years, and then you have a weapon you never dreamed of. Now, run along home before someone sees you here.'

Pleasure Mouse did as she was told, but as she was speeding along the Dragon Way, trying to reach the eastern Sun Gate of the estate before she was seen, she had the bad fortune to run smack into the sedan chair procession of her father's older sister, Lao Bing. Her old auntie had come all the way from the city for the footbinding, and when she peered out of the window of her sedan chair and saw Pleasure Mouse, she bellowed in an imperious tone, 'Halt!'

The bearers halted abruptly and set the sedan chair down in the middle of the Dragon Way. An enormous donkey cart, that of the night-soil collector, which had been following a few lengths behind the procession, now was forced to halt also, and a vicious verbal battle ensued between the chair bearers and the night-soil collector and his men as to who had the right of way. Lao Bing paid no attention to this mêlée. She opened the door of the sedan chair and cried out, 'All right, Pleasure Mouse, I see you. Come over here this minute.'

Pleasure Mouse ran to the sedan chair and scampered inside. As she closed the door, Lao Bing bellowed, 'Drive on!' and the bearers stopped quarrelling with the collector, hoisted the sedan chair poles onto their knobby-muscled shoulders and continued in a silent run to the estate.

The sedan chair rocked like a rowboat on a storm-tossed sea. Pleasure Mouse began to feel queasy inside the dark box. The odour of Lao Bing's hair oil permeated the heavy brocades, and the atmosphere was cloying. The old one's hair ornaments jiggled in emphasis as she spoke.

'Really, Pleasure Mouse, young maidens of good family are not allowed outdoors much less outside the estate grounds. Oh, if your father knew I had found you on the Dragon Way . . .'

'Dearest Auntie,' entreated Pleasure Mouse, 'please don't tell. I only thought since the footbinder is coming tomorrow and I'll no longer be able to –'

'Footbinder?' Lao Bing seemed perturbed. 'What footbinder? You don't mean to tell me your mother has *hired* a footbinder for tomorrow?' Pleasure Mouse nodded.

'Really, that woman spends like a spoiled concubine!' Lao Bing peeked through the curtain on the window and sighed in resignation. 'All right, Pleasure Mouse, we are inside the Sun Gate now. You may get down. Halt!' The bearers halted and Lao Bing opened the door.

'Auntie?' Pleasure Mouse hesitated before the door. 'What is it like?'

Lao Bing mulled the question over for a moment and then replied briskly, 'It is something a woman must endure in order to make a good marriage. No more. No less, Pleasure Mouse.

If you wish to live at court, you must have tiny feet. Logic, indubitable logic.'

'And does it hurt, Lao Bing?' Pleasure Mouse gazed stoically into her aunt's eyes and prepared herself for the reply. The old lady never minced words.

'Beauty is the stillbirth of suffering, every woman knows that. Now scamper away, little mouse, and dream your girlish dreams, for tomorrow you will learn some secret things that will make you feel old.'

Lao Bing closed the door of the sedan chair and gave the order: 'Drive on!' Pleasure Mouse circled the Meadow of One Hundred Orchids, traversed The Heavenly Thicket, and made her way to the recently constructed Avenue of Lifelong Misconceptions, where she passed the afternoon contemplating her future footsize.

Lady Guo Guo was receiving in her burial chamber. It was bleak in the dense stone edifice, dim, musty and airless, but it was cool and the flaming torches affixed to the walls gave off a flickering, dangerous light. A party of silk weavers from Shantung milled nervously in one corner while their agent haggled with Lady Guo Guo over the quantity of mouse-vein-blue silk. In another corner, the head caterer waited to discuss the banquet of the dead and dodged attempts by a group of nosy flower arrangers to guess the menu. There were poetry chanters, trainers of performing insects, literary men – throngs of humanity of every occupation crammed into the burial chamber and its anteroom, hoping to be hired for a day's labour. And many had been. And many were. One local gluemaker had quite literally made his fortune off Lady Guo Guo in the last sixteen years. He had retired early, well-fed and happy. And he was but one among many.

It was through this teeming mass of gilders, cutlers, jugglers, sackmakers, pork butchers and pawnshop owners, that Lao Bing now made her way preceded by three servants who, rather noisily and brutishly, made a path. Lady Guo Guo, distracted by the commotion, looked up from her bargaining, recognised her sister-in-law, and hurried to greet her.

'Welcome, venerable husband's sister, to my recently completed burial chamber. Majestic, is it not? I shall enter the afterlife like a princess wearing a gown of,' Lady Guo Guo snapped the bolt of silk and it unrolled like a snake across the cold stone floor, 'this blue silk. My colour, I think you'll admit. Thank goodness you have come with all your years of wisdom behind you,' Lao Bing sniffed audibly, 'for I need your advice, Lao Bing. Do we do the wall hangings in the blue with a border in a green of new apples or a green of old lizards who have recently sluffed their skin? Question two: Who shall do my death mask and who my ancestor portrait? Should the same man do both?'

'Old lizards and different men,' said Lao Bing decisively, and tottered over to a sandalwood stool and sat on it. 'Little Sister,' she began, a note of warning in her voice, 'these days the Lord, your husband, reminds me of a thunderclap in clothes. Day and night the creditors camp outside the door of the prefecture. He asks why you do not use the rents from the rooming houses you inherited from your father to pay these merchants?'

'What? And deplete my family's coffers? The lord, my husband, is as tight with cash as the strings on a courtesan's purse, Lao Bing, and no tighter. Do not deceive yourself.'

'Well, really,' said Lao Bing, her sensibilities offended, and her message delivered, abruptly changed the subject. 'They say that the fallow deer sold in the market is actually donkey flesh. It's a dreadful scandal. The city is buzzing with it. And as if that weren't enough –' Lao Bing lowered her voice, rose from her seat, and ushered Lady Guo Guo away from the throngs and down into the depression in the vast stone floor where her coffin would eventually lie. 'As if that weren't enough,' Lao Bing continued, sotto voce, 'the emperor is using his concubines to hunt rabbits.'

Lady Guo Guo was horror-struck. 'What? Instead of dogs?'

Lao Bing nodded solemnly.

'But they cannot run.'

'Ah, well, that's the amusement in it, don't you see? They cannot possibly keep up with the horses. They stumble and fall – '

Lady Guo Guo swayed from side to side. 'No more please. I feel faint.'

'You are too delicate, younger brother's wife.'

'For this world but not for the next.' Lady Guo Guo patted the lip of the depression to emphasise her point.

'Hmm, yes,' said Lao Bing, 'if it is up to you. All of which brings me to the subject of tomorrow's footbinding. Pleasure Mouse tells me you've *hired* a footbinder.'

'Really, Lao Bing, expense is no object when my daughter's feet —'

'I have no concern with the expense, Little Sister. It is simply that the Guo Guo women have been binding their daughters' feet themselves for centuries. To pay an outsider to perform such an intimate, such a traditional, such an honourable and serious act is an outrage, a travesty, a shirking of responsibility, unlucky, too arrogant and a dreadful loss of face.'

'Lao Bing.' Lady Guo Guo climbed out of the depression with the help of a sackmaker who hurried over to ingratiate himself. 'You are like an old donkey on the Dragon Way, unable to forge a new path, stubbornly treading the muddy ruts of the previous donkey and cart. This footbinder is a specialist, an artist, renowned throughout the district. And what is more important in this mortal world, I'm sure you'll agree, is not who does or does not do the binding, but the size of Pleasure Mouse's feet once it's done.'

Lao Bing clapped her hands, and her servants appeared by her side, hoisted her out of the depression and set her down once again on the cold stone floor. Her hair ornaments spun with the impact. 'Very well,' she said after some moments of icy reflection. 'But let us hope that with your modern ways you have not offended any household spirits.'

A breeze of fear gusted across Lady Guo Guo's features. 'I am not a fool, Lao Bing,' she said quietly. 'In the last few days I have burned enough incense to propitiate the entire netherworld. I have begged the blessing of ancestors so long departed they failed to recognise our family name and had to be reminded. The geomancer claimed he had never seen anything like it — before he collapsed from exhaustion.'

'And he is sure about tomorrow?' Lao Bing asked, and then regretted it.

'Really, Lao Bing.' Lady Guo Guo turned on a tiny heel and scurried back to her bargaining table. With a snap of her fingers, she summoned two maids and instructed them to show Lao Bing to her apartments in the Red Dust Pavilion. The old lady, suddenly fatigued by her journey, waddled slowly over to her sister-in-law's side and said gently, 'Forgive me, Little Sister. It is a festival fraught with sentiments, worse this time perhaps because it is my perky Pleasure Mouse.'

But Lady Guo Guo had returned to her business. 'I'll take the green of old lizards,' she was saying to the silk weavers' agent, 'at three cash per yard and not a penny more.' Haggling began anew and echoed off the great stone walls. Lao Bing departed, preceded by her servants, who elbowed her way into the crowd, which parted for a moment to admit her and then closed behind her again. Just like, thought Lady Guo Guo, a python who swallows whole its prey.

In the hot, dry centre of the oven-baked night, Pleasure Mouse tossed and turned and glowed with tiny drops of baby sweat. Ordinarily, the nightly strumming of the zither players out in the courtyard would have long since lulled her to sleep, but not this night. She was far too excited.

She sat up on her lacquered bed, crossed her legs, and removed from beneath her pillow, the tiny pair of shoes she had stolen from her sister. She stroked them for a moment, deep red satin with sky-blue birds and lime-green buds embroidered over all, and then placed them on the coverlet in the strongest of rays of blue moonlight.

'How sweet,' she murmured to herself, 'how beauteous. Soon I will embroider some for myself and I will choose . . . cats and owls. So tiny, I do not see how –'

And she glanced around to make sure she was alone and unseen, and stealthily picked up one shoe and tried to slip it on her foot. But it would not fit, in any way whatsoever. Most of her toes, her heel and half of her foot spilled over the sides. She was very disappointed. 'Perhaps my feet are already too big,' she sighed aloud, and might have tried once more like panicked birds who fly into the window mat and though they've gained no exit, fly again, but just then the jagged sound of breaking glass shattered her reverie, and up she sprang and hid the tiny shoes beneath her pillow.

'Who goes there?' she cried, and ran to the door of her chamber.

'Oh, great heavens, Pleasure Mouse, it's I,' came the whispered reply, and Pleasure Mouse sighed with relief and slipped into the corridor. There, crisscrossed by moonlight, on her knees before a broken vial, her father's concubine, Warm Milk, aged nineteen and great with child for lo these six long moons, looked up at her and wept. 'Oh, Pleasure Mouse,' she managed through her tears, 'I've ruined the decoction. I'll never get more dog flies now in time, or earthworms, for that matter. It took weeks to collect the ingredients and I've dropped them. It's my legs. They're swollen like dead horses in the mud. And as for my feet, well, they're no longer of this earth, Pleasure Mouse.' Warm Milk rolled off her knees and sat squarely on the floor, her eyes tightly shut and soft moans of agony escaping her lips as she stretched her legs out in front of her. Pleasure Mouse stared at her opulent stomach, which looked like a giant peach protruding through Warm Milk's bedclothes and wondered what creature was inside. Warm Milk bent over and began to massage her legs. Her tiny white-bandaged feet stuck out beyond the hem of her nightgown like standards of surrender at a miniature battle. 'They cannot bear the weight of two, Pleasure Mouse, but never say I said so. Promise?'

Pleasure Mouse nodded solemnly. 'Promise,' she replied, and examined Warm Milk's feet out of the corner of her eyes.

'They stink, Pleasure Mouse, that's the worst of it, like a pork butcher's hands at the end of a market day. It frightens me, Pleasure Mouse, but never say I said so. Promise?'

Pleasure Mouse nodded furiously. She would have liked to speak but when she tried, no voice was forthcoming. Her little girl's body had begun to contract with a terrible heat and in the pit of her stomach, feelings cavorted like the boxers she had heard of at the pleasure grounds.

Warm Milk leaned back on her hands and was silent for a moment. Her waist-length blue-black hair fell about her swollen little body and gleamed in the moonlight. Her flat, round face was blue-white, as pale and ghostlike as pure white jade. So too her hands.

'I was going to the shrine of the Moon Goddess to beg her for a boy. The decoction,' she sat up and gestured at the oozy pink puddle that was beginning to travel along the corridor floor, 'was to drink during the supplication. They say it always works, a male child is assured. Perhaps –' Warm Milk cupped her hands in the pink slime and brought it to her lips.

'No,' cried Pleasure Mouse, horrified at such intimacy with dirt. 'Please don't. You will be sick. Tomorrow I will run and find you many spiders and new dog flies too!' Warm Milk smiled gratefully at the little girl. 'Will you, Pleasure Mouse?' she asked. And Pleasure Mouse remembered.

'Oh, no, I can't,' she cried, blushing deeply. Her slanted eyes welled up with tears like tiny diamonds in the blue moonlight. 'Tomorrow, the footbinder comes to bind my feet and –'

'You shan't be running anywhere.' Warm Milk sighed resignedly and sucked the liquid from the palms of her hands. 'What bad fortune, Pleasure Mouse, for us both, as it turns out. For us both. But never say I said so.'

'Where are your toes?' Pleasure Mouse asked suddenly and without advance thought. It was just that she had glanced at Warm Milk's feet and finally realised what was different about them.

'My what?' asked Warm Milk nervously.

'Your toes.' Pleasure Mouse squatted down before the bandaged feet and pointed a tiny finger at them. 'I have five toes. You have one. Did they cut the others off?' Her eyes were wide with terror.

'No.' Warm Milk pulled her nightgown over her feet. 'No, of course not.'

'Well, what happened to them?' Pleasure Mouse looked directly into Warm Milk's kind black eyes and awaited an answer.

Warm Milk dropped her head and basked for a moment in the blue moonlight. Out in the courtyard, the zither players were at their height, their instruments warm and responsive, their male hearts carried away by the loveliness of the tune. At length, Warm Milk spoke.

'When I was but five seasons old, the elegance of my carriage and the delicacy of my stature were already known far and wide. And so my mother, on the counsel of my father, bound my feet, which was an unusual occurrence for a maid of my then lowly peasant status. I could not run. I could not play. The other girls made mockery of my condition. But when I was ten, your father spied my little shrew-nosed feet and bought me from my father for his honourable concubine. Beneath your venerable father's wing I have nestled healthfully and prosperously for many seasons but never so happily as when I see, from the heights of my sedan chair, my big-footed playmates now turned flower-drum girls hawking their wanton wares by the river's edge.'

Warm Milk laughed modestly. 'Do you understand me, Pleasure Mouse?' Pleasure Mouse nodded, but she wasn't sure. 'Yes, Honourable Concubine, but about your toes, where –' She began again but was interrupted by the appearance of six horrified maids who should have been on duty throughout the pavilion but who, because of the closeness of the evening, had ventured into the courtyard to watch the zither players, and had quite forgotten their charges in the romance of the moonlight and song.

The corridor rang with noises of reproach and then, like ants with a cake crumb, four of the maids quickly lifted up the concubine Warm Milk and bore her away to her apartments. The remaining two hurried Pleasure Mouse into her chamber and into her bed.

'I want my dolly,' said Pleasure Mouse mournfully, and the maid brought it to her. The big rag doll, fashioned for her by aged Fen Wen, with the lovely hand-painted face of the Moon Goddess, black hair of spun silk, and masterfully embroidered robes, came to her anxious mistress with open arms. Pleasure Mouse hugged her close and sniffed deeply at her silken hair. Then she slid her hand under the pillow, pulled out the tiny shoes and slipped them on the dolly's rag feet. After a bit of stuffing and pushing, the shoes fitted perfectly. And Spring Rain, for that was the dolly's name, looked so lady-like and harmonious of spirit in the tiny shoes, that Pleasure Mouse forgot her fears and soon was sound asleep.

The footbinder was late. Already it was two hours past cock-crow, and the courtyard outside the Temple of Two Thousand Ancestors was buzzing with anticipation and excitement. The man with the performing fish had arrived early and so was understandably perturbed about the wait. So too the tellers of obscene stories and the kiteflyer. Had it been another season, they might have chatted away the time, but it was mid-summer and as the hours dragged by, the day grew hotter and the energy for physical performance ebbed slowly away. The zither players were doing their best to keep up spirits, strumming at first soothingly and then rousingly in celebration of the occasion. Hands holding fans wafted back and forth in tempo to the music, pausing only to pluck cloying hair and clothing from damp and heated skin.

Inside the dark, hot temple, Lady Guo Guo stamped her tiny foot. The din from the courtyard resounded through the walls, and she was dreadfully embarrassed before her ancestors. The geomancer, a thin, effeminate young man, shook his head and wrists.

'The propitious hour is upon us, Lady. After it passes, I cannot be responsible for the consequences.'

Lao Bing, suffering mightily from the heat and certainly tired of waiting, concurred, 'Really, Little Sister, we must get on with it. This is exactly what happens when you pay an outsider — oh!' Lao Bing, frustrated beyond words, ceased speaking and fanned herself wildly.

Before the altar, Pleasure Mouse sat on a stool with her feet soaking in a broth of monkey bones. She stared up at the portraits of her most recently departed ancestors, solemn in the yellow light of the prayer candles. Occasionally, her eyes travelled about the walls of the great chamber and met those of hundreds of other ancestors whom she had never known in life and of whom she had never heard.

Just after cockcrow, she had entered the temple and with the female members of her family, she had prayed to the Little-Footed Miss for the plumpest and softest and finest of Lotus Hooks. You could, Lao Bing informed her, end up with either Long Hairpins, Buddha's Heads or Red Cocoons. It all depended on the expertise of the binding, the favour of the ancestral and household spirits, and the propitiousness of the hour at which the feet were bound. The broth of monkey bones was to soften her feet, to make them malleable enough to fit into the tiny pair of red satin boots that her mother had made for her and which now sat upon the altar like an offering to the gods.

'I have paid for the footbinder, and I shall have one!' snarled Lady Guo Guo, and followed by her maids, she lurched angrily from the temple.

The sunlight caught her unawares. It struck her like the projectile of a crossbow, and she was momentarily blinded and confused. She and her small procession immediately snapped open their fans, shielded their eyes from above and held this pose, unmoving, like an operatic tableau. Those in the courtyard pushed forward and back, chattering among themselves, eagerly awaiting instructions. The zither players struck up Lady Guo Guo's favourite tune, and as her eyes adjusted to the light, she dimly perceived members of the crowd being shoved to and fro and finally propelled to one side to permit the entrance of, she focused her eyes sharply to make sure, her husband and master, the prefect, Lord Guo Guo.

Lady Guo Guo bowed as did the entire crowd and said, 'Welcome, my lord, an unexpected pleasure. I had no idea you were in the neighbourhood. You are stopping at The Five Enjoyments Tea House, I presume?'

'Ah, if only I could afford to,' he replied pointedly. 'But alas, I'm just passing through on a visit to the sub-prefect.'

'Let us climb the belvedere,' began Lady Guo Guo nervously, 'for there we can speak in private.' She hurried toward the turret, which was hard by the temple. 'I call it Hereafter-View, for its beauty is quite suffocating.' Lord Guo Guo followed and then stopped, carefully examining the stones at the belvedere's base.

'What stone is this?' he asked. His copyist followed, taking notes.

'Marble,' Lady Guo Guo answered nonchalantly as if he ought to know.

'From?'

'From . . .' Lady Guo Guo concentrated intently. 'From, from, from – forgive me, husband, I have forgotten the name. I am overwrought. Your arrival has coincided with Pleasure Mouse's footbinding. The propitious hour is upon us; I cannot –'

'Perhaps I can help you remember. It is a Chinese name?'

'No,' snapped the Lady, and fled into the belvedere and up the winding marble steps. The Lord followed.

'No? Not a Chinese name, then presumably not from China. Imported then. Let me think. Annam? Champa?'

Lady Guo Guo disappeared beyond the next turn in the stairs. The Lord stayed behind.

'What?' he cried out. 'Not even from the East? How luxurious! From the West, then. Ah, I know! Egypt!' Lord Guo Guo removed a knife from his sash and proceeded to carve a message into the marble wall. The knife scraped unpleasantly against the stone, and curious as to the noise, Lady Guo Guo reappeared around the bend. The message read: 'Paid for by the prefect, Lord Guo Guo,' and the date, '1260'. The Lady gasped. 'How dare you deface my belvedere?' she demanded.

'How dare you use my wealth to make the merchants rich? Pretty soon there will be no aristocracy left. At the rate you are spending, I shall be the first to go.' Lord Guo Guo put away his knife.

'If you are so fearful, why do you not impose excessive taxes or put a ceiling on prices as you did last year when you bought yourself your title? As it is, I must purchase everything from the shops you own under a fraudulent name, and shoddy merchandise it is too! This marble was my one extravagance –'

'No more credit,' Lord Guo Guo said simply, and Lady Guo Guo sank to her knees and sobbed.

'You men are so cruel,' she cried, her tears dropping to the marble step. 'Building this tomb is my one last pleasure, and you will take it from me just as you took from me my ability to walk. Well, let me tell you, you may cripple me in this endeavour, but you will never stop me.'

'Men took from you your ability to walk?' the Lord said incredulously. 'Is it the man who pulls the binding cloth to cripple a daughter's feet? No man could do a thing like that. No man could bear it.'

'No man would marry a natural-footed woman. There is more to binding feet than just the binding!'

'If all women were natural-footed, a man would have no choice,' Lord Guo Guo concluded and began descending the stairs.

Lady Guo Guo shook with fury and called after him. 'Shall I leave your daughter natural-footed then? Yes. Yes. You are quite right and logical. Let our family be the one to begin the new fashion, and we shall begin it with the perky Pleasure Mouse!' In her anger, the Lady called out theatrically to her maid, 'Wild Mint! Tell the footbinder to go away; we shall not need her.'

'The footbinder?' asked Lord Guo Guo quietly. 'Then you will not do the binding yourself?'

'Shall the prefect Lord Guo Guo's daughter be natural-footed? Your choice, my lord.'

'So.' The Lord grinned. 'You've hired another to do the job for you? An interesting twist.'

'Natural feet or lotus hooks? Be quick, my husband, the propitious hour is passing and will not come again for a full twelve seasons of growth.'

Lord Guo Guo grew impatient at this last and turned his back. 'These are women's things, your affairs, wife, not mine,' he muttered sullenly.

Lady Guo Guo tapped her tiny foot. 'What if I were to fall ill, creating a disturbance, right this moment and allow the propitious hour to pass?'

'I wouldn't let you,' Lord Guo Guo snarled.

'You could not prevent me. It is a women's ritual, my husband, and as such, depends on the good omen. A mother's falling ill during a ceremony at which no man can show his face, even a father, especially a father –'

'Would you harm your daughter to harm me? What is it you seek, wife?'

'Unlimited credit, sir. Decide quickly; there is little time left.'

Lord Guo Guo's nostrils flared. 'You have it, ma'am' were the words that he spat out as, robes flying, he hurled through the belvedere door. Lady Guo Guo smiled to herself and followed quickly behind.

'Here, wife.' The Lord spoke through gritted teeth and thrust a walking stick into the Lady's arms. 'An ebony cane. Also imported like your marble from Africa. For the Pleasure Mouse, for after.'

'Thank you, my lord,' said Lady Guo Guo, bowing low, 'and a good journey, sir. Please come again.' And with that she was off, hobbling swiftly toward the temple courtyard before Wild Mint could send the footbinder away.

Pleasure Mouse looked around nervously at Lao Bing and the geomancer, who were whispering together.

'Well,' sniffed Lao Bing, 'if it comes to it, I'll do it myself then. I bound three daughters of my own with perfect success. Autumn Surprise won the Emperor's commendation for the most beauteous hooks at the Hu Street small foot contest. Now she's his concubine-in-waiting, if you don't mind.'

'Exquisite,' said the geomancer in his whiny voice. 'But did you hear about the Sung sisters?'

'What?'

'Rivals for the same young man, Black Mist cut up all of Blue Jade's tiny shoes and heaped them in the courtyard for all to see!'

'No!'

'Yes. And speaking of concubines-in-waiting, I hear the Emperor often keeps them waiting for years, and in the harems with only each other for company, I hear they use each other's hooks for –'

'The footbinder has arrived,' announced Lady Guo Guo as she entered the chamber. 'Let us begin.'

Lao Bing sent the geomancer a parting glance of daggers. 'Leave us,' she hissed and then turned to inspect the famous footbinder.

'Forgive me, everyone,' the footbinder waved heartily at those assembled as she strode into the temple. 'The youngest daughter of the Wang family persists in unbinding on the sly. Each time she does this I tell her I shall only have to pull the bindings tighter. After all, we have two reputations to think of, hers and mine. But you can't tell a child about Lotus Boats, as you all know. They never believe it can happen to them.'

Lao Bing, Lady Guo Guo, and the various maidservants in the chamber nodded in understanding.

'Children think we are born with small feet,' began Lao Bing.

'Oh, if only we were,' sighed Lady Guo Guo, interrupting.

Lao Bing continued. 'But once in Shensi Province, I saw a natural-footed peasant girl, well, you talk of Lotus Boats, but really Fox Paws would be more accurate. Feet as large as a catapult repairman's.'

Pleasure Mouse twisted around and stared at the footbinder. Barely four feet high and as round as a carved ivory ball, the tiny woman removed her pointy-hooded homespun cloak and revealed herself to be a Buddhist nun. Shaved head and eyebrows, saffron robes, face unadorned by powder or blush, the little fat turnip of a woman bent down and picked up her basket and hurried toward the altar.

Lao Bing gasped in horror and took Lady Guo Guo roughly to one side. 'What is the meaning of this? She's not wearing shoes! She's barefooted and natural-footed. I've never been so embarrassed, and what about Pleasure Mouse? I –'

'Shh!' Lady Guo Guo took Lao Bing's hands and tried to explain. 'Not having bound feet herself, she is better able to make a really good job of binding others. It is an aesthetic act to her, objective, don't you see? For us it is so much more, so clouded. Our sympathy overcomes our good judgement. Pleasure Mouse's feet will be as hummingbirds, you'll see.'

'All right,' sniffed Lao Bing. 'I suppose it makes some sense.

But my aunt did my bindings, and merciless she was.' Lao Bing's voice had risen as she remembered. 'I have always felt that had it been my own mama, some sympathy might have been shown for my agony.'

'Perhaps,' called the footbinder from across the room. 'Perhaps not.'

'At any rate,' Lao Bing, outraged at the interruption, went on, 'I blame such newfangled notions on the barbarians from the North, the Mongol hordes. I pray such contaminate influences do not sully my perky Pleasure Mouse. But if they do, I personally —'

'Silence, please,' boomed the footbinder. And then, 'Send away the throngs outside the temple!'

'No kiteflyer?' asked Lady Guo Guo timidly. 'But we have always had a kiteflyer for before. It is the last time —'

'No. No. The feet swell from the running and it is far too difficult. As for the teller of obscene stories, he was present when I bound the Wang girls and, sadly, he is simply neither obscene nor funny.'

'He seemed amply disgusting to me,' mused Lady Guo Guo as she padded toward the chamber door.

'Yes, foul,' agreed Lao Bing.

'Wild Mint.' Lady Guo Guo's number one maidservant rushed foward and curtsied. 'Clear the courtyard.'

'But the man with the performing fish?'

'Keep him on retainer. Perhaps for the inaugural ceremonies.'

Wild Mint nodded and rushed out. Some angry murmurs rose and fell, but soon there was bright, hot quiet outside, disturbed now and then only by the buzz of insects. Wild Mint re-entered the chamber and took up her post behind a red-lacquered pillar.

'Where is Tiger Mouse?' Lao Bing was whispering to Lady Guo Guo.

'I am afraid she is still too delicate to attend the ritual. She cannot as yet see the humour in it.' Lady Guo Guo placed her finger across her lips to command silence then and turned her attention to what the footbinder was doing.

'What are you doing?' Pleasure Mouse was asking.

The footbinder trained her beady eyes on the child and answered directly, 'I am tying you to the chair with leather thongs.' She finished securing the last arm and leg and paused to examine her handiwork.

'Why?' asked Pleasure Mouse, pulling a bit against the bonds.

'It hurts, Pleasure Mouse, and if you writhe all over the place you will interfere with perfection of the binding. Now here, grasp these water chestnuts in each hand and when it hurts, squeeze them with all your might and if you are lucky, your feet will turn out no bigger than they are.'

Pleasure Mouse took the water chestnuts and squeezed them in her palms. The footbinder scurried around in front of the altar, head bent to her task and mumbling to herself.

'Here's a handkerchief to wipe the tears. Here's my knife. The binding cloth. Alum. Red jasmine powder. All right. I think we are all ready. Is it the propitious hour?' The footbinder glanced at Lady Guo Guo, who nodded and came forward to one side of Pleasure Mouse's chair. She patted the little girl on the shoulder and smiled weakly. Lao Bing came forward as well and stood on the opposite side. 'If we begin just at the propitious hour, it won't hurt,' the old lady said without much conviction.

Warm Milk entered at this moment by the side door of the temple and sat without comment next to Lao Bing on a stool carried in by her maidservants. Warm Milk did not look well, so swollen was she with womanly waters pressurised by the heat. But she smiled at Pleasure Mouse and waved one of her long, long sleeves.

The footbinder took up the knife and knelt down in front of the chair and concentrated on the broth of monkey bones and Pleasure Mouse's feet. She draped a towel over her knees and picked up one foot and dried it. She then took the knife and brought it toward Pleasure Mouse's toes. The little girl shrieked with terror and fought against her bonds. Her mother and her aunt held her down and tried to placate her. Warm Milk stood up hurriedly and cried out.

'Do not be afraid, Pleasure Mouse. She means only to cut your toenails. Truly, little one, truly.'

Pleasure Mouse relaxed and tears ran down her face and on

to the new silk robe that her mother had embroidered just for this occasion. The footbinder grabbed Pleasure Mouse's handkerchief, dabbed her cheeks and proceeded to cut her toenails.

'Now, what are the rules that all ladies must obey? Let me hear them while I cut.'

Pleasure Mouse recited in a clear, sad voice:

Do not walk with toes pointed upwards.
Do not stand with heels in mid-air.
Do not move skirt when sitting.
Do not move feet when lying down.
Do not remove the binding for there is
nothing aesthetic beneath it.

'And because, once bound, a foot does not feel well unbound. Excellent, Pleasure Mouse,' said the footbinder setting down her knife and rubbing the child's feet with alum. 'I can see that once your hooks are formed, you will be quite a little temptress.' The footbinder winked lewdly at Lao Bing and Lady Guo Guo. 'I predict buttocks like giant pitted plums, thighs like sacks of uncombed wool, a vagina with more folds than a go-between's message, and a nature as subdued as a eunuch's desire.'

The women in the temple tittered modestly, and Pleasure Mouse blushed and squirmed beneath the bonds.

Suddenly, Pleasure Mouse became mesmerised by a beauteous ring on the right index finger of the footbinder's dimpled hand. It flashed in the light of the prayer candles, and as the footbinder laid out the silk binding cloths, it created, in mid-air, a miniature fireworks display.

'What a splendid ring,' murmured Pleasure Mouse.

'What ring, dear?' asked Lady Guo Guo.

'That one, there – ' Pleasure Mouse indicated the footbinder's right hand with a bob of her head, but the ring had gone, vanished.

'Never mind,' said Pleasure Mouse, and squeezed the chestnuts in her tiny hands.

The footbinder took hold of the child's right foot and, leaving the big toe free, bent the other toes beneath the foot and bound them down with the long, silk cloth. The women gathered around the chair and watched the process intently. She then took a second cloth and bound, as tightly as she could, around the heel of the foot and down, again over and around the now bent toes, with the result that the heel and the toes were brought as close together as they could go, and the arch of the foot was forced upward in the knowledge that eventually it would break, restructure itself and foreshorten the foot. The last binding was applied beneath the big toe and around the heel, pushing the appendage up and inward like the point of a moon sickle. When the right foot was done, the footbinder bound the left foot in the same manner, removed the basin of monkey bone broth and retrieved the tiny shoes from the altar. She knelt before the Pleasure Mouse and, as she forced her bound feet into the shoes, Lady Guo Guo intoned a prayer: 'Oh, venerable ancestors, smile favourably upon my perky Pleasure Mouse, that she may marry well and one day see her own daughter's entry into womanhood. Take the first step, my child. Take the first step.'

Lady Guo Guo, Lao Bing and the footbinder untied the leather thongs and released Pleasure Mouse's arms and legs. Pleasure Mouse was silent and rigid in the chair.

'Up, dear,' said Lao Bing, taking the child's elbow. 'Up, you must walk.'

'Take the first step,' said Lady Guo Guo, grasping the other elbow.

'Up, child,' said the footbinder, and she stood Pleasure Mouse on her newly fashioned feet.

Pleasure Mouse screamed. She looked down at the tiny shoes and on her now strangely shaped feet and she screamed again. She jerked toward her mother and screamed a third time and tried to throw herself to the ground. The women held her up. 'Walk,' they chanted all together, 'you must walk or you will sicken. The pain goes away in time.'

'In about two years' time,' crooned the courtesan, Honey Tongue. She had suddenly appeared in place of the footbinder who seemed to have vanished.

'Walk, little one, no matter how painful,' Lao Bing grabbed the flailing child and shook her by the shoulders. 'We have all been through it, can't you see that? You must trust us. Now walk!'

The women stepped back, and Pleasure Mouse hobbled two or three steps. Waves of agony as sharp as stiletto blades traversed the six-year-old's legs and thighs, her spine and head. She bent over like an aged crone and staggered around, not fully comprehending why she was being forced to crush her own toes with her own body weight.

Pleasure Mouse lunged toward the apparition and fell on the altar, sobbing and coughing. Honey Tongue enveloped her in a warm and perfumed aura.

'Do you wish to stay on earth, or do you wish to come with me?' Honey Tongue waved her long, long sleeve, and for a moment all was still. The women froze in their positions. Time was suspended in the temple.

'You can be a constellation, a profusion of stars in the summer sky, a High Lama in the great mountains to the East – a man, but holy. Or an orchid in the Perfect Afterlife Garden. Or you may stay as you are. It is your choice, Pleasure Mouse.'

The little girl thought for a long while and then answered, 'The only way to escape one's destiny is to enjoy it. I will stay here.'

Honey Tongue vanished, and in her place reappeared the small, fat cabbage of a footbinder. The women wept and chattered, Pleasure Mouse moaned and bellowed in agony, and Time, its feet unbound, bounded on.

'Come, Pleasure Mouse. Sit,' said the footbinder, and with her strong, muscled arms, she lifted the little girl and set her in the chair before the altar. The child sighed with relief and hung her head. The tiny shoes were stained with blood, as were her dreams of ladyhood. She whimpered softly. Warm Milk lurched painfully to her side, bent down and began to massage Pleasure Mouse's small burning legs. The women gathered around the altar, and the footbinder lit two prayer strips and recited:

Oh, Little Footed Miss, Goddess of our female fate, keep

the Pleasure Mouse healthy and safe. Let her hooks be as round, white dumplings. Let them not turn to dead, brown shreds at the end of her legs. Let her blood not be poisoned or her spirit. Let her learn to walk daintily without pain, and let her not envy those who can run for they are lowly and abused. Ay, let her never forget: for them, running is not luxury but necessity. Let her marry a relative of the Emperor, if not the Emperor himself. And let her have many sons that, when the season comes, she might enter the afterlife like a princess.

Lady Guo Guo snapped her fingers. 'Wild Mint, escort our new lady back to her chambers, if you please. I will come later, Pleasure Mouse, when the sun goes down, and I will bring with me an ebony cane sent by your father from the city. Look, little one, here is Spring Rain. Wild Mint sent for her that she might see you in your lady-like mantle.'

'My word,' gasped Lao Bing, 'the doll wears the tiny shoes!'

Lady Guo Guo laughed. 'So she does. How odd. Perhaps Tiger Mouse –'

Pleasure Mouse grabbed Spring Rain and ripped the shoes off her feet. She clasped the rag doll to her chest and stumbled from the temple.

Lady Guo Guo took the footbinder aside and paid her. The women wandered aimlessly from the temple into the sunlight.

'Oh dear,' sighed Lao Bing. 'I hurt all over again. As if fifty years ago were yesterday.' She shielded her eyes from the sun with her fan.

'Must it always be so violent?' murmured Warm Milk.

'I don't know if it must be, but it always is,' said the footbinder as she and Lady Guo Guo emerged from the temple.

'Have many young girls . . . died?' asked Lady Guo Guo.

'Some prefer death, Lady Gee, it is the way of the world.' The footbinder climbed into her sedan chair. 'I must be off,' she said. 'Keep the child on her hooks. I shall return in one week to wash and rebind. Please have the next smallest pair of shoes ready for my return. Goodbye.'

Warm Milk curtsied to Lao Bing and Lady Guo Guo and with the aid of her maids, tottered past the departing procession toward her apartments.

Lao Bing and Lady Guo Guo watched the footbinder's sedan chair disappear through the Sun Gate, and when it was gone, Lao Bing clucked and said, 'A footbinder. A footbinder. Ah, the seasons do change. I feel old, Little Sister. My toes are flattened out like cat tongues. The soles of my feet rise and fall like mountain peaks. How much did you pay her?'

'Thirty cash.'

'Thirty cash!'

'It was worth it not to be the cause of pain,' Lady Guo Guo said simply.

'Ah yes, I see,' sighed Lao Bing. 'Well then, perhaps she won't blame you although –'

'After Tiger Mouse, I could not bear – you understand?'

'Of course.' Lao Bing patted her brother's wife on the shoulder and, with a nod of her head, summoned her sedan chair.

'Farewell, Little Sister. We shall meet again in the city. I shall regale the Lord, your husband, with tales of the magnificence of your burial tomb, but be frugal, child, his patience falters.'

'Thank you for your counsel, Lao Bing. It is well taken.'

Lady Guo Guo closed the door of the sedan chair and waited until the pole bearers hoisted up the old lady and trotted away down the temple path.

The sun was iron-hot and glaring. Lady Guo Guo swept into a shadow of the temple eaves and stood there by herself, staring into nothingness, occasionally and absentmindedly waving her fan. After a time she ventured out into the sunlight, determined to make her way to the Pavilion of Coolness, where, she had decided, today she would take her rest. She padded past the Hereafter-View belvedere, across the Courtyard of a Thousand Fools, and right in front of the Zither Players' Wing, where the zither players caught sight of her and at once struck up her favourite tune. 'China Nights' was the name of the song, and she waited politely in the white-hot sunlight until the final pings had died away. After bowing in thanks, she continued on, slower now, as she was losing strength. By the time she reached the Pavilion of Coolness, her hooks were puffy and throbbing like beating hearts.

The Pangs of Love

Jane Gardam

It is not generally known that the good little mermaid of Hans Christian Andersen, who died for love of the handsome prince and allowed herself to dissolve in the foam of the ocean, had a younger sister, a difficult child of very different temper.

She was very young when the tragedy occurred, and was only told it later by her five elder sisters and her grandmother, the Sea King's mother with the twelve important oyster shells in her tail. They spent much of their time, all these women, mourning the tragic life of the little mermaid in the Sea King's palace below the waves, and a very dreary place it had become in consequence.

'I don't see what she did it for,' the seventh little mermaid used to say. 'Love for a man – ridiculous,' and all the others would sway on the tide and moan, 'Hush, hush – you don't know how she suffered for love.'

'I don't understand this "suffered for love,"' said the seventh mermaid. 'She sounds very silly and obviously spoiled her life.'

'She may have spoiled her life,' said the Sea King's mother, 'but think how good she was. She was given the chance of saving her life, but because it would have harmed the prince and his earthly bride she let herself die.'

'What had he done so special to deserve that?' asked the seventh mermaid.

'He had *done* nothing. He was just her beloved prince to whom she would sacrifice all.'

'What did he sacrifice for her?' asked Signorina Settima.

'Not a lot,' said the Sea King's mother, 'I believe they don't on the whole. But it doesn't stop us loving them.'

'It would me,' said the seventh mermaid. 'I must get a look

at some of this mankind, and perhaps I will then understand more.'

'You must wait until your fifteenth birthday,' said the Sea King's mother. 'That has always been the rule with all your sisters.'

'Oh, shit,' said the seventh mermaid (she was rather coarse). 'Times change. I'm as mature now as they were at fifteen. Howsabout tomorrow?'

'I'm sure I don't know what's to be done with you,' said the Sea King's mother, whose character had weakened in later years. 'You are totally different from the others and yet I'm sure I brought you all up the same.'

'Oh no you didn't,' said the five elder sisters in chorus, 'she's always been spoiled. We'd never have dared talk to you like that. Think if our beloved sister who died for love had talked to you like that.'

'Maybe she should have done,' said the dreadful seventh damsel officiously, and this time in spite of her grandmother's failing powers she was put in a cave for a while in the dark and made to miss her supper.

Nevertheless, she was the sort of girl who didn't let other people's views interfere with her too much, and she could argue like nobody else in the sea, so that in the end her grandmother said, 'Oh for goodness' sake then – go. Go now and don't even wait for your *fourteenth* birthday. Go and look at some men and don't come back unless they can turn you into a mermaid one hundredth part as good as your beloved foamy sister.'

'Whoops,' said Mademoiselle Sept, and she flicked her tail and was away up out of the Sea King's palace, rising through the coral and the fishes that wove about the red and blue seaweed trees like birds, up and up until her head shot out into the air and she took a deep breath of it and said, 'Wow!'

The sky, as her admirable sister had noticed stood above the sea like a large glass bell, and the waves rolled and lifted and tossed towards a green shore where there were fields and palaces and flowers and forests where fish with wings and legs wove about the branches of green and so forth trees, singing at the tops of their voices. On a balcony sticking out from the best palace stood, as he had stood before his marriage when the immaculate sister had first seen him, the wonderful prince with his chin resting on his hand as it often did of an evening – and indeed in the mornings and afternoons, too.

'Oh help!' said the seventh mermaid, feeling a queer twisting around the heart. Then she thought, 'Watch it.' She dived under water for a time and came up on a rock on the shore, where she sat and examined her sea-green finger nails and smoothed down the silver scales of her tail.

She was sitting where the prince could see her and after a while he gave a cry and she looked up. 'Oh,' he said, 'how you remind me of someone. I thought for a moment you were my lost love.'

'Lost love,' said the seventh mermaid. 'And whose fault was that? She was my sister. She died for love of you and you never gave her one serious thought. You even took her along on your honeymoon like a pet toy. I don't know what she saw in you.'

'I always loved her,' said the prince. 'But I didn't realise it until too late.'

'That's what they all say,' said Numera Septima. 'Are you a poet? They're the worst. Hardy, Tennyson, Shakespeare, Homer. Homer was the worst of all. And he hadn't a good word to say for mermaids.'

'Forgive me,' said the prince, who had removed his chin from his hand and was passionately clenching the parapet. 'Every word you speak reminds me more and more –'

'I don't see how it can,' said the s.m., 'since for love of you and because she was told it was the only way she could come to you, she let them cut out her tongue, the silly ass.'

'And your face,' he cried, 'your whole aspect, except of course for the tail.'

'She had that removed, too. They told her it would be agony and it was, so my sisters tell me. It shrivelled up and she got two ugly stumps called legs – I dare say you've got them under that parapet. When she danced, every step she took was like knives.'

'Alas, alas!'

'Catch me getting rid of my tail,' said syedmaya krasavitsa, twitching it seductively about, and the prince gave a great sprint from the balcony and embraced her on the rocks. It was all right until half way down but the scales were cold and prickly. Slimy too, and he shuddered.

'How dare you shudder,' cried La Septième. 'Go back to your earthly bride.'

'She's not here at present,' said the p., 'she's gone to her mother for the weekend. Won't you come in? We can have dinner in the bath.'

The seventh little mermaid spent the whole weekend with the prince in the bath, and he became quite frantic with desire by Monday morning because of the insurmountable problem below the mermaid's waist. 'Your eyes, your hair,' he cried, 'but that's about all.'

'My sister did away with her beautiful tail for love of you,' said the s.m., reading a volume of Descartes over the prince's shoulder as he lay on her sea-green bosom. 'They tell me she even wore a disgusting harness on the top half of her for you, and make-up and dresses. She was the saint of mermaids.'

'Ah, a saint,' said the prince. 'But without your wit, your spark. I would do anything in the world for you.'

'So what about getting rid of your legs?'

'Getting rid of my *legs*?'

'Then you can come and live with me below the waves. No one has legs down there and there's nothing wrong with any of us. As a matter of fact, aesthetically we're a very good species.'

'Get rid of my *legs*?'

'Yes – my grandmother, the Sea King's mother, and the Sea Witch behind the last whirlpool who fixed up my poor sister, silly cow, could see to it for you.'

'Oh, how I love your racy talk,' said the prince. 'It's like nothing I ever heard before. I should love you even with my eyes shut. Even at a distance. Even on the telephone.'

'No fear,' said the seventh m., 'I know all about this waiting by the telephone. All my sisters do it. It never rings when they want it to. It has days and days of terrible silence and they all roll about weeping and chewing their handkerchieves. You don't catch me getting in that condition.'

'Gosh, you're marvellous,' said the prince, who had been to an old-fashioned school, 'I'll do anything –'

'The legs?'

'Hum. Ha. Well – the legs.'

'Carry me back to the rocks,' said the seventh little mermaid, 'I'll leave you to think about it. What's more I hear a disturbance in the hall which heralds the return of your wife. By the way, it wasn't your wife, you know, who saved you from drowning when you got ship-wrecked on your sixteenth birthday. It was my dear old sister once again. "She swam among the spars and planks which drifted on the sea, quite forgetting they might crush her. Then she ducked beneath the water, and rising again on the billows managed at last to reach you who by now" (being fairly feeble in the muscles I'd guess, with all the stately living) "was scarcely able to swim any longer in the raging sea. Your arms, your legs" (ha!) "began to fail you and your beautiful eyes were closed and you must surely have died if my sister had not come to your assistance. She held your head above the water and let the billows drive her and you together wherever they pleased."'

'What antique phraseology.'

'It's a translation from the Danish. Anyway, "when the sun rose red and beaming from the water, your cheeks regained the hue of life but your eyes remained closed. My sister kissed – "

('No!')

'"– your lofty handsome brow and stroked back your wet locks . . . She kissed you again and longed that you might live." What's more if you'd only woken up then she could have spoken to you. It was when she got obsessed by you back down under the waves again that she went in for all this tongue and tail stuff with the Sea Witch.'

'She was an awfully nice girl,' said the prince, and tears came into his eyes – which was more than they ever could do for a mermaid however sad, because as we know from H. C. Andersen, mermaids can never cry which makes it harder for them.

'The woman I saw when I came to on the beach,' said the prince, 'was she who is now my wife. A good sort of woman but she drinks.'

'I'm not surprised,' said the seventh mermaid. 'I'd drink if I was married to someone who just stood gazing out to sea thinking of a girl he had allowed to turn into foam,' and she flicked her tail and disappeared.

'Now then,' she thought, 'what's to do next?' She was not to go back, her grandmother had said, until she was one hundredth part as good as the little m. her dead sister, now a spirit of air, and although she was a tearaway and, as I say, rather coarse, she was not altogether untouched by the discipline of the Sea King's mother and her upbringing. Yet she could not say that she exactly yearned for her father's palace with all her melancholy sisters singing dreary stuff about the past. Nor was she too thrilled to return to the heaviness of water with all the featherless fishes swimming through the amber windows and butting in to her, and the living flowers growing out of the palace walls like dry rot. However, after flicking about for a bit, once coming up to do an inspection of a fishing boat in difficulties with the tide and enjoying the usual drop-jawed faces, she took a header home into the front room and sat down quietly in a corner.

'You're back,' said the Sea King's mother. 'How was it? I take it you now feel you are a hundredth part as good as your sainted sister?'

'I've always tried to be good,' said the s.m., 'I've just tried to be rationally good and not romantically good, that's all.'

'Now don't start again. I take it you have seen some men?'

'I saw the prince.'

At this the five elder sisters set up a wavering lament.

'Did you feel for him —'

'Oh, feelings, feelings,' said the seventh and rational mermaid, 'I'm sick to death of feelings. He's good looking, I'll give you that, and rather sweet-natured and he's having a rough time at home, but he's totally self-centred. I agree that my sister must have been a true sea-saint to listen to him dripping on about himself all day. He's warm-hearted though, and not at all bad in the bath.'

The Sea King's mother fainted away at this outspoken and uninhibited statement, and the five senior mermaids fled in

shock. The seventh mermaid tidied her hair and set off to find
the terrible cave of the Sea Witch behind the last whirlpool,
briskly pushing aside the disgusting polypi, half plant, half
animal, and the fingery seaweeds that had so terrified her dead
sister on a similar journey.

'Aha,' said the Sea Witch, stirring a pot of filthy black
bouillabaisse, 'you, like your sister, cannot do without me. I
suppose you also want to risk body and soul for the human
prince up there on the dry earth?'

'Good afternoon, no,' said the seventh mermaid. 'Might I sit
down?' (For even the seventh mermaid was polite to the Sea
Witch.) 'I want to ask you if, when the prince follows me down
here below the waves, you could arrange for him to live with
me until the end of time?'

'He'd have to lose his legs. What would he think of that?'

'I think he might consider it. In due course.'

'He would have to learn to sing and not care about clothes
or money or possessions or power – what would he think of
that?'

'Difficult, but not impossible.'

'He'd have to face the fact that if you fell in love with one of
your own kind and married him he would die and also lose his
soul as your sister did when he wouldn't make an honest woman
of her.'

'It was not,' said the seventh mermaid, 'that he wouldn't
make an honest woman of her. It just never occurred to him.
After all – she couldn't speak to him about it. You had cut out
her tongue.'

'Aha,' said the s.w., 'it's different for a man, is it? Falling in
love, are you?'

'Certainly not,' said Fräulein Sieben. 'Certainly not.'

'Cruel then, eh? Revengeful? Or do you hate men? It's very
fashionable.'

'I'm not cruel. Or revengeful. I'm just rational. And I don't
hate men. I think I'd probably like them very much, especially
if they are all as kind and as beautiful as the prince. I just don't
believe in falling in love with them. It is a burden and it spoils
life. It is a mental illness. It killed my sister and it puts women

in a weak position and makes us to be considered second class.'

'They fall in love with us,' said the Sea Witch. 'That's to say, with women. So I've been told. Sometimes. Haven't you read the sonnets of Shakespeare and the poems of Petrarch?'

'The sonnets of Shakespeare are hardly all about one woman,' said the bright young mermaid. 'In fact some of them are written to a man. As for Petrarch, (there was scarcely a thing this girl hadn't read) he only saw his girl once, walking over a bridge. They never exactly brushed their teeth together.'

'Well, there are the Brownings.'

'Yes. The Brownings were all right,' said the mermaid. 'Very funny looking though. I don't suppose anyone else ever wanted them.'

'You are a determined young mermaid,' said the Sea Witch. 'Yes, I'll agree to treat the prince if he comes this way. But you must wait and see if he does.'

'Thank you, yes I will,' said the seventh mermaid. 'He'll come,' and she did wait, quite confidently, being the kind of girl well-heeled men do run after because she never ran after them, very like Elizabeth Bennet.

So, one day, who should come swimming down through the wonderful blue water and into the golden palaces of the Sea King and floating through the windows like the fish and touching with wonder the dry-rot flowers upon the walls, but the prince, his golden hair floating behind him and his golden hose and tunic stuck tight to him all over like a wet-suit, and he looked terrific.

'Oh, princess, sweet seventh mermaid,' he said, finding her at once (because she was the sort of girl who is always in the right place at the right time). 'I have found you again. Ever since I threw you back in the sea I have dreamed of you. I cannot live without you. I have left my boozy wife and have come to live with you for ever.'

'There are terrible conditions,' said the seventh mermaid. 'Remember. The same conditions which my poor sister accepted in reverse. You must lose your legs and wear a tail.'

'This I will do.'

'You must learn to sing for hours and hours in unison with the other mermen, in wondrous notes that hypnotise simple sailors up above and make them think they hear faint sounds from Glyndebourne or Milan.'

'As to that,' said the prince, 'I always wished I had a voice.'

'And you must know that if I decide that I want someone more than you, someone of my own sort, and marry him, you will lose everything, as my sister did – your body, your immortal soul and your self-respect.'

'Oh well, that's quite all right,' said the prince. He knew that no girl could ever prefer anyone else to him.

'*Right*,' said the mermaid. 'Well, before we go off to the Sea Witch, let's give a party. And let me introduce you to my mother and sisters.'

Then there followed a time of most glorious celebration, similar only to the celebration some years back for the prince's wedding night when the poor little mermaid now dead had had to sit on the deck of the nuptial barque and watch the bride and groom until she had quite melted away. Then the cannons had roared and the flags had waved and a royal bridal tent of cloth of gold and purple and precious furs had been set upon the deck and when it grew dark, coloured lamps had been lit and sailors danced merrily and the bride and groom had gone into the tent without the prince giving the little mermaid a backward glance.

Now, beneath the waves the sea was similarly alight with glowing corals and brilliant sea-flowers and a bower was set up for the seventh mermaid and the prince and she danced with all the mermen who had silver crowns on their heads and St Christophers round their necks, very trendy like the South of France, and they all had a lovely time.

And the party went on and on. It was beautiful. Day after day and night after night and anyone who was anyone was there, and the weather was gorgeous – no storms below or above and it was exactly as Hans Christian Andersen said: 'a wondrous blue tint lay over everything; one would be more inclined to fancy one was high up in the air and saw nothing but sky above and below than that one was at the bottom of the sea. During a calm, too, one could catch a glimpse of the sun. It looked like a crimson flower from the cup of which, light streamed forth.' The seventh mermaid danced and danced, particularly with a handsome young merman with whom she seemed much at her ease.

'Who is that merman?' asked the prince. 'You seem to know him well.'

'Oh – just an old friend,' said the seventh m., 'he's always been about. We were in our prams together.' (This was not true. The seventh m. was just testing the prince. She had never bothered with mermen even in her pram.)

'I'm sorry,' said the prince, 'I can't have you having mermen friends. Even if there's nothing in it.'

'We must discuss this with the Sea Witch,' said the seventh mermaid, and taking his hand she swam with him out of the palace and away and away through the dreadful polypi again. She took him past the last whirlpool to the cave where the Sea Witch was sitting eating a most unpleasant-looking type of caviar from a giant snail shell and stroking her necklace of sea snakes.

'Ha,' said the Sea Witch, 'the prince. You have come to be rid of your legs?'

'Er – well –'

'You have come to be rid of your earthly speech, your clothes and possessions and power?'

'Well, it's something that we might discuss.'

'And you agree to lose soul and body and self-respect if this interesting mermaid goes off and marries someone?'

There was a very long silence and the seventh mermaid closely examined some shells round her neck, tiny pale pink oyster shells each containing a pearl which would be the glory of a Queen's crown. The prince held his beautiful chin in his lovely, sensitive hand. His gentle eyes filled with tears. At last he took the mermaid's small hand and kissed its palm and folded the sea-green nails over the kiss (he had sweet ways) and said, 'I must not look at you. I must go at once,' and he pushed off. That is to say, he pushed himself upwards off the floor of the sea and shot up and away and away through the foam, arriving home in time for tea and early sherry with his wife, who was much relieved.

It was a very long time indeed before the seventh little mermaid returned to the party. In fact the party was all but over. There was only the odd slithery merman twanging a harp of dead fisherman's bones and the greediest and grubbiest of the deep water fishes eating up the last of the sandwiches. The Sea King's old mother was asleep, her heavy tail studded with important oyster shells coiled round the legs of her throne.

The five elder sisters had gone on somewhere amusing.

The seventh mermaid sat down at the feet of her grandmother and at length the old lady woke up and surveyed the chaos left over from the fun. 'Hullo, my child,' she said. 'Are you alone?'

'Yes. The prince has gone. The engagement's off.'

'My dear – what did I tell you? Remember how your poor sister suffered. I warned you.'

'Pooh – I'm not suffering. I've just proved my point. Men aren't worth it.'

'Maybe you and she were unfortunate,' said the Sea King's mother. 'Which men you meet is very much a matter of luck, I'm told.'

'No – they're all the same,' said the mermaid who by now was nearly fifteen years old. 'I've proved what I suspected. I'm free now – free of the terrible pangs of love which put women in bondage, and I shall dedicate my life to freeing and instructing other women and saving them from humiliation.'

'Well, I hope you don't become one of those frowsty little women who don't laugh and have only one subject of conversation,' said the Sea Witch. 'It is a mistake to base a whole philosophy upon one disappointment.'

'Disappointment – pah!' said the seventh mermaid. 'When was I ever negative?'

'And I hope you don't become aggressive.'

'When was I ever aggressive?' said Senorita Septima ferociously.

'That's a good girl then,' said the Sea King's mother, 'So now – unclench that fist.'

The Shining Mountain

Alison Fell

Once there was a Scottish girl with a strange name and a father who was always on television. The girl was called Pangma-La, and of course she was teased about it. At first she cried, but her father scolded her.

'Pangma-La,' he said, 'I called you after a shining mountain so that you would stand tall and be proud. Pangma-La,' he said, 'Scotland has enough ordinary Morags and Janets already.'

And he pinned a picture of the Shining Mountain on her wall, and told her that one day they would climb it together.

For Pangma-La's father was a famous mountaineer. She would come home from an ordinary school day and there he would be on the BBC news, planting the Union Jack on a far, far mountain peak. She would sit on an ordinary bus, and hear people say, 'Now there's a hard man, there's a hero.'

So Pangma-La dried her tears and vowed never to be ordinary and disappoint him.

As the years passed and Pangma-La grew bigger, her father taught her to balance finely on the high tops of walls, and shin up sheer rocks by toe- and finger-holds. Her mother shook her head and fussed.

'Pangma-La,' she said, 'you'll tear your good jumper. Pangma-La,' she said, 'you'll fall and hurt yourself.'

But her father only laughed and said, 'Let her be, she's tough and hard as nails,' and Pangma-La was proud.

At last it was time to set out for the Shining Mountain. Pangma-La and her father took off in a white plane. Below them the houses and cars and her mother waving were small and bright as Smarties. Then the earth disappeared and they were high in the crystal blue sky where the sun hurts your eyes.

Pangma-La fell asleep and dreamt a bad dream. She was a white swan flying high above the Shining Mountain, with no father or mother anywhere. She was tired, she wanted to land on the top of the mountain and rest her wings. But the mountain turned its back on her, saying, Pangma-La, you cannot land here and you cannot rest. You must fly on until your white wings freeze and you tumble down to the hard ground.

Pangma-La woke up frightened and wanting her mother, but she said nothing, for she was afraid her father would be disappointed in her.

When the plane landed, Pangma-La and her father set out for the mountains. The villagers, hearing that the young girl was called after their shining mountain, smiled and gave her sherbet and figs. But then Pangma-La and her father came to the last village, where the trees stopped and the snows began. There Sherpa men crowded round, offering to carry their loads at a price.

'My daughter and I do not need porters,' Pangma-La's father said proudly. 'We are strong and we will climb the mountain alone.'

The Sherpa men were angry.

'The mountain goddess will send winds to tear at you,' they said, 'and spindrift snow to sting your face, and avalanche to toss and tumble you.'

But Pangma-La's father turned away and laughed. 'Only weak men believe in old wives' tales,' he said scornfully.

Above them the mountain rose like a tall white tower. At first Pangma-La climbed happily, smelling the clear air, while up ahead her father's feet made deep blue prints in the snow.

But soon she began to grow weary.

Just then an old Sherpa woman appeared, in a ragged brown cloak.

'Let me carry your heavy sack, daughter,' said the woman, but Pangma-La shook her head, for she was afraid that her father would be disappointed in her. That night under the bright stars she told him about the Sherpa woman, but her father looked at her strangely.

'I saw no woman,' he said. And he made Pangma-La promise

that she would speak to no one, no matter what they asked or what help they offered.

On the second day, Pangma-La set out boldly and well. Then a strong wind blew up to tear at her, and the going was hard. She began to feel weak and ill under the weight of the rucksack, but she would not stop, for her father would be disappointed in her.

Just then the Sherpa woman appeared, and pulled a handful of swan's feathers from under her ragged cloak.

'Take out your heavy things from the sack, daughter,' she said, 'and fill it with this swan'sdown. Then you will get to the top of the mountain, and your father will never tell the difference.'

Pangma-La thought of her promise, but she had such a bad sick feeling everywhere in her, that she did what the woman asked. The Sherpa woman carried the heavy things under her ragged cloak, and Pangma-La carried a light rucksack full of swan'sdown, and her father never told the difference. And at sunset, the woman gave back her heavy things, and Pangma-La lay down to sleep.

On the third day she set off with a weary feeling already in her bones. Spindrift snow blew up to sting her face, and just when she was sure she could go no further, the Sherpa woman appeared.

'Take off your heavy, heavy clothes, daughter, and I will cover you with swan's feathers, and you will get to the top of the mountain.'

And so Pangma-La did, and once again, as the sun went down, the woman gave her back the heavy clothes, and her father never told the difference.

On the fourth day the roar of an avalanche thundered past them, and this time Pangma-La's father walked beside her.

Oh, father, she thought to herself, my boots are too big and I can't fill them, and I want to go home to my mother more than anything in the world. And a tear escaped and ran down her nose.

'Pangma-La,' her father scolded, 'Look at the mountain I named you for, is it not beautiful?' Pangma-La felt so ill she could hardly bear to look up at it, so crystal-cold and merciless above her. She hung her head, ashamed.

'Yes father,' she said, and the tear froze to an icicle on her face.

Her father climbed on and on, and Pangma-La tried hard to keep up with him. Soon her legs could not go another step, and a dizziness took her, and she fell down in the snow.

Just then the Sherpa woman appeared, kneeling over her.

'Give me your heavy, heavy heart, daughter', she said, 'and I will fill you with swan'sdown. Then you will get to the top of the mountain, and your father will never tell the difference.'

So Pangma-La gave up her heart, and the lungs which panted and hurt, and the bones which weighed like iron, and flew easily to the top of the mountain in all her light swan's feathers.

But this time when it came to sunset the Sherpa woman did not give back Pangma-La's heavy, heavy heart, and Pangma-La's father stood at the top of the Shining Mountain, calling wildly for his daughter, but she was nowhere to be seen.

Then the Sherpa woman appeared in her ragged cloak.

'Here is your Pangma-La,' she said, pointing to the white swan which fluttered beside her, 'But now she is my daughter for ever and always.'

Pangma-La's father cried out in anger and cursed the hag for her cruel spell. He raised his ice-axe to strike the woman down, but just then a peal of thunder shook the mountain and threw him to the ground.

And there in front of him stood no hag, but the mountain goddess herself, tall and straight, with skin of darkest gleaming gold, and eyes yellow and far-seeing as a snow-leopard. She wore a cloak of swan's feathers, and blue lightning-fire danced at her finger ends.

'You wanted your daughter to get to the top of the mountain,' said the goddess, 'and I have given you your heart's desire. You named your daughter after me, to be strong and light as the gods, and feel no human pain, and weep no human tears. And I have given you your heart's desire.'

Then Pangma-La's father saw that his daughter had given her life away just to please him, and he cursed himself and his heart's desire, and ran to the edge of the mountain to cast himself off.

But the goddess barred his way easily with a bolt of blue lightning.

'Not so hasty to make an end of it, brave hero,' she said. She brought Pangma-La's heavy sack and heavy clothes from under her cloak and gave them to him. 'First you must feel the weight of your heavy, heavy burden,' she said. Then she brought out Pangma-La's heart, and gave it to him. 'And now you must feel the weight of your heavy, heavy heart,' she said.

At this Pangma-La's father fell on his knees and for the first time wept hot tears like any human.

The mountain goddess, seeing this, was satisfied.

'You have learned your lesson,' she said, and was gone in a swirl of swan's feathers.

Pangma-La's father looked down to see his daughter alive and heavy and human in his arms.

Feeling the wet drops on her face, Pangma-La opened her eyes. When she saw that her father the hero was crying she was no longer ashamed, and a great weight lifted from her. She jumped up and pulled him strongly to his feet. Then, skidding and sliding, Pangma-La and her father ran all the way to the bottom of the Shining Mountain, while the snow flew up behind them like sherbet or swan's feathers, and never again was Pangma-La afraid that her father would be disappointed in her.

My Mother

Jamaica Kincaid

Immediately on wishing my mother dead and seeing the pain it caused her, I was sorry and cried so many tears that all the earth around me was drenched. Standing before my mother, I begged her forgiveness, and I begged so earnestly that she took pity on me, kissing my face and placing my head on her bosom to rest. Placing her arms around me, she drew my head closer and closer to her bosom, until finally I suffocated. I lay on her bosom, breathless, for a time uncountable, until one day, for a reason she has kept to herself, she shook me out and stood me under a tree and I started to breathe again. I cast a sharp glance at her and said to myself, 'So.' Instantly I grew my own bosoms, small mounds at first, leaving a small, soft place between them, where, if ever necessary, I could rest my own head. Between my mother and me now were the tears I had cried, and I gathered up some stones and banked them in so that they formed a small pond. The water in the pond was thick and black and poisonous, so that only unnamable invertebrates could live in it. My mother and I now watched each other carefully, always making sure to shower the other with words and deeds of love and affection.

I was sitting on my mother's bed trying to get a good look at myself. It was a large bed and it stood in the middle of a large, completely dark room. The room was completely dark because all the windows had been boarded up and all the crevices stuffed with black cloth. My mother lit some candles and the room burst into a pink-like, yellow-like glow. Looming over us, much larger than ourselves, were our shadows. We sat mesmerised because our shadows had made a place between themselves, as if they were making room for someone else. Nothing filled up the space between them, and the shadow of my mother sighed. The shadow of my mother danced around the room to a tune that my own shadow sang, and then they stopped. All along, our shadows had grown thick and thin, long and short, had fallen at every angle, as if they were controlled by the light of day. Suddenly my mother got up and blew out the candles and our shadows vanished. I continued to sit on the bed, trying to get a good look at myself.

My mother removed her clothes and covered thoroughly her skin with a thick gold-colored oil, which had recently been rendered in a hot pan from the livers of reptiles with pouched throats. She grew plates of metal-colored scales on her back, and light, when it collided with this surface, would shatter and collapse into tiny points. Her teeth now arranged themselves into rows that reached all the way back to her long white throat. She uncoiled her hair from her head and then removed her hair altogether. Taking her head into her large palms, she flattened it so that her eyes, which were by now ablaze, sat on top of her head and spun like two revolving balls. Then, making two lines on the soles of each foot, she divided her feet into crossroads. Silently, she had instructed me to follow her example, and now I too travelled along on my white underbelly, my tongue darting and flickering in the hot air. 'Look,' said my mother.

My mother and I were standing on the seabed side by side, my arms laced loosely around her waist, my head resting securely on her shoulder, as if I needed the support. To make sure she believed in my frailness, I sighed occasionally – long soft sighs, the kind of sigh she had long ago taught me could evoke sympathy. In fact, how I really felt was invincible. I was no longer a child but I was not yet a woman. My skin had just blackened and cracked and fallen away and my new impregnable carapace had taken full hold. My nose had flattened; my hair curled in and stood out straight from my head simultaneously; my many rows of teeth in their retractable trays were in place. My mother and I wordlessly made an arrangement – I sent out my beautiful sighs, she received them; I leaned ever more heavily on her for support, she offered her shoulder, which shortly grew to the size of a thick plank. A long time passed, at the end of which I had hoped to see my mother permanently cemented to the seabed. My mother reached out to pass a hand over my head, a pacifying gesture, but I laughed and, with great agility, stepped aside. I let out a horrible roar, then a self-pitying whine. I had grown big, but my mother was bigger, and that would always be so. We walked to the Garden of Fruits and there ate to our hearts' satisfaction. We departed through the southwesterly gate, leaving as always, in our trail, small colonies of worms.

With my mother, I crossed, unwillingly, the valley. We saw a lamb grazing and when it heard our footsteps it paused and looked up at us. The lamb looked cross and miserable. I said to my mother, 'The lamb is cross and miserable. So would I be, too, if I had to live in a climate not suited to my nature.' My mother and I now entered the cave. It was the dark and cold cave. I felt something growing under my feet and I bent down to eat it. I stayed that way for years, bent over eating whatever I found growing under my feet. Eventually, I grew a special lens that would allow me to see in the darkest of darkness; eventually, I grew a special coat that kept me warm in the coldest of coldness. One day I saw my mother sitting on a rock. She said, 'What a strange expression you have on your face. So cross, so miserable, as if you were living in a climate not suited to your nature.' Laughing, she vanished. I dug a deep, deep hole. I built a beautiful house, a floorless house, over the deep, deep hole. I put in lattice windows, most favored of windows by my mother, so perfect for looking out at people passing by without her being observed. I painted the house itself yellow, the windows green, colors I knew would please her. Standing just outside the door, I asked her to inspect the house. I said, 'Take a look. Tell me if it's to your satisfaction.' Laughing out of the corner of a mouth I could not see, she stepped inside. I stood just outside the door, listening carefully, hoping to hear her land with a thud at the bottom of the deep, deep hole. Instead she walked up and down in every direction, even pounding her heel on the air. Coming outside to greet me, she said, 'It is an excellent house. I would be honored to live in it,' and then vanished. I filled up the hole and burnt the house to the ground.

My mother has grown to an enormous height. I have grown to an enormous height also, but my mother's height is three times mine. Sometimes I cannot see from her breasts on up, so lost is she in the atmosphere. One day, seeing her sitting on the seashore, her hand reaching out in the deep to caress the belly of a striped fish as he swam through a place where two seas met, I glowed red with anger. For a while then I lived alone on the island where there were eight full moons and I adorned the face of each moon with expressions I had seen on my mother's face. All the expressions favored me. I soon grew tired of living in this way and returned to my mother's side. I remained, though glowing red with anger, and my mother and I built houses on opposite banks of the dead pond. The dead pond lay between us; in it, only small invertebrates with poisonous lances lived. My mother behaved toward them as if she had suddenly found herself in the same room with relatives we had long since risen above. I cherished their presence and gave them names. Still I missed my mother's close company and cried constantly for her, but at the end of each day when I saw her return to her house, incredible and great deeds in her wake, each of them singing loudly her praises, I glowed and glowed again, red with anger. Eventually, I wore myself out and sank into a deep, deep sleep, the only dreamless sleep I have ever had.

One day my mother packed my things in a grip and, taking me by the hand, walked me to the jetty, placed me on board a boat, in care of the captain. My mother, while caressing my chin and cheeks, said some words of comfort to me because we had never been apart before. She kissed me on the forehead and turned and walked away. I cried so much my chest heaved up and down, my whole body shook at the sight of her back turned toward me, as if I had never seen her back turned toward me before. I started to make plans to get off the boat, but when I saw that the boat was encased in a large green bottle, as if it were about to decorate a mantelpiece, I fell asleep, until I reached my destination, the new island. When the boat stopped, I got off and I saw a woman with feet exactly like mine, especially around the arch of the instep. Even though the face was completely different from what I was used to, I recognised this woman as my mother. We greeted each other at first with great caution and politeness, but as we walked along, our steps became one, and as we talked, our voices became one voice, and we were in complete union in every other way. What peace came over me then, for I could not see where she left off and I began, or where I left off and she began.

My mother and I walk through the rooms of her house. Every crack in the floor holds a significant event: here, an apparently healthy young man suddenly dropped dead; here a young woman defied her father and, while riding her bicycle to the forbidden lovers' meeting place, fell down a precipice, remaining a cripple for the rest of a very long life. My mother and I find this a beautiful house. The rooms are large and empty, opening on to each other, waiting for people and things to fill them up. Our white muslin skirts billow up around our ankles, our hair hangs straight down our backs as our arms hang straight at our sides. I fit perfectly in the crook of my mother's arm, on the curve of her back, in the hollow of her stomach. We eat from the same bowl, drink from the same cup; when we sleep, our heads rest on the same pillow. As we walk through the rooms, we merge and separate, merge and separate; soon we shall enter the final stage of our evolution.

The fishermen are coming in from sea; their catch is bountiful, my mother has seen to that. As the waves plop, plop against each other, the fishermen are happy that the sea is calm. My mother points out the fishermen to me, their contentment is a source of my contentment. I am sitting in my mother's enormous lap. Sometimes I sit on a mat she has made for me from her hair. The lime trees are weighed down with limes – I have already perfumed myself with their blossoms. A hummingbird has nested on my stomach, a sign of my fertileness. My mother and I live in a bower made from flowers whose petals are imperishable. There is the silvery blue of the sea, crisscrossed with sharp darts of light, there is the warm rain falling on the clumps of castor bush, there is the small lamb bounding across the pasture, there is the soft ground welcoming the soles of my pink feet. It is in this way my mother and I have lived for a long time now.

Given Names

Sue Miller

My aunt's last words were characteristic. My uncle, her brother, to whom she had spoken them, repeated them compulsively to everyone who would listen at the memorial service a week later. My aunt had drowned. She had been drunk, which was not unusual for her, and she and my uncle were rowing home together in the dark from a family picnic. She objected to the way he rowed. 'My God, Orrie, look at you, batting at the water in that half-assed way,' she had said. 'Jesus, put a little life into it. I could *swim* home faster than this.'

Orrie said she sat still for a minute after this, and the only sound was of the oars slipping in and out of the black water. Then she stood up, kicked off her shoes, and dove in.

The boat rocked violently after she sprang off. My uncle thinks he might have jerked his hand off the oar to pull back from her splash, or maybe just the rocking bounced the oar out of the oarlock and his hand. It slid off into the water at any rate, and he spent several minutes retrieving it. My aunt floated on her back near the boat briefly, and he said he spoke sharply to her, told her she was 'a damn fool or some such thing.' She laughed at him and blew an arc of water up into the moonlight, 'a great jet,' he called it, then rolled over and swam off. By the time he got the oar back into the oarlock, he could barely hear her in the distance. He tried to row in her direction. He said he would row for a few strokes, pulling hard for speed, then coast and listen for her. By the third or fourth interval he knew he'd lost her. All he could hear was the gentle rush of water against the bow of the coasting boat. He rowed around in wide circles in the moonlight for a while, and then he had to row home and tell his parents. She was forty-two. They found her two days later.

The rowboat wasn't used until three days after that when my grandparents headed into town to retrieve her ashes. As my grandfather carefully handed my grandmother in, she spotted Babe's Papagallo shoes in the stern of the boat where she'd kicked them off before her dive. At this my grandmother, who'd taken it all 'like a brick, a real brick' in my uncle's words, became hysterical. She began to scream rhythmically, steady bursts of sound. When my grandfather tried to loosen her hands from the edge of the boat, she hit him several times. She broke his glasses. Dr Burns had to be summoned from his cottage across the lake to administer a sedative. 'My baby, my baby,' she whimpered, until she fell into her chemical sleep.

My aunt was my mother's youngest sister, my grandparents' youngest child. She had been an afterthought of one sort or another; everyone always had known it. But no one had ever dared to ask, and so no one knew, whether she was a mistake or one last yearning look back at a stage in their lives already well past for my grandparents. My mother was twenty-two years older than her sister. She told me once that she had at first thought her mother was joking when she said she was going to have another child; and then was ashamed and embarrassed by it. She said it ruined her senior year of college.

They were full of nicknames in my mother's family. The brother who rowed home alone in the moonlight had been christened Frank Junior. But because of a prematurely lugubrious nature, he was called Eeyore as a boy, short for Junior. That eventually became Or, which grew back again into Orrie.

My aunt's name was Edith, but she was 'the baby' while she grew up, and this shortened easily to Babe. My mother was Bunny, and the two middle sisters were Rain and Weezie, for Lorraine and Louise.

They were a handsome, high-strung group, dominated by my grandfather, who was at once expansive and authoritarian. His parents had been immigrants. As a young man he had patented a wear-resisting heel for shoes, then sold the patent to B. F. Goodrich, and learned to make money from money. Each of the daughters had, in turn, married a man of great business promise, but somehow each one got stuck as a middle-level executive, none so gloriously successful as my grandfather.

My grandmother seemed overwhelmed in their company. In the few remaining pictures of her alone, without the family, she is a radiant debutante, a smiling, confident bride. But in even my earliest memories she is mostly just a silent presence: a cool hand on my forehead through a feverish night, or someone to make intercession with Grandfather over a minor infraction of the rules; but of herself, inexpressive.

I was the oldest grandchild, five years younger than my Aunt Babe. I spent every childhood summer with her on the lake where my grandparents had their summer home, and where she died. In her isolation Babe befriended me. Reciprocally, I adored her. I had no siblings. I was dominated completely by my mother, and Babe seemed the ideal older sister, glamorous, strong, and defiant.

My grandparents' summer home was really what used to be called a camp, of several buildings on the far shore of an inland lake in Maine. The road ended on the near side, so the first people to open camp in the summer had to bushwhack their way around the lake, open the shed and lower the leaky rowboats into the water; then return for the boxes and trunks and whining, dusty children. Subsequent arrivals would park and honk their horns, one long, three short. There was always some eager cousin waiting to row across and fetch them.

My grandparents' summer home had no electricity, no running water, no telephone. We used only canoes or rowboats for transportation. There was an unspoken contempt for those weekend families across the lake, whose clusters of electric lights twinkled merrily at us after dark while we huddled around kerosene lamps; who polluted the late with motorboats, and had names on their cabins like Bide-a-Wee, or Cee-the-Vue. In the last several years, because they are old now, and made more uncomfortable by the camp's inconveniences, my grandparents have paid to have electric wires run around and bought a small powerboat. On the night Babe died, my younger cousins were using the powerboat to ferry the rest of the family home.

There were four separate family cottages at camp, but most of us cousins slept together on the sleeping porch of the large main house, the only one with a kitchen. Each child had an iron hospital bed, and we were grouped by families. Since I was an only child and Babe an aberration, we slept together. Babe had rigged up a curtain to separate our corner of the porch from the rest. She didn't mind my hanging around watching her paint her toenails or curl her hair. But if one of the younger cousins poked a head under the curtain, she was harsh. 'No brats!' she'd snap.

In the early morning the sunlight reflected off the lake onto the whitewashed ceiling of the sleeping porch. As the air began to stir, the motion of the ripples increased until the ceiling shimmered with golden lights. I lay still and watched them; watched my beautiful aunt sleep; until my grandmother arrived from her cottage to the kitchen. With the smell of coffee and bacon, the squeak of the pump by the kitchen sink, I'd get up, easing my weight slowly off the steel mesh which supported my mattress so as not to disturb Babe, and go to help Grandmother make breakfast for the fifteen or twenty cousins and aunts and uncles who would rise when she rang the bell.

The buildings were all painted white, with dark green trim. Years later, newly divorced, with a one-year teaching appointment in the Midwest, I chose those colours to paint my daughter's bedroom; and it was only as I recognised their source in the finished job that I realised how frightened and homesick I was for something familiar and safe.

My mother always sent me to my grandparents' for the whole summer. She herself would come up only for a month or so. My father stayed in Schenectady for all but the two weeks GE allowed him. He seemed uncomfortable when he did come up, as did the other brothers-in-law. They spent their time growing beards and fishing. The walls of the main house were dotted with birch bark reproductions of record catches, traced by the men in an unspoken competition that had developed over the years.

The sisters grew more expansive and thick as thieves as the summer wore on, seeming to pull away from us children. They told secrets, laughed at private things, often made fun of Uncle Orrie's wife, who clearly was never to be one of them. In general they seemed transformed into people we had never known, could never know. Into girls, in a sense, but girls whose club was private and exclusive and cruel.

Babe was, of course, not a part of the club. But she was also clearly not one of us cousins. Her singular status was a constant irritant to my aunts and my mother. They wanted someone to be in charge of Babe, her appearance, her language, her behavior towards the nieces and nephews. They turned in vain to my grandmother. She was in her silent way, almost proud of Babe's eccentricities. She'd say, 'Oh, that's just Babe's way.' Or, 'But you know, dearest, *I* can't do a thing with her.' Neither could they, so she existed in a no man's land, nobody's child, nobody's mother.

She was sometimes a leader of the cousins, and sometimes tormented them. I was honored to be her ally in whichever direction she went. I felt I had no choice, and didn't want any. To be more than just myself, to be like her, that was the opportunity she offered me. Even now I feel I would have been a fool to say no. And when I occasionally tried, she made me ashamed of myself. 'But, Babe,' I'd say, 'Aunt Rain *said* . . .'

'You want to grow up to be a creep like Rain?' she interrupted. 'The most exciting thing she's done in the last ten years, she finished that thousand piece jigsaw puzzle last week?'

And so I was her accomplice, for instance, when she decided we should haunt the outhouse. It was an ideal spot, in some ways. The path out to it was curved and tortuous. Roots leaped up from its surface to trip you. Industrious spiders could spin a web in the tiny building in the span of an hour to catch at your face as you stepped into the dark, reeking room. I was always terrified of the idea, of animals biting me from below, and could never resist turning my flashlight into the hole to check for them; the sight of the lime-sprinkled turds of three generations invariably caused my stomach to clench.

Babe and I alternated stationing ourselves behind the building in the evening, just as the cousins were trooping out one by one with their flashlights for their last visit of the day. She was good at animal-like noises. I was less inventive, and would merely scratch at the walls, or throw pebbles from a little distance once the cousin was settled inside.

Soon several of the cousins stopped going to the outhouse at night. Peering around the corner of the building, I could watch their approach, the tiny pajamaed figures stumbling along with the little circle of light dancing in front of them on the path. Now I would watch the light beam swerve off the path, stop, and then I could hear the steady stream of piss hitting the forest floor.

It was not long before the first droppings were found. 'Distinctly humanoid,' Aunt Rain pronounced, and there could be no arguing. It suddenly occurred to several others that the traces of deer or bear they'd thought they'd seen could have been humanoid also. Grandfather organised an inspection tour of suspicious droppings. Then a family council was called.

There were seven children at camp that summer, including Babe and me. One, Agatha, was exonerated because she wore diapers. We assembled on the porch with my grandfather who, as usual, took over the actual administration of the punishment. Some person or persons, Grandfather said, had been going to the bathroom around camp. There was no excuse for this, and he wanted the guilty party or parties to speak up. If they didn't, they would have to bear the additional guilt of knowing they had caused all of us to be punished equally. We would wait.

In the distance the loons called tragically to each other. My grandfather was reading. My aunts' voices in the kitchen rose and fell as they prepared supper, and the water lapped steadily on the tiny rocky beach where the rowboats were pulled up on their rotting slips.

There was a little whispering among the seven-year-olds. My grandfather's eyes did not rise from the page, but his voice was sharp. 'There will be no collusion!' The profound silence fell again. Grandmother brought him out a cup of tea and looked worriedly around at us all, her eyes resting an instant longer on Babe than on anyone else. Finally, after about fifteen minutes, one seven-year-old capitulated.

'I did some of 'em Gramps.' He could barely be heard. A rush to confess followed, and three of the boys admitted responsibility.

Their punishment was twofold. They had to clean up all the piles. (They were heard grumbling, 'Geez, we didn't do *all* these!') And they had to scrape and repaint the peeling, stinking outhouse, inside and out. Babe claimed she felt no remorse and curled up on her bed with *Jane Eyre*, but I went out several times and helped them. Once my grandfather, coming out to check on the work, caught me wielding the scraper and gave me a hard look, but nothing was ever said.

If the cousins ever guessed Babe's part in this or other misfortunes that befell them, it didn't alter their feelings for her. She was their heroine too. She was a born teacher, Babe, and she bound them to her through crime and her own special insights into the adult world. She swiped food regularly, and kept a supply in the ice house which she sometimes shared. She pilfered cigarettes and taught us all to smoke. We had a meeting place, a dappled clearing far back in the woods; and I can see her now, sitting on a rock, puffing a Pall Mall, her fuchsia toenails glimmering on her dirty bare feet, and pronouncing all the aunts and uncles, our parents, a bunch of fucking assholes. She didn't even cough.

Another time she pulled down her pants and showed us where the hair was going to grow when we were as old as she was. We thought it was disgusting, ugly. We hoped she was wrong, that it wouldn't happen that way to us. But we adored her for doing it.

A few years after this Babe grew more remote from me. Her adolescence fell like a shadow between us. She was simply gone a good deal of the time, off with young men in powerboats from the other side of the lake where the houses clustered close to the shoreline. They would come swooping into our inlet to get her, shearing off endless cotter pins on the unmarked rocks which studded it, and then hover helplessly fifteen feet from shore. We had only rowboats, so no need of docks. Sometimes I or a cousin would row her out the little distance, but often she waded out, holding a bundle of dry clothes out of the water with one hand, swimming the last few feet awkwardly. She often came back after dark, and occasionally so late that she swam in quite a distance, theoretically so that the noise of the boat wouldn't wake the family. The lake was so still at night, though, that I'm sure my grandparents lay in their beds listening, as I did, to the dying whine of the motor's approach, the murmur of voices, laughter, carrying over the still water, and the splash as she dived in. Her teeth sometimes chattered a long time after she slid under the layers of covers on the cold sleeping porch. Later I wondered if she were thinking of all those nights when she dove out of Uncle Orrie's rowboat.

My grandfather was always angry at her now, but his methods of punishment had no effect on Babe. He was stony with her. I heard him talk more than once of her betraying his trust. He withdrew his charm and warmth, of which he had a considerable supply, from her. She simply didn't care. Occasionally he would force her to stay home in the evening. She would pace around the sitting-room of the main house, where we all passed evenings together, occasionally stopping to try and fit a piece into whatever the ongoing puzzle was, sighing, picking up and putting down whatever book she was reading. She made everyone nervous, and we were all just as happy, in truth, to have her gone.

Two summers after this, my mother enrolled me in music camp, so I saw Babe only for a week or so at the ends. When I again spent all summer at my grandparents', she was nineteen, in college, and I was fourteen. From the start of the summer she was preoccupied and dreamy. She wrote long letters daily, and usually made the trip into town herself to get the mail in my grandparents' old Packard. Sometimes I accompanied her, as she seemed to be at a stage again where she didn't mind my presence. Once or twice we sat in the car for a long time listening to popular songs on the radio while the battery ran down. There was no radio allowed at camp.

She seemed plumper, softer, tamed. Yet, mysteriously to me, she still seemed to create a furor in the family. There was constant tension between her and my grandfather and aunts. Sudden silences would fall when I or the cousins came around. Yet her behavior by contrast with previous summers seemed impeccable.

I was myself preoccupied because of the music camp. Somehow, it was clear to me, the decision had been made that I was not, as my mother had hoped, musically gifted. My teacher's attitude had shifted during the previous year, from that of rigorous demand to a kind of tensionless approval. I knew she and Mother had talked. I would not go to the camp again. Mother said it seemed a waste of money, when I could have such a good time at my grandparents'. I don't remember that the decision about music had ever been mine, but I had accepted it and wanted to be good. Now I felt that my life as a serious person was over.

Near the end of August, Babe and I went on a picnic together to Blueberry Island. I swam briefly, feeling my usual anxiety about brushing against unfamiliar rocks or trees in the strange water. Babe lay in shorts and a man's shirt, with sleeves rolled up, and sunbathed.

I came out of the water and dried off. Babe sat up. We chatted briefly, about my mother, about how disappointed she was in me. Babe offered the theory that she probably lost interest in my musical career when she discovered you didn't wear little white gloves to play in concerts. I went down to the rowboat we'd pulled up onto the shoreline and brought back a sweatshirt for myself, and two blueberry pails. We walked into the center of the small island, screened from the lake by trees and brush, and knelt down to pick the berries. After a while, I asked Babe why everyone seemed so angry with her, why all the doors kept slamming shut on family conferences. Babe's lips and teeth were stained blue and she leaned back on her heels and said, 'You might as well know now, I guess. I'm going to have a baby. I'm almost three months pregnant. They're all in a twit. They *hate* my boyfriend, he's not *respectable* enough. They think I'm too young. Daddy brought me up here this summer to get me away, to bring me to my senses he said. They want me to go to Europe next year.' Tears began to slide down her face. 'All I want is just to be with Richard.'

I was stunned and appalled and thrilled, just as I had been

when she had shown us the secrets of her adolescent body. I remember I asked her why she and Richard didn't run away, and she said he had no money. He needed to finish college. He was ambitious and poor, and besides, he didn't know she was pregnant.

I asked her how *she* knew, and, eternally the teacher, she wiped her nose on her sleeve and carefully explained to me the way. Then she said she also knew almost right away by her body, how it looked and felt, and that was how Aunt Wizzy had found out about it – by seeing Babe naked and guessing.

'How *does* it feel, Babe?' I asked, knowing she would tell me. She smiled. 'Oh, wonderful. Kind of ripe and full. Like this.' She held up a fat berry. Then she put it between her teeth and popped it and we both laughed. A sudden shy silence fell between us. Then she said, 'Do you want to see?'

'Sure.' I said, trying to sound casual.

Babe stood up and stepped out of her shorts and underpants. The big shirt covered her to mid-thigh. She unbuttoned it ceremoniously, top to bottom, and took it off. Then undid her bra and let it drop. I was silent, embarrassed and aroused. Babe was beautiful. She had been beautiful even at my age, but now she looked like a woman to me. If her waist had thickened at all, it was just slightly, but a kind of heaviness seemed to pull her belly lower so it had a curve downward, and her thick fleecy hair seemed tucked underneath it. But her breasts were what most stirred me. They were still smallish, but they seemed fat, and the nipples had widened out like two silver dollars. She looked down at herself with satisfaction, and began, unselfconsciously, to explain the sequence of changes she was going through. I remember she held one breast fondly and set two fingers gently across the pale disc in the centre as she talked. If Norman Rockwell had ever gone in for the mildly erotic, he might have found a subject in us: Babe, beautiful anyway, and now lush, standing in a pool of discarded clothing, representing a womanhood I felt was impossible for me; and me, all acute angles, caught on the edge of pubescence, gaping at her in amazement. She smiled at me.

'Do you want to feel?'

I nodded, though I wasn't sure what I wanted. She stepped towards me, reaching for my paralysed hands, and raised them to her breasts. Her skin was softer even than it looked. My skinny brown hands, laced with tiny white scratches from the blueberry bushes, the nails clipped short out of habit for piano practice, seemed hard, male, by contrast with her silken perfection. Her voice was excited, telling me – what? I can't remember. She moved my hands down to her waist, then to her abdomen. I felt her fur brush against my fingertips, dry, and yet soft. As soon as she loosened her grip on me, I pulled my hands back.

When we returned, my grandmother uncharacteristically kissed Babe to thank her for the berries. She cooked them in pancakes for everyone the next morning, and suddenly the whole family, with their blue teeth, seemed part of Babe's secret to me. Except my grandfather. His breakfast was invariable, grapefruit and poached egg on wholewheat toast, and his smile stayed impeccably his own.

Less than a week later, Babe left, abruptly and tearfully, for Europe, accompanied by Aunt Rain. I rowed them across, facing my grandfather in the stern of the boat. He was to drive them to the train station in town. They each had only a small suitcase, but my grandmother was going to ship Babe's things to her later. As we walked up the path to the road where the car was parked, my grandfather pointed out places where it was growing over and suggested I bring the scythe with me when I rowed back to pick him up again.

Babe hugged me hard, and kissed me once, on the mouth, as though it were Richard she were saying goodbye to, not her niece. I noticed I was taller than she and the taste of her tears stayed in my mouth until I swallowed. I waved to the retreating car until all I could see was the dust settling behind it.

That fall and winter I waited for news of Babe's baby. From the family came reports of her adventures in Europe. She was doing well in school in Switzerland. She had enjoyed learning to ski in the Alps. She stayed with friends of the family in Paris at Christmas. She sent me a card from Paris. It showed the Madonna and Child on the front – the child a fat, real, mischievous boy, penis and all. Inside it said 'Noel'. She had written on the back: 'Life goes on, Europe isn't quite all it's cracked up to be, but the wine is wonderful, and I go through the days here agreeably, as I'm supposed to, a Jack O'Lantern's grin carved on my face. Keep up the good fight. Love, Babe.'

In the spring, striving to sound casual, I finally asked, 'Mother, was Aunt Babe ever going to have a baby?' She was sewing, and she looked up for a minute over the edge of her glasses. Her mouth pulled tight, and then she smiled.

'Of course not, dear. Aunt Babe's never even been *married*. You knew that.'

I recall that I blushed uncomfortably. My mother looked at me sharply, but then turned back to her sewing and nothing more was ever said.

My life went on also. My body changed in some of the ways Babe had promised, and I grew more comfortable in it, though not as comfortable as she would once have liked me to be. She seemed to shun most family gatherings. On those infrequent occasions when I did see her, she was usually fortified by a fair amount of booze and a new man. For a while after college she had a job in an art gallery in New York, and later at the Whitney Museum. Over the years I have drifted away more from the family, but apparently Babe had begun to effect a ginger reconciliation. The family party which was the occasion of her death was my grandparents' sixty-fifth wedding anniversary. I was absent, but I did make it a point to come to Babe's memorial service the next week.

We were lined up in generations in the church, my mother and aunts in the row in front of me and the other cousins. I could watch my grandparents sharing a hymnal in the front row, the one ahead of my mother. It seemed a reminder of our mortality, this arrangement; the blonde and jet black of my row giving way to the gray of our parents, and then to the yellowish white of Grandmother and Grandfather and the two extant great-aunts. My grandfather's voice sang out bravely and joyously the words to the hymn. My grandmother, I noticed, did not sing at all. The eulogy was short and somewhat impersonal, focussing on the untimely nature of Babe's passing, instead of saying anything about who she was.

My mother and her sisters seemed to be crying occasionally in the church, but in the car on the way to the family luncheon, Mother expressed what seemed like resentment over my grandmother's grief for Babe. 'After all,' she said, 'it isn't as though Babe were the one who did *anything* for her or Daddy all these years.'

For a little while, there was a kind of deliberate sobriety to the luncheon, but shortly after the fruit cup the aunts began to chatter, and my cousins to compare house purchases, pregnancies, and recipes. Only Orrie, sitting on my right, who couldn't stop telling his awful story over and over; and Grandmother, stony at the end of the table, seemed affected.

I had to leave early. I'd left my daughter with friends overnight, and needed to catch the afternoon plane home. I went around the table, whispering goodbyes to those who might be hurt if I didn't – my mother, grandfather, and the aunts; then I stopped at my grandmother's chair, and knelt next to her. She swung her head slowly towards me like someone hearing a distant call. I realised she was still strongly sedated.

'Gram?' I said. 'It's Anna. I came to say goodbye to you. I have to go.' I spoke clearly and slowly.

She reached out and touched my face in a kind of recognition. 'Say goodbye,' she repeated.

'Yes, I have to go. I'm sorry I can't stay longer. But I wanted just to come, to remember Babe today.' She kept nodding her assent.

'Edith,' she said mournfully.

'Yes, Edith. I was so sorry, Gram.' She nodded.

'I'm going now Gram. Goodbye.' She stopped nodding as I leaned forward to kiss her. Her hand clutched at mine. Her grip was bony and tight.

'Don't go,' she whispered.

'I'd like to stay, Gram, but my plane . . .'

'Don't leave me.' I looked at her face. It stayed inexpressive, but tears sat waiting in her eyes. Impulsively I put my free arm around her and held her. 'I can stay just a minute, Gram,' I said, patting her back.

She whispered in my ear, 'Don't leave me alone.'

Her body felt empty but for the frame of bones. I held her until her hand loosened its grip on mine. When I leaned back away from her, her face was completely blank again. I kissed her cheek. 'Goodbye, Gram.'

I sat alone on the plane. I ordered a drink, but even before it arrived I had begun to cry. The stewardess was concerned; asked me if I were all right. I assured her I would be, I had just been to a funeral. As I sipped the drink and stared out into the blank sky, I realised that I had never before heard anyone in the family call Babe by her christened name.

The Unnatural Mother
Charlotte Perkins Gilman

'Don't tell me!' said old Mis' Briggs, with a forbidding shake of the head. 'No mother that was a mother would desert her own child for anything on earth!'

'And leaving it a care on the town, too!' put in Susannah Jacobs. 'As if we hadn't enough to do to take care of our own!'

Miss Jacobs was a well-to-do old maid, owning a comfortable farm and homestead, and living alone with an impoverished cousin acting as general servant, companion, and protégée. Mis' Briggs, on the contrary, had had thirteen children, five of whom remained to bless her, so that what maternal feeling Miss Jacobs might lack, Mis' Briggs could certainly supply.

'I should think,' piped little Martha Ann Simmons, the village dressmaker, 'that she might 'a saved her young one first and then tried what she could do for the town.'

Martha had been married, had lost her husband, and had one sickly boy to care for.

The youngest Briggs girl, still unmarried at thirty-six, and in her mother's eyes a most tender infant, now ventured to make a remark.

'You don't any of you seem to think what she did for all of us – if she hadn't left hers we should all have lost ours, sure.'

'You ain't no call to judge, Maria 'Melia,' her mother hastened to reply. 'You've no children of your own, and you can't judge of a mother's duty. No mother ought to leave her child, whatever happens. The Lord gave it to her to take care of – he never gave her other people's. You needn't tell me!'

'She was an unnatural mother,' repeated Miss Jacobs harshly, 'as I said to begin with!'

'What is the story?' asked the City Boarder. The City Boarder was interested in stories from a business point of view, but they did not know that. 'What did this woman do?' she asked.

There was no difficulty in eliciting particulars. The difficulty was rather in discriminating amidst their profusion and contradictoriness. But when the City Boarder got it clear in her mind, it was somewhat as follows:

The name of the much-condemned heroine was Esther Greenwood, and she lived and died here in Toddsville.

Toddsville was a mill village. The Todds lived on a beautiful eminence overlooking the little town, as the castles of robber barons on the Rhine used to overlook their little towns. The mills and the mill hands' houses were built close along the bed of the river. They had to be pretty close, because the valley was a narrow one, and the bordering hills were too steep for travel, but the water power was fine. Above the village was the reservoir, filling the entire valley save for a narrow road beside it, a fair blue smiling lake, edged with lilies and blue flag, rich in pickerel and perch. This lake gave them fish, it gave them ice, it gave the power that ran the mills that gave the town its bread. Blue Lake was both useful and ornamental.

In this pretty and industrious village Esther had grown up, the somewhat neglected child of a heart-broken widower. He had lost a young wife, and three fair babies before her – this one was left him, and he said he meant that she should have all the chance there was.

'That was what ailed her in the first place!' they all eagerly explained to the City Boarder. 'She never knew what 'twas to have a mother, and she grew up a regular tomboy! Why, she used to roam the country for miles around, in all weather like an Injun! And her father wouldn't take no advice!'

This topic lent itself to eager discussion. The recreant father, it appeared, was a doctor, not their accepted standby, the resident physician of the neighborhood, but an alien doctor, possessed of 'views.'

'You never heard such things as he advocated,' Miss Jacobs explained. 'He wouldn't give no medicines, hardly; said "nature" did the curing – he couldn't.'

'And he couldn't either – that was clear,' Mrs Briggs agreed.

'Look at his wife and children dying on his hands, as it were! "Physician, heal thyself," I say.'

'But, Mother,' Maria Amelia put in, 'she was an invalid when he married her, they say; and those children died of polly – polly – what's that thing that nobody can help?'

'That may all be so,' Miss Jacobs admitted, 'but all the same, it's a doctor's business to give medicine. If "nature" was all that was wanted, we needn't have any doctor at all!'

'I believe in medicine and plenty of it. I always gave my children a good clearance, spring and fall, whether anything ailed 'em or not, just to be on the safe side. And if there was anything the matter with 'em, they had plenty more. I never had anything to reproach myself with on that score,' stated Mrs Briggs, firmly. Then as a sort of concession to the family graveyard, she added piously, 'The Lord giveth and the Lord taketh away.'

'You should have seen the way he dressed that child!' pursued Miss Jacobs. 'It was a reproach to the town. Why, you couldn't tell at a distance whether it was a boy or a girl. And barefoot! He let that child go barefoot till she was so big we was actually mortified to see her.'

It appeared that a wild, healthy childhood had made Esther very different in her early womanhood from the meek, well-behaved damsels of the little place. She was well enough liked by those who knew her at all, and the children of the place adored her, but the worthy matrons shook their heads and prophesied no good of a girl who was 'queer.'

She was described with rich detail in reminiscence, how she wore her hair short till she was fifteen – 'just shingled like a boy's – it did seem a shame that girl had no mother to look after her – and her clo'se was almost a scandal, even when she did put on shoes and stockings. Just gingham – brown gingham – and *short!*'

'I think she was a real nice girl,' said Maria Amelia. 'I can remember her just as well! She was *so* nice to us children. She was five or six years older than I was, and most girls that age won't have anything to do with little ones. But she was kind and pleasant. She'd take us berrying and on all sorts of walks, and teach us new games and tell us things. I don't remember anyone that ever did us the good she did!'

Maria Amelia's thin chest heaved with emotion, and there were tears in her eyes; but her mother took her up somewhat sharply.

'That sounds well I must say – right before your own mother that's toiled and slaved for you! It's all very well for a young thing that's got nothing on earth to do to make herself agreeable to young ones. That poor blinded father of hers never taught her to do the work a girl should – naturally he couldn't.'

'At least he might have married again and given her another mother,' said Susannah Jacobs, with decision, with so much decision, in fact, that the City Boarder studied her expression for a moment and concluded that if this recreant father had not married again it was not for lack of opportunity.

Mrs Simmons cast an understanding glance upon Miss Jacobs, and nodded wisely.

'Yes, he ought to have done that, of course. A man's not fit to bring up children, anyhow. How can they? Mothers have the instinct – that is, all natural mothers have. But, dear me! There's some as don't seem to *be* mothers – even when they have a child!'

'You're quite right, Mis' Simmons,' agreed the mother of thirteen. 'It's a divine instinct, I say. I'm sorry for the child that lacks it. Now this Esther. We always knew she wan't like other girls – she never seemed to care for dress and company and things girls naturally do, but was always philandering over the hills with a parcel of young ones. There wan't a child in town but would run after her. She made more trouble 'n a little in families, the young ones quotin' what Aunt Esther said, and tellin' what Aunt Esther did to their own mothers, and she only a young girl. Why, she actually seemed to care more for them children than she did for beaux or anything – it wasn't natural!'

'But she did marry?' pursued the City Boarder.

'Marry! Yes, she married finally. We all thought she never would, but she did. After the things her father taught her, it did seem as if he'd ruined *all* her chances. It's simply terrible the way that girl was trained.'

'Him being a doctor,' put in Mrs Simmons, 'made it different, I suppose.'

'Doctor or no doctor,' Miss Jacobs rigidly interposed, 'it was a crying shame to have a young girl so instructed.'

'Maria 'Melia,' said her mother, 'I want you should get me my smelling salts. They're up in the spare chamber, I believe. When your Aunt Marcia was here she had one of her spells – don't you remember? – and she asked for salts. Look in the top bureau drawer – they must be there.'

Maria Amelia, thirty-six but unmarried, withdrew dutifully, and the other ladies drew closer to the City Boarder.

'It's the most shocking thing I ever heard of,' murmured Mrs Briggs. 'Do you know he – a father – actually taught his daughter how babies come!'

There was a breathless hush.

'He did,' eagerly chimed in the little dressmaker. 'All the particulars. It was perfectly awful!'

'He said,' continued Mrs Briggs, 'that he expected her to be a mother and that she ought to understand what was before her!'

'He was waited on by a committee of ladies from the church, married ladies, all older than he was,' explained Miss Jacobs severely. 'They told him it was creating a scandal in the town – and what do you think he said?'

There was another breathless silence.

Above, the steps of Maria Amelia were heard, approaching the stairs.

'It ain't there, Ma!'

'Well, you look in the highboy and in the top drawer; they're somewhere up there,' her mother replied.

Then, in a sepulchral whisper:

'He told us – yes, ma'am, I was on that committee – he told us that until young women knew what was before them as mothers, they would not do their duty in choosing a father for their children! That was his expression – "choosing a father"! A nice thing for a young girl to be thinking of – a father for her children!'

'Yes, and more than that,' inserted Miss Jacobs, who, though not on the committee, seemed familiar with its workings. 'He told them –' But Mrs Briggs waved her aside and continued swiftly –

'He taught that innocent girl about – the Bad Disease! Actually!'

'He did!' said the dressmaker. 'It got out, too, all over town. There wasn't a man here would have married her after that.'

Miss Jacobs insisted on taking up the tale. 'I understand that he said it was "to protect her"! Protect her, indeed! Against matrimony! As if any man alive would want to marry a young girl who knew all the evil of life! I was brought up differently, I assure you!'

'Young girls should be kept innocent!' Mrs Briggs solemnly proclaimed. 'Why, when I was married I knew no more what was before me than a babe unborn, and my girls were all brought up so, too!'

Then, as Maria Amelia returned with the salts, she continued more loudly. 'But she did marry after all. And a mighty queer husband she got, too. He was an artist or something, made pictures for the magazines and such as that, and they do say she met him first out in the hills. That's the first 'twas known of it here, anyhow – them two traipsing about all over; him with his painting things! They married and just settled down to live with her father, for she vowed she wouldn't leave him; and he said it didn't make no difference where he lived, he took his business with him.'

'They seemed very happy together,' said Maria Amelia.

'Happy! Well, they might have been, I suppose. It was a pretty queer family, I think.' And her mother shook her head in retrospection. 'They got on all right for a while; but the old man died, and those two – well, I don't call it housekeeping – the way they lived!'

'No,' said Miss Jacobs. 'They spent more time out-of-doors than they did in the house. She followed him around everywhere. And for open lovemaking –'

They all showed deep disapproval at this memory. All but the City Boarder and Maria Amelia.

'She had one child, a girl,' continued Mrs Briggs, 'and it was just shocking to see how she neglected that child from the beginnin'. She never seemed to have no maternal feelin' at all!'

'But I thought you said she was very fond of children,' remonstrated the City Boarder.

'Oh, *children*, yes. She'd take up with any dirty-faced brat in town, even them Canucks. I've seen her again and again with a whole swarm of the mill hands' young ones round her, goin' on some picnic or other – "open air school", she used to call it – *such* notions as she had. But when it come to her own child! Why – ' Here the speaker's voice sank to a horrified hush. 'She never had no baby clo'se for it! Not a single sock!'

The City Boarder was interested. 'Why, what did she do with the little thing?'

'The Lord knows!' answered old Mis' Briggs. 'She never would let us hardly see it when 'twas little. 'Shamed too, I don't doubt. But that's strange feelin's for a mother. Why, I was so proud of my babies! And I kept 'em lookin' so pretty! I'd 'a sat up all night and sewed and washed, but I'd 'a had my children look well!' And the poor old eyes filled with tears as she thought of the eight little graves in the churchyard, which she never failed to keep looking pretty, even now. 'She just let that young one roll round in the grass like a puppy with hardly nothin' on! Why, a squaw does better. She does keep 'em done up for a spell! That child was treated worse 'n an Injun! We all done what we could, of course. We felt it no more 'n right. But she was real hateful about it, and we had to let her be.'

'The child died?' asked the City Boarder.

'Died! Dear no! That's it you saw going by; a great strappin' girl she is, too, and promisin' to grow up well, thanks to Mrs Stone's taking her. Mrs Stone always thought a heap of Esther. It's a mercy to the child that she lost her mother, I do believe! How she ever survived that kind of treatment beats all! Why, that woman never seemed to have the first spark of maternal feeling to the end! She seemed just as fond of the other young ones after she had her own as she was before, and that's against nature. The way it happened was this. You see, they lived up the valley nearer to the lake than the village. He was away, and was coming home that night, it seems, driving from Drayton along the lake road. And she set out to meet him. She must 'a walked up to the dam to look for him; and we think maybe she saw the team clear across the lake. Maybe she thought he could get to the house and save little Esther in time – that's the only explanation we ever could put on it. But this is what she did; and you can judge for yourselves if any mother in her senses *could* 'a done such a thing! You see 'twas the time of that awful disaster, you've read of it, likely, that destroyed three villages. Well, she got to the dam and seen that 'twas givin' way – she was always great for knowin' all such things. And she just turned and ran. Jake Elder was up on the hill after a stray cow, and he seen her go. He was too far off to imagine what ailed her, but he said he never saw a woman run so in his life.

'And, if you'll believe it, she run right by her own house – never stopped – never looked at it. Just run for the village. Of course, she may have lost her head with the fright, but that wasn't like her. No, I think she had made up her mind to leave that innocent baby to die! She just ran down here and give warnin', and, of course, we sent word down valley on horseback, and there was no lives lost in all three villages. She started to run back as soon as we was 'roused, but 'twas too late then.

'Jake saw it all, though he was too far off to do a thing. He said he couldn't stir a foot, it was so awful. He seen the wagon drivin' along as nice as you please till it got close to the dam, and then Greenwood seemed to see the danger and shipped up like mad. He was the father, you know. But he wasn't quite in time – the dam give way and the water went over him like a tidal wave. She was almost to the gate when it struck the house and her – and we never found her body nor his for days and days. They was washed clear down river.

'Their house was strong, and it stood a little high and had some big trees between it and the lake, too. It was moved off the place and brought up against the side of the stone church down yonder, but 'twant wholly in pieces. And that child was found swimmin' round in its bed, most drowned, but not quite. The wonder is, it didn't die of a cold, but it's here yet – must have a strong constitution. Their folks never did nothing for it – so we had to keep it here.'

'Well, now, Mother,' said Maria Amelia Briggs. 'It does seem to me that she did her duty. You know yourself that if she hadn't give warnin' all three of the villages would 'a been cleaned out – a matter of fifteen hundred people. And if she'd stopped to lug that child, she couldn't have got here in time. Don't you believe she was thinkin' of those mill hands' children?'

'Maria 'Melia, I'm ashamed of you!' said old Mis' Briggs. 'But you ain't married and ain't a mother. A mother's duty is to her own child! She neglected her own to look after other folks' – the Lord never gave her them other children to care for!'

'Yes,' said Miss Jacobs, 'and here's her child, a burden on the town! She was an unnatural mother!'

The Late Bud

Ama Ata Aidoo

'The good child who willingly goes on errands eats the food of peace.' This was a favourite saying in the house. Maami, Aunt Efua, Aunt Araba . . . oh, they all said it especially when they had prepared something delicious like cocoyam porridge and seasoned beef. You know how it is.

First, as they stirred it with the ladle, its scent rose from the pot and became a little cloud hanging over the hearth. Gradually, it spread through the courtyard and entered the inner and outer rooms of the women's apartments. This was the first scent that greeted the afternoon sleeper. She stretched herself luxuriously, inhaled a large quantity of the sweet scent, cried 'Mm' and either fell back again to sleep or got up to be about her business. The aroma did not stay. It rolled into the next house and the next, until it filled the whole neighbourhood. And Yaaba would sniff it.

As usual, she would be playing with her friends by the Big Trunk. She would suddenly throw down her pebbles even if it was her turn, jump up, shake her cloth free of sand and announce, 'I am going home.'

'Why?'

'Yaaba, why?'

But the questions of her amazed companions would reach her faintly like whispers. She was flying home. Having crossed the threshold, she then slunk by the wall. But there would be none for her.

Yaaba never stayed at home to go on an errand. Even when she was around, she never would fetch water to save a dying soul. How could she then eat the food of peace? Oh, if it was a formal meal, like in the morning or evening, that was a different matter. Of that, even Yaaba got her lawful share . . . But not this sweet-sweet porridge. 'Nsia, Antobam, Naabanyin, Adwoa, come for some porridge.' And the other children trooped in with their little plates and bowls. But not the figure by the wall. They chattered as they came and the mother teased as she dished out their titbits.

'Is yours alright, Adwoa? . . . and yours, Tawia? . . . yours is certainly sufficient, Antobam . . . But my child, this is only a titbit for us, the deserving. Other people,' and she would squint at Yaaba, 'who have not worked will not get the tiniest bit.' She then started eating hers. If Yaaba felt that the joke was being carried too far, she coughed. 'Oh,' the mother would cry out, 'people should be careful about their throats. Even if they coughed until they spat blood none of this porridge would touch their mouths.'

But it was not things and incidents like these which worried Yaaba. For inevitably, a mother's womb cried out for a lonely figure by a wall and she would be given some porridge. Even when her mother could be bile-bellied enough to look at her and dish out all the porridge, Yaaba could run into the doorway and ambush some child and rob him of the greater part of his share. No, it was not such things that worried her. Every mother might call her a bad girl. She enjoyed playing by the Big Trunk, for instance. Since to be a good girl, one had to stay by the hearth and not by the Big Trunk throwing pebbles, but with one's hands folded quietly on one's lap, waiting to be sent everywhere by all the mothers, Yaaba let people like Adwoa who wanted to be called 'good' be good. Thank you, she was not interested.

But there was something which disturbed Yaaba. No one knew it did, but it did. She used to wonder why, every time Maami called Adwoa, she called her 'My child Adwoa', while she was always merely called 'Yaaba'.

'My child Adwoa, pick me the drinking can . . . My child you have done well . . .'

Oh, it is so always. Am I not my mother's child?

'Yaaba, come for your food.' She always wished in her heart that she could ask somebody about it . . . Paapa . . . Maami

. . . Nana, am I not Maami's daughter? Who was my mother?

But you see, one does not go round asking elders such questions. Take the day Antobam asked her grandmother where her own mother was. The grandmother also asked Antobam whether she was not being looked after well, and then started weeping and saying things. Other mothers joined in the weeping. Then some more women came over from the neighbourhood and her aunts and uncles came too and there was more weeping and there was also drinking and libation-pouring. At the end of it all, they gave Antobam a stiff talking-to.

No, one does not go round asking one's elders such questions.

But Adwoa, my child, bring me the knife . . . Yaaba . . . Yaaba, your cloth is dirty. Yaaba, Yaaba . . .

It was the afternoon of the Saturday before Christmas Sunday. Yaaba had just come from the playgrounds to gobble down her afternoon meal. It was kenkey and a little fish stewed in palm oil. She had eaten in such a hurry that a bone had got stuck in her throat. She had drunk a lot of water but still the bone was sticking there. She did not want to tell Maami about it. She knew she would get a scolding or even a knock on the head. It was while she was in the outer room looking for a bit of kenkey to push down the troublesome bone that she heard Maami talking in the inner room.

'Ah, and what shall I do now? But I thought there was a whole big lump left . . . O . . . O! Things like this irritate me so. How can I spend Christmas without varnishing my floor?'

Yaaba discovered a piece of kenkey which was left from the week before, hidden in its huge wrappings. She pounced upon it and without breaking away the mildew, swallowed it. She choked, stretched her neck and the bone was gone. She drank some water and with her cloth, wiped away the tears which had started gathering in her eyes. She was about to bounce away to the playgrounds when she remembered that she had heard Maami speaking to herself.

Although one must not stand by to listen to elders if they are not addressing one, yet one can hide and listen. And anyway, it would be interesting to hear the sort of things our elders say to themselves. 'And how can I celebrate Christmas on a hardened, whitened floor?' Maami's voice went on. 'If I could only get a piece of red earth. But I cannot go round my friends begging, "Give me a piece of red earth." No. O . . . O! And it is growing dark already. If only my child Adwoa was here. I am sure she could have run to the red-earth pit and fetched me just a hoeful. Then I could varnish the floor before the church bells ring tomorrow.' Yaaba was thinking she had heard enough.

After all, our elders do not say anything interesting to themselves. It is their usual complaints about how difficult life is. If it is not the price of cloth or fish, then it is the scarcity of water. It is all very uninteresting. I will always play with my children when they grow up. I will not grumble about anything . . .

It was quite dark. The children could hardly see their own hands as they threw up the pebbles. But Yaaba insisted that they go on. There were only three left of the eight girls who were playing *soso-mba*. From time to time mothers, fathers or elder sisters had come and called to the others to go home. The two still with Yaaba were Panyin and Kakra. Their mother had travelled and that was why they were still there. No one came any longer to call Yaaba. Up till the year before, Maami always came to yell for her when it was sundown. When she could not come, she sent Adwoa. But of course, Yaaba never listened to them.

What is the point in breaking a game to go home? She stayed out and played even by herself until it was dark and she was satisfied. And now, at the age of ten, no one came to call her.

The pebble hit Kakra on the head.

'*Ajii.*'

'What is it?'

'The pebble has hit me.'

'I am sorry. It was not intentional.' Panyin said, 'But it is dark. Kakra, let us go home.' So they stood up.

'Panyin, will you go to church tomorrow?'

'No.'

'Why? You have no new cloths?'

'We have new cloths but we will not get gold chains or earrings. Our mother is not at home. She has gone to some place and will only return in the afternoon. Kakra, remember we will get up very early tomorrow morning.'

'Why?'

'Have you forgotten what mother told us before she went away? Did she not tell us to go and get some red earth from the pit? Yaaba, we are going away.'

'*Yoo.*'

And the twins turned towards home.

Red earth! The pit! Probably, Maami will be the only woman in the village who will not have red earth to varnish her floor. *Oo!*

'Panyin! Kakra! Panyin!'

'Who is calling us?'

'It is me, Yaaba. Wait for me.'

She ran in the darkness and almost collided with someone who was carrying food to her husband's house.

'Panyin, do you say you will go to the pit tomorrow morning?'

'Yes, what is it?'

'I want to go with you.'

'Why?'

'Because I want to get some red earth for my mother.'

'But tomorrow you will go to church.'

'Yes, but I will try to get it done in time to go to church as well.'

'See, you cannot. Do you not know the pit? It is very far away. Everyone will already be at church by the time we get back home.'

Yaaba stood quietly digging her right toe into the hard ground beneath her. 'It doesn't matter, I will go.'

'Do you not want to wear your gold things? Kakra and I are very sorry that we cannot wear ours because our mother is not here.'

'It does not matter. Come and wake me up.'

'Where do you sleep?'

'Under my mother's window. I will wake up if you hit the window with a small pebble.'

'*Yoo* . . . We will come to call you.'

'Do not forget your *apampa* and your hoe.'

'*Yoo.*'

When Yaaba arrived home, they had already finished eating the evening meal. Adwoa had arrived from an errand it seemed. In fact she had gone on several others. Yaaba was slinking like a cat to take her food which she knew would be under the wooden bowl, when Maami saw her. 'Yes, go and take it. You are hungry, are you not? And very soon you will be swallowing all that huge lump of fufu as quickly as a hen would swallow corn.' Yaaba stood still.

'*Aa.* My Father God, who inflicted on me such a child? Look here, Yaaba. You are growing, so be careful how you live your life. When you are ten years old you are not a child any more. And a woman that lives on the playground is not a woman. If you were a boy, it would be bad enough, but for a girl, it is a curse. The house cannot hold you. *Tchia.*'

Yaaba crept into the outer room. She saw the wooden bowl. She turned it over and as she had known all the time, her food was there. She swallowed it more quickly than a hen would have swallowed corn. When she finished eating, she went into the inner room, she picked her mat, spread it on the floor, threw herself down and was soon asleep. Long afterwards, Maami came in from the conversation with the other mothers. When she saw the figure of Yaaba, her heart did a somersault. Pooh, went her fists on the figure in the corner. Pooh, 'You lazy lazy thing.' Pooh, pooh! 'You good-for-nothing, empty-corn husk of a daughter . . . ' She pulled her ears, and Yaaba screamed. Still sleepy-eyed, she sat up on the mat.

'If you like, you scream, and watch what I will do to you. If I do not pull your mouth until it is as long as a pestle, then my name is not Benyiwa.'

But Yaaba was now wide awake and tearless. Who said she was screaming, anyway? She stared at Maami with shining tearless eyes. Maami was angry at this too.

'I spit in your eyes, witch! Stare at me and tell me if I am going to die tomorrow. At your age . . .' and the blows came pooh, pooh, pooh. 'You do not know that you wash yourself before your skin touches the mat. And after a long day in the sand, the dust and filth by the Big Trunk. *Hoo! Pooh!* You moth-bitten grain. *Pooh!'*

The clock in the chief's house struck twelve o'clock midnight. Yaaba never cried. She only tried, without success, to ward off the blows. Perhaps Maami was tired herself, perhaps she was satisfied. Or perhaps she was afraid she was putting herself in the position of Kweku Ananse tempting the spirits to carry their kindness as far as to come and help her beat her daughter. Of course, this would kill Yaaba. Anyway, she stopped beating her and lay down by Kofi, Kwame and Adwoa. Yaaba saw the figure of Adwoa lying peacefully there. It was then her eyes misted. The tears flowed from her eyes. Every time, she wiped them with her cloth but more came. They did not make any noise for Maami to hear. Soon the cloth was wet. When the clock struck one, she heard Maami snoring. She herself could not sleep even when she lay down.

Is this woman my mother?

Perhaps I should not go and fetch her some red earth. But the twins will come . . .

Yaaba rose and went into the outer room. There was no door between the inner and outer rooms to creak and wake anybody. She wanted the *apampa* and a hoe. At ten years of age, she should have had her own of both, but of course, she had not. Adwoa's hoe, she knew, was in the corner left of the door. She groped and found it. She also knew Adwoa's *apampa* was on the bamboo shelf. It was when she turned and was groping towards the bamboo shelf that she stumbled over the large water-bowl. Her chest hit the edge of the tray. The tray tilted and the water poured on the floor. She could not rise up. When Maami heard the noise her fall made, she screamed 'Thief! Thief! Thief! Everybody, come, there is a thief in my room.'

She gave the thief a chance to run away since he might attack her before the men of the village came. But no thief rushed through the door and there were no running footsteps in the courtyard. In fact, all was too quiet.

She picked up the lantern, pushed the wick up to blazing point and went gingerly to the outer room. There was Yaaba, sprawled like a freshly-killed overgrown cock on the tray. She screamed again.

'Ah Yaaba, why do you frighten me like this? What were you looking for? That is why I always say you are a witch. What do you want at this time of the night that you should fall on a water-bowl? And look at the floor. But of course, you were playing when someone lent me a piece of red earth to polish it, eh?' The figure in the tray just lay there. Maami bent down to help her up and then she saw the hoe. She stood up again.

'A hoe! I swear by all that be that I do not understand this.' She lifted her up and was carrying her to the inner room when Yaaba's lips parted as if to say something. She closed the lips again, her eyelids fluttered down and the neck sagged. 'My Saviour!' There was nothing strange in the fact that the cry was heard in the north and south of the village. Was it not past midnight?

People had heard Maami's first cry of 'Thief' and by the time she cried out again, the first men were coming from all directions. Soon the courtyard was full. Questions and answers went round. Some said Yaaba was trying to catch a thief, others that she was running from her mother's beating. But the first thing was to wake her up.

'Pour anowata into her nose!' – and the mothers ran into their husbands' chambers to bring their giant-sized bottles of the sweetest scents. 'Touch her feet with a little fire' . . . 'Squeeze a little ginger juice into her nose.'

The latter was done and before she could suffer further ordeals, Yaaba's eyelids fluttered up.

'Aa . . . Oo . . . we thank God. She is awake, she is awake.' Everyone said it. Some were too far away and saw her neither in the faint nor awake. But they said it as they trooped back to piece together their broken sleep. Egya Yaw, the village medicine-man, examined her and told the now-mad Maami that she should not worry. 'The impact was violent but I do not think anything has happened to the breast-bone. I will bind her up in beaten herbs, and she should be all right in a few days.' 'Thank you, Egya,' said Maami, Paapa, her grandmother, the other mothers and all her relatives. The medicine-man went

to his house and came back. Yaaba's brawniest uncles beat up
the herbs. Soon, Yaaba was bound up. The cock had crowed
once, when they laid her down. Her relatives then left for their
own homes. Only Maami, Paapa and the other mothers were
left. 'And how is she?' one of the women asked.

'But what really happened?'

'Only Benyiwa can answer you.'

'Benyiwa, what happened?'

'But I am surprised myself. After she had eaten her kenkey
this afternoon, I heard her movements in the outer room but I
did not mind her. Then she went away and came back when it
was dark to eat her food. After our talk, I went to sleep. And
there she was lying. As usual, she had not had a wash, so I just
held her . . .'

'You held her what? Had she met with death you would have
been the one that pushed her into it – beating a child in the
night!'

'But Yaaba is too troublesome!'

'And so you think every child will be good? But how did she
come to fall in the tray?'

'That is what I cannot tell. My eyes were just playing me
tricks when I heard some noise in the outer room.'

'Is that why you cried "Thief"?'

'Yes. When I went to see what it was, I saw her lying in the
tray, clutching a hoe.'

'A hoe?'

'Yes, Adwoa's hoe.'

'Perhaps there was a thief after all? She can tell us the truth
. . . but . . .'

So they went on through the early morning. Yaaba slept. The
second cock-crow came. The church bell soon did its Christmas
reveille. In the distance, they heard the songs of the dawn
procession. Quite near in the doorway, the regular pat, pat of
the twins' footsteps drew nearer towards the elderly group by
the hearth. Both parties were surprised at the encounter.

'Children, what do you want at dawn?'

'Where is Yaaba?'

'Yaaba is asleep.'

'May we go and wake her, she asked us to.'

'Why?'

'She said she will go with us to the red-earth pit.'

'O . . . O!' The group around the hearth was amazed but they did not show it before the children.

'*Yoo*. You go today. She may come with you next time.'

'*Yoo*, Mother.'

'Walk well, my children. When she wakes up, we shall tell her you came.'

'We cannot understand it. Yaaba? What affected her head?'

'My sister, the world is a strange place. That is all.'

'And my sister, the child that will not do anything is better than a sheep.'

'Benyiwa, we will go and lie down a little.'

'Good morning.'

'Good morning.'

'Good morning.'

'*Yoo*. I thank you all.'

So Maami went into the apartment and closed the door. She knelt by the sleeping Yaaba and put her left hand on her bound chest. 'My child, I say thank you. You were getting ready to go and fetch me red earth? Is that why you were holding the hoe? My child, my child, I thank you.'

And the tears streamed down her face. Yaaba heard 'My child' from very far away. She opened her eyes. Maami was weeping and still calling her 'My child' and saying things which she did not understand.

Is Maami really calling me that? May the twins come. Am I Maami's own child?

'My child Yaaba . . .'

But how will I get red earth?

But why can I not speak . . .?

'I wish the twins would come . . .'

I want to wear the gold earrings . . .

I want to know whether Maami called me her child. Does it mean I am her child like Adwoa is? But one does not ask our elders such questions. And anyway, there is too much pain. And there are barriers where my chest is.

Probably tomorrow ... but now Maami called me 'My child!' ...

And she fell asleep again.

Everyday Use

Alice Walker

for your grandmama

I will wait for her in the yard that Maggie and I made so clean and wavy yesterday afternoon. A yard like this is more comfortable than most people know. It is not just a yard. It is like an extended living-room. When the hard clay is swept clean as a floor and the fine sand around the edges lined with tiny, irregular grooves, anyone can come and sit and look up into the elm tree and wait for the breezes that never come inside the house.

Maggie will be nervous until after her sister goes: she will stand hopelessly in corners, homely and ashamed of the burn scars down her arms and legs, eyeing her sister with a mixture of envy and awe. She thinks her sister has held life always in the palm of one hand, that 'no' is a word the world never learned to say to her.

You've no doubt seen those TV shows where the child who has 'made it' is confronted, as a surprise, by her own mother and father, tottering in weakly from backstage. (A pleasant surprise, of course: What would they do if parent and child came on the show only to curse out and insult each other?) On TV mother and child embrace and smile into each other's faces. Sometimes the mother and father weep, the child wraps them in her arms and leans across the table to tell how she would not have made it without their help. I have seen these programmes.

Sometimes I dream a dream in which Dee and I are suddenly brought together on a TV programme of this sort. Out of a dark and soft-seated limousine I am ushered into a bright room filled with many people. There I meet a smiling, grey, sporty man like Johnny Carson who shakes my hand and tells me what a fine girl I have. Then we are on the stage and Dee is embracing me with tears in her eyes. She pins on my dress a large orchid, even though she has told me once that she thinks orchids are tacky flowers.

In real life I am a large, big-boned woman with rough, man-working hands. In the winter I wear flannel night-gowns to bed and overalls during the day. I can kill and clean a hog as mercilessly as a man. My fat keeps me hot in zero weather. I can work outside all day, breaking ice to get water for washing; I can eat pork liver cooked over the open fire minutes after it comes steaming from the hog. One winter I knocked a bull calf straight in the brain between the eyes with a sledge hammer and had the meat hung up to chill before nightfall. But of course all this does not show on television. I am the way my daughter would want me to be: a hundred pounds lighter, my skin like an uncooked barley pancake. My hair glistens in the hot bright lights. Johnny Carson has much to do to keep up with my quick and witty tongue.

But that is a mistake. I know even before I wake up. Who ever knew a Johnson with a quick tongue? Who can even imagine me looking a strange white man in the eye? It seems to me I have talked to them always with one foot raised in flight, with my head turned in whichever way is farthest from them. Dee, though. She would always look anyone in the eye. Hesitation was no part of her nature.

'How do I look, Mama?' Maggie says, showing just enough of her thin body enveloped in pink skirt and red blouse for me to know she's there, almost hidden by the door.

'Come out into the yard,' I say.

Have you ever seen a lame animal, perhaps a dog run over by some careless person rich enough to own a car, sidle up to someone who is ignorant enough to be kind to him? That is the way my Maggie walks. She has been like this, chin on chest, eyes on ground, feet in shuffle, ever since the fire that burned the other house to the ground.

Dee is lighter than Maggie, with nicer hair and a fuller figure. She's a woman now, though sometimes I forget. How long ago was it that the other house burned? Ten, twelve years? Sometimes I can still hear the flames and feel Maggie's arms sticking to me, her hair smoking and her dress falling off her in little black papery flakes. Her eyes seemed stretched open, blazed open by the flames reflected in them. And Dee. I see her standing off under the sweet gum tree she used to dig gum out of; a look of concentration on her face as she watched the last dingy grey board of the house fall in toward the red-hot brick chimney. Why don't you do a dance around the ashes? I'd wanted to ask her. She had hated the house that much.

I used to think she hated Maggie, too. But that was before we raised the money, the church and me, to send her to Augusta to school. She used to read to us without pity; forcing words, lies, other folks' habits, whole lives upon us two, sitting trapped and ignorant underneath her voice. She washed us in a river of make-believe, burned us with a lot of knowledge we didn't necessarily need to know. Pressed us to her with the serious way she read, to shove us away at just the moment, like dimwits, we seemed about to understand.

Dee wanted nice things. A yellow organdie dress to wear to her graduation from high school; black pumps to match a green suit she'd made from an old suit somebody gave me. She was determined to stare down any disaster in her efforts. Her eyelids would not flicker for minutes at a time. Often I fought off the temptation to shake her. At sixteen she had a style of her own: and knew what style was.

I never had an education myself. After second grade the school was closed down. Don't ask me why: in 1927 coloured asked fewer questions than they do now. Sometimes Maggie reads to me. She stumbles along good-naturedly but can't see well. She knows she is not bright. Like good looks and money, quickness passed her by. She will marry John Thomas (who has mossy teeth in an earnest face) and then I'll be free to sit here and I guess just sing church songs to myself. Although I never was a good singer. Never could carry a tune. I was always better at a man's job. I used to love to milk till I was hooked in the side in '49. Cows are soothing and slow and don't bother you, unless you try to milk them the wrong way.

I have deliberately turned my back on the house. It is three rooms, just like the one that burned, except the roof is tin; they don't make shingle roofs any more. There are no real windows, just some holes cut in the sides, like the portholes in a ship, but not round and not square, with rawhide holding the shutters up on the outside. This house is in a pasture, too, like the other one. No doubt when Dee sees it she will want to tear it down. She wrote me once that no matter where we 'choose' to live, she will manage to come see us. But she will never bring her friends. Maggie and I thought about this and Maggie asked me, 'Mama, when did Dee ever *have* any friends?'

She had a few. Furtive boys in pink shirts hanging about on washday after school. Nervous girls who never laughed. Impressed with her they worshipped the well-turned phrase, the cute shape, the scalding humour that erupted like bubbles in lye. She read to them.

When she was courting Jimmy T she didn't have much time to pay to us, but turned all her faultfinding power on him. He *flew* to marry a cheap city girl from a family of ignorant flashy people. She hardly had time to recompose herself.

When she comes I will meet – but there they are!

Maggie attempts to make a dash for the house, in her shuffling way, but I stay her with my hand. 'Come back here,' I say. And she stops and tries to dig a well in the sand with her toe.

It is hard to see them clearly through the strong sun. But even the first glimpse of leg out of the car tells me it is Dee. Her feet were always neat-looking, as if God himself had shaped them with a certain style. From the other side of the car comes a short, stocky man. Hair is all over his head a foot long and hanging from his chin like a kinky mule tail. I hear Maggie suck in her breath. 'Uhnnnh', is what it sounds like. Like when you see the wriggling end of a snake just in front of your foot on the road. 'Uhnnnh.'

Dee next. A dress down to the ground, in this hot weather. A dress so loud it hurts my eyes. There are yellows and oranges enough to throw back the light of the sun. I feel my whole face warming from the heat waves it throws out. Earrings gold, too, and hanging down to her shoulders. Bracelets dangling and making noises when she moves her arm up to shake the folds of the dress out of her armpits. The dress is loose and flows, and as she walks closer, I like it. I hear Maggie go 'Uhnnnh' again. It is her sister's hair. It stands straight up like the wool on a sheep. It is black as night and around the edges are two long pigtails that rope about like small lizards disappearing behind her ears.

'Wa-su-zo-Tean-o!' she says, coming on in that gliding way the dress makes her move. The short stocky fellow with the hair to his navel is all grinning and he follows up with 'Asalamalakim, my mother and sister!' He moves to hug Maggie but she falls back, right up against the back of my chair. I feel her trembling there and when I look up I see the perspiration falling off her chin.

'Don't get up,' says Dee. Since I am stout it takes something of a push. You can see me trying to move a second or two before I make it. She turns, showing white heels through her sandals, and goes back to the car. Out she peeks next with a Polaroid. She stoops down quickly and lines up picture after picture of me sitting there in front of the house with Maggie cowering behind me. She never takes a shot without making sure the house is included. When a cow comes nibbling around the edge of the yard she snaps it and me and Maggie *and* the house. Then she puts the Polaroid in the back seat of the car, and comes up and kisses me on the forehead.

Meanwhile Asalamalakim is going through motions with Maggie's hand. Maggie's hand is as limp as a fish, and probably as cold, despite the sweat, and she keeps trying to pull it back. It looks like Asalamalakim wants to shake hands but wants to do it fancy. Or maybe he don't know how people shake hands. Anyhow, he soon gives up on Maggie.

'Well,' I say. 'Dee.'

'No, Mama,' she says. 'Not "Dee", Wangero Leewanika Kemanjo!'

'What happened to "Dee"?' I wanted to know.

'She's dead,' Wangero said. 'I couldn't bear it any longer, being named after the people who oppress me.'

'You know as well as me you was named after your aunt Dicie,' I said. Dicie is my sister. She named Dee. We called her 'Big Dee' after Dee was born.

'But who was *she* named after?' asked Wangero.

'I guess after Grandma Dee,' I said.

'And who was she named after?' asked Wangero.

'Her mother,' I said, and saw Wangero was getting tired. 'That's about as far back as I can trace it,' I said. Though, in fact, I probably could have carried it back beyond the Civil War through the branches.

'Well,' said Asalamalakim, 'there you are.'

'Uhnnnh,' I heard Maggie say.

'There I was not,' I said, 'before "Dicie" cropped up in our family, so why should I try to trace it that far back?'

He just stood there grinning, looking down on me like somebody inspecting a Model A car. Every once in a while he and Wangero sent eye signals over my head.

'How do you pronounce this name?' I asked.

'You don't have to call me by it if you don't want to,' said Wangero.

'Why shouldn't I?' I asked. 'If that's what you want us to call you, we'll call you.'

'I know it might sound awkward at first,' said Wangero.

'I'll get used to it,' I said. 'Ream it out again.'

Well, soon we got the name out of the way. Asalamalakim had a name twice as long and three times as hard. After I tripped over it two or three times he told me to just call him Hakim-a-barber. I wanted to ask him was he a barber, but I didn't really think he was, so I didn't ask.

'You must belong to those beef-cattle peoples down the road,' I said. They said 'Asalamalakim' when they met you, too, but they didn't shake hands. Always too busy: feeding the cattle, fixing the fences, putting up salt-lick shelters, throwing down hay. When the white folks poisoned some of the herd the men stayed up all night with rifles in their hands. I walked a mile and a half just to see the sight.

Hakim-a-barber said, 'I accept some of their doctrines, but farming and raising cattle is not my style.' (They didn't tell me, and I didn't ask, whether Wangero (Dee) had really gone and married him.)

We sat down to eat and right away he said he didn't eat collards and pork was unclean. Wangero, though, went on through the chitlins and corn bread, the greens and everything else. She talked a blue streak over the sweet potatoes. Everything delighted her. Even the fact that we still used the benches her daddy made for the table when we couldn't afford to buy chairs.

'Oh, Mama!' she cried. Then turned to Hakim-a-barber. 'I never knew how lovely these benches are. You can feel the rump prints,' she said, running her hands underneath her and along the bench. Then she gave a sigh and her hand closed over Grandma Dee's butter dish. 'That's it!' she said. 'I knew there was something I wanted to ask you if I could have.' She jumped up from the table and went over in the corner where the churn stood, the milk in it clabber by now. She looked at the churn and looked at it.

'This churn top is what I need,' she said. 'Didn't Uncle Buddy whittle it out of a tree you all used to have?'

'Yes,' I said.

'Uh huh,' she said happily. 'And I want the dasher, too.'

'Uncle Buddy whittle that, too?' asked the barber.

Dee (Wangero) looked up at me.

'Aunt Dee's first husband whittled the dash,' said Maggie so low you almost couldn't hear her. 'His name was Henry, but they called him Stash.'

'Maggie's brain is like an elephant's,' Wangero said, laughing. 'I can use the churn top as a centrepiece for the alcove table,' she said, sliding a plate over the churn, 'and I'll think of something artistic to do with the dasher.'

When she finished wrapping the dasher the handle stuck out. I took it for a moment in my hands. You didn't even have to look close to see where hands pushing the dasher up and down to make butter had left a kind of sink in the wood. In fact, there were a lot of small sinks; you could see where thumbs and fingers had sunk into the wood. It was beautiful light yellow wood, from a tree that grew in the yard where Big Dee and Stash had lived.

After dinner Dee (Wangero) went to the trunk at the foot of my bed and started rifling through it. Maggie hung back in the kitchen over the dishpan. Out came Wangero with two quilts. They had been pieced by Grandma Dee and then Big Dee and me had hung them on the quilt frames on the front porch and quilted them. One was in the Lone Star pattern. The other was Walk Around the Mountain. In both of them were scraps of dresses Grandma Dee had worn fifty and more years ago. Bits and pieces of Grandpa Jarrell's Paisley shirts. And one teeny faded blue piece, about the size of a penny matchbox, that was from Great Grandpa Ezra's uniform that he wore in the Civil War.

'Mama,' Wangero said sweet as a bird. 'Can I have these old quilts?'

I heard something fall in the kitchen, and a minute later the kitchen door slammed.

'Why don't you take one or two of the others?' I asked. 'These old things was just done by me and Big Dee from some tops your grandma pieced before she died.'

'No,' said Wangero. 'I don't want those. They are stitched around the borders by machine.'

'That'll make them last better,' I said.

'That's not the point,' said Wangero. 'These are all pieces of dresses Grandma used to wear. She did all this stitching by hand. Imagine!' She held the quilts securely in her arms, stroking them.

'Some of the pieces, like those lavender ones, come from old clothes her mother handed down to her,' I said, moving up to touch the quilts. Dee (Wangero) moved back just enough so that I couldn't reach the quilts. They already belonged to her.

'Imagine!' she breathed again, clutching them closely to her bosom.

'The truth is,' I said, 'I promised to give them quilts to Maggie, for when she marries John Thomas.'

She gasped like a bee had stung her.

'Maggie can't appreciate these quilts!' she said. 'She'd probably be backward enough to put them to everyday use.'

'I reckon she would,' I said. 'God knows I been saving 'em for long enough with nobody using 'em. I hope she will!' I didn't want to bring up how I had offered Dee (Wangero) a quilt when she went away to college. Then she had told me they were old-fashioned, out of style.

'But they're *priceless*!' she was saying now, furiously; for she has a temper. 'Maggie would put them on the bed and in five years they'd be in rags. Less than that!'

'She can always make some more,' I said. 'Maggie knows how to quilt.'

Dee (Wangero) looked at me with hatred. 'You just will not understand. The point is these quilts, *these* quilts!'

'Well,' I said, stumped. 'What would *you* do with them?'

'Hang them,' she said. As if that was the only thing you could do with quilts.

Maggie by now was standing in the door. I could almost hear the sound her feet made as they scraped over each other.

'She can have them, Mama,' she said, like somebody used to never winning anything, or having anything reserved for her. 'I can 'member Grandma Dee without the quilts.'

I looked at her hard. She had filled her bottom lip with checkerberry snuff and it gave her face a kind of dopey, hangdog look. It was Grandma Dee and Big Dee who taught her how to quilt herself. She stood there with her scarred hands hidden in the folds of her skirt. She looked at her sister with something like fear but she wasn't mad at her. This was Maggie's portion. This was the way she knew God to work.

When I looked at her like that something hit me in the top of my head and ran down to the soles of my feet. Just like when I'm in church and the spirit of God touches me and I get happy and shout. I did something I never had done before: hugged Maggie to me, then dragged her on into the room, snatched the quilts out of Miss Wangero's hands and dumped them into Maggie's lap. Maggie just sat there on my bed with her mouth open.

'Take one or two of the others,' I said to Dee.

But she turned without a word and went out to Hakim-a-barber.

'You just don't understand,' she said, as Maggie and I came out to the car.

'What don't I understand?' I wanted to know.

'Your heritage,' she said. And then she turned to Maggie, kissed her, and said, 'You ought to try to make something of yourself, too, Maggie. It's really a new day for us. But from the way you and Mama still live you'd never know it.'

She put on some sunglasses that hid everything above the tip of her nose and her chin.

Maggie smiled; maybe at the sunglasses. But a real smile, not scared. After we watched the car dust settle I asked Maggie to bring me a dip of snuff. And then the two of us sat there just enjoying, until it was time to go in the house and go to bed.

The Day
Mr Prescott Died

Sylvia Plath

It was a bright day, a hot day, the day old Mr Prescott died.
Mama and I sat on the side seat of the rickety green bus from
the subway station to Devonshire Terrace and jogged and
jogged. The sweat was trickling down my back, I could feel it,
and my black linen was stuck solid against the seat. Every time
I moved it would come loose with a tearing sound, and I gave
Mama an angry 'so there' look, just like it was her fault, which
it wasn't. But she only sat with her hands folded in her lap,
jouncing up and down, and didn't say anything. Just looked
resigned to fate is all.

'I say, Mama,' I'd told her after Mrs Mayfair called that
morning, 'I can see going to the funeral even though I don't
believe in funerals, only what do you mean we have to sit up
and watch with them?'

'It is what you do when somebody close dies,' Mama said,
very reasonable. 'You go over and sit with them. It is a bad
time.'

'So it is a bad time,' I argued. 'So what can I do, not seeing
Liz and Ben Prescott since I was a kid except once a year at
Christmas time for giving presents at Mrs Mayfair's. I am
supposed to sit around hold handkerchiefs, maybe?'

With that remark, Mama up and slapped me across the
mouth, the way she hadn't done since I was a little kid and very
fresh. 'You are coming with me,' she said in her dignified tone
that means definitely no more fooling.

So that is how I happened to be sitting in this bus on the

hottest day of the year. I wasn't sure how you dressed for waiting up with people, but I figured as long as it was black it was all right. So I had on this real smart black linen suit and a little veil hat, like I wear to the office when I go out to dinner nights, and I felt ready for anything.

Well, the bus chugged along and we went through the real bad parts of East Boston I hadn't seen since I was a kid. Ever since we moved to the country with Aunt Myra, I hadn't come back to my home town. The only thing I really missed after we moved was the ocean. Even today on this bus I caught myself waiting for that first stretch of blue.

'Look, Mama, there's the old beach,' I said, pointing.

Mama looked and smiled. 'Yes.' Then she turned around to me and her thin face got very serious. 'I want you to make me proud of you today. When you talk, talk. But talk nice. None of this fancy business about burning people up like roast pigs. It isn't decent.'

'Oh, Mama,' I said, very tired. I was always explaining. 'Don't you know I've got better sense. Just because old Mr Prescott had it coming. Just because nobody's sorry, don't think I won't be nice and proper.'

I knew that would get Mama. 'What do you mean nobody's sorry?' she hissed at me, first making sure people weren't near enough to listen. 'What do you mean, talking so nasty?'

'Now, Mama,' I said, 'you know Mr Prescott was twenty years older than Mrs Prescott and she was just waiting for him to die so she could have some fun. Just waiting. He was a grumpy old man even as far back as I remember. A cross word for everybody, and he kept getting that skin disease on his hands.'

'That was a pity the poor man couldn't help,' Mama said piously. 'He had a right to be crotchety over his hands itching all the time, rubbing them the way he did.'

'Remember the time he came to Christmas Eve supper last year?' I went on stubbornly. 'He sat at the table and kept rubbing his hands so loud you couldn't hear anything else, only the skin like sandpaper flaking off in little pieces. How would you like to live with *that* every day?'

I had her there. No doubt about it, Mr Prescott's going was no sorrow for anybody. It was the best thing that could have happened all around.

'Well,' Mama breathed, 'we can at least be glad he went so quick and easy. I only hope I go like that when my time comes.'

Then the streets were crowding up together all of a sudden, and there we were by old Devonshire Terrace and Mama was pulling the buzzer. The bus dived to a stop, and I grabbed hold of the chipped chromium pole behind the driver just before I would have shot out the front window. 'Thanks, mister,' I said in my best icy tone, and minced down from the bus.

'Remember,' Mama said as we walked down the sidewalk, going single file where there was a hydrant, it was so narrow, 'remember, we stay as long as they need us. And no complaining. Just wash dishes, or talk to Liz, or whatever.'

'But Mama,' I complained, 'how can I say I'm sorry about Mr Prescott when I'm really not sorry at all? When I really think it's a good thing?'

'You can say it is the mercy of the Lord he went so peaceful,' Mama said sternly. 'Then you will be telling the honest truth.'

I got nervous only when we turned up the little gravel drive by the old yellow house the Prescotts owned on Devonshire Terrace. I didn't feel even the least bit sad. The orange-and-green awning was out over the porch, just like I remembered, and after ten years it didn't look any different, only smaller. And the two poplar trees on each side of the door had shrunk, but that was all.

As I helped Mama up the stone steps onto the porch, I could hear a creaking and sure enough, there was Ben Prescott sitting and swinging on the porch hammock like it was any other day in the world but the one his Pop died. He just sat there, lanky and tall as life. What really surprised me was he had his favorite guitar in the hammock beside him. Like he'd just finished playing 'The Big Rock Candy Mountain', or something.

'Hello Ben,' Mama said mournfully. 'I'm so sorry.'

Ben looked embarrassed. 'Heck, that's all right,' he said. 'The folks are all in the living-room.'

I followed Mama in through the screen door, giving Ben a

little smile. I didn't know whether it was all right to smile because Ben was a nice guy, or whether I shouldn't, out of respect for his Pop.

Inside the house, it was like I remembered too, very dark so you could hardly see, and the green window blinds didn't help. They were all pulled down. Because of the heat or the funeral, I couldn't tell. Mama felt her way to the living-room and drew back the portières, 'Lydia?' she called.

'Agnes?' There was this little stir in the dark of the living-room and Mrs Prescott came out to meet us. I had never seen her looking so well, even though the powder on her face was all streaked from crying.

I only stood there while the two of them hugged and kissed and made sympathetic little noises to each other. Then Mrs Prescott turned to me and gave me her cheek to kiss. I tried to look sad again but it just wouldn't come, so I said, 'You don't know how surprised we were to hear about Mr Prescott.' Really, though, nobody was at all surprised, because the old man only needed one more heart attack and that would be that. But it was the right thing to say.

'Ah, yes,' Mrs Prescott sighed. 'I hadn't thought to see this day for many a long year yet.' And she led us into the living-room.

After I got used to the dim light, I could make out the people sitting around. There was Mrs Mayfair, who was Mrs Prescott's sister-in-law and the most enormous woman I've ever seen. She was in the corner by the piano. Then there was Liz, who barely said hello to me. She was in shorts and an old shirt, smoking one drag after the other. For a girl who had seen her father die that morning, she was real casual, only a little pale is all.

Well, when we were all settled, no one said anything for a minute, as if waiting for a cue, like before a show begins. Only Mrs Mayfair, sitting there in her layers of fat, was wiping away her eyes with a handkerchief, and I was reasonably sure it was sweat running down and not tears by a long shot.

'It's a shame,' Mama began then, very low, 'It's a shame, Lydia, that it had to happen like this. I was so quick in coming I didn't hear tell who found him even.'

Mama pronounced 'him' like it should have a capital H, but I guessed it was safe now that old Mr Prescott wouldn't be bothering anybody again, with that mean temper and those raspy hands. Anyhow, it was just the lead that Mrs Prescott was waiting for.

'Oh, Agnes,' she began, with a peculiar shining light to her face, 'I wasn't even here. It was Liz found him, poor child.'

'Poor child,' sniffed Mrs Mayfair into her handkerchief. Her huge red face wrinkled up like a cracked watermelon. 'He dropped dead right in her arms he did.'

Liz didn't say anything, but just ground out one cigarette only half smoked and lit another. Her hands weren't even shaking. And believe me, I looked real carefully.

'I was at the rabbi's,' Mrs Prescott took up. She is a great one for these new religions. All the time it is some new minister or preacher having dinner at her house. So now it's a rabbi, yet. 'I was at the rabbi's, and Liz was home getting dinner when Pop came home from swimming. You know the way he always loved to swim, Agnes.'

Mama said yes, she knew the way Mr Prescott always loved to swim.

'Well,' Mrs Prescott went on, calm as this guy on the Dragnet program, 'it wasn't more than eleven-thirty. Pop always liked a morning dip, even when the water was like ice, and he came up and was in the yard drying off, talking to our next door neighbor over the hollyhock fence.'

'He just put up that very fence a year ago,' Mrs Mayfair interrupted, like it was an important clue.

'And Mr Gove, this nice man next door, thought Pop looked funny, blue, he said, and Pop all at once didn't answer him but just stood there staring with a silly smile on his face.'

Liz was looking out of the front window where there was still the sound of the hammock creaking on the front porch. She was blowing smoke rings. Not a word the whole time. Smoke rings only.

'So Mr Gove yells to Liz and she comes running out, and Pop falls like a tree right to the ground, and Mr Gove runs to

get some brandy in the house while Liz holds Pop in her
arms . . .'

'What happened then?' I couldn't help asking, just the way I
used to when I was a kid and Mama was telling burglar
stories.

'Then,' Mrs Prescott told us, 'Pop just . . . passed away, right
there in Liz's arms. Before he could even finish the brandy.'

'Oh, Lydia,' Mama cried. 'What you have been through!'

Mrs Prescott didn't look as if she had been through much of
anything. Mrs Mayfair began sobbing in her handkerchief and
invoking the name of the Lord. She must have had it in for the
old guy, because she kept praying, 'Oh, forgive us our sins,' like
she had up and killed him herself.

'We will go on,' Mrs Prescott said, smiling bravely. 'Pop
would have wanted us to go on.'

'That is all the best of us can do,' Mama sighed.

'I only hope I go as peacefully,' Mrs Prescott said.

'Forgive us our sins,' Mrs Mayfair sobbed to no one in
particular.

At this point, the creaking of the hammock stopped outside
and Ben Prescott stood in the doorway, blinking his eyes behind
the thick glasses and trying to see where we all were in the dark.
'I'm hungry,' he said.

'I think we should all eat now,' Mrs Prescott smiled on us.
'The neighbors have brought over enough to last a week.'

'Turkey and ham, soup and salad,' Liz remarked in a bored
tone, like she was a waitress reading off a menu. 'I just didn't
know where to put it all.'

'Oh, Lydia,' Mama exclaimed, 'Let *us* get it ready. Let *us*
help. I hope it isn't too much trouble . . .'

'Trouble, no,' Mrs Prescott smiled her new radiant smile.
'We'll let the young folks get it.'

Mama turned to me with one of her purposeful nods and
I jumped up like I had an electric shock. 'Show me where
the things are, Liz,' I said, 'and we'll get this set up in no
time.'

Ben tailed us out to the kitchen, where the black old gas stove
was, and the sink, full of dirty dishes. First thing I did was pick

up a big heavy glass soaking in the sink and run myself a long drink of water.

'My, I'm thirsty,' I said and gulped it down. Liz and Ben were staring at me like they were hypnotised. Then I noticed the water had a funny taste, as if I hadn't washed out the glass well enough and there were drops of some strong drink left in the bottom to mix with the water.

'That,' said Liz after a drag on her cigarette, 'is the last glass Pop drank out of. But never mind.'

'Oh Lordy, I'm sorry,' I said, putting it down fast. All at once I felt very much like being sick because I had a picture of old Mr Prescott, drinking his last from the glass and turning blue. 'I really am sorry.'

Ben grinned 'Somebody's got to drink out of it someday.' I liked Ben. He was always a practical guy when he wanted to be.

Liz went upstairs to change then, after showing me what to get ready for supper.

'Mind if I bring in my guitar?' Ben asked, while I was starting to fix up the potato salad.

'Sure, it's okay by me,' I said. 'Only won't folks talk? Guitars being mostly for parties and all?'

'So let them talk. I've got a yen to strum.'

I made tracks around the kitchen and Ben didn't say much, only sat and played these hillbilly songs very soft, that made you want to laugh and sometimes cry.

'You know, Ben,' I said, cutting up a plate of cold turkey, 'I wonder, are you really sorry.'

Ben grinned, that way he has. 'Not really sorry, now, but I could have been nicer. Could have been nicer, that's all.'

I thought of Mama, and suddenly all the sad part I hadn't been able to find during the day came up in my throat. 'We'll go on better than before,' I said. And then I quoted Mama like I never thought I would: 'It's all the best of us can do.' And I went to take the hot pea soup off the stove.

'Queer, isn't it,' Ben said. 'How you think something is dead and you're free, and then you find it sitting in your own guts laughing at you. Like I don't feel Pop has really died. He's down there somewhere inside of me, looking at what's going on. And grinning away.'

'That can be the good part,' I said, suddenly knowing that it really could. 'The part you don't have to run from. You know you take it with you, and then when you go any place, it's not running away. It's just growing up.'

Ben smiled at me, and I went to call the folks in. Supper was kind of a quiet meal, with lots of good cold ham and turkey. We talked about my job at the insurance office, and I even made Mrs Mayfair laugh, telling about my boss Mr Murray and his trick cigars. Liz was almost engaged, Mrs Prescott said, and she wasn't half herself unless Barry was around. Not a mention of old Mr Prescott.

Mrs Mayfair gorged herself on three desserts and kept saying, 'Just a sliver, that's all. Just a sliver!' when the chocolate cake went round.

'Poor Henrietta,' Mrs Prescott said, watching her enormous sister-in-law spooning down ice cream. 'It's that psychosomatic hunger they're always talking about. Makes her eat so.'

After coffee which Liz made on the grinder, so you could smell how good it was, there was an awkward little silence. Mama kept picking up her cup and sipping from it, although I could tell she was really all through. Liz was smoking again, so there was a small cloud of haze around her. Ben was making an airplane glider out of his paper napkin.

'Well,' Mrs Prescott cleared her throat, 'I guess I'll go over to the parlor now with Henrietta. Understand, Agnes, I'm not old-fashioned about this. It said definitely no flowers and no one needs to come. It's only a few of Pop's business associates kind of expect it.'

'I'll come,' said Mama staunchly.

'The children aren't going,' Mrs Prescott said. 'They've had enough already.'

'Barry's coming over later,' Liz said. 'I have to wash up.'

'I will do the dishes,' I volunteered, not looking at Mama. 'Ben will help me.'

'Well, that takes care of everybody, I guess.' Mrs Prescott

helped Mrs Mayfair to her feet, and Mama took her other arm. The last I saw of them, they were holding Mrs Mayfair while she backed down the front steps, huffing and puffing. It was the only way she could go down safe, without falling, she said.

Hostages

Fay Zwicky

I think I began to hate when I was twelve. Consciously, I mean. The war was then in its fourth year, there was no chocolate and my father was still away in Borneo. I barely knew him. Till then I had learnt to admire what my mother believed to be admirable. Striving to please with ascetic rigour, I practised scales and read Greek myths. Morality hinged on hours of piano practice achieved or neglected. I knew no evil. The uncommon neutrality of my existence as a musical child in wartime was secured in a world neither good nor malevolent. My place among men was given. Did I have feelings? I was not ready to admit them for there seemed to be rules governing their revelation which I either could not or would not grasp. Nameless, passionless, and without daring I repressed deepest candour. But *tout comprendre c'est tout pardonner*; what was once self-indulgence is now permissible revelation. Why, then, should shame crimp the edge of my reflection so many years after the event?

It all started with the weekly visit to our house of a German refugee piano teacher, Sophie Lindauer-Grunberg. Poor fat sentimental Sophie, grateful recipient of my mother's pity. I was to be her first Australian pupil.

'But why me?'

'Because she needs help. She has nothing and you, thank God, have everything. She's been a very fine musician in her own country. You have to understand that this is someone who has lost everything. Yes, you can roll your eyes. *Everything*, I said. Something I hope, please God, will never happen to you. So you'll be nice to her and pay attention to what she says. I've told Mr Grover he lives too far away for me to go on taking you to lessons twice a week.'

Suddenly dull and bumbling Mr Grover in his music room smelling of tobacco and hair oil seemed like my last contact with the outside world. I was to be corralled into the tight, airless circle of maternal philanthropy.

The day of my first lesson a hot north wind was tearing at the huge gum in front of the house. Blinds and curtains were drawn against the promised heat. The house stood girded like an island under siege. My younger brother and sister had gone swimming. I watched them go, screwing up my eyes with the beginnings of a headache, envying their laughter and the way they tore sprigs off the lantana plants lining the driveway. I awaited my teacher, a recalcitrant hostage. The rooms were generous and high-ceilinged but I prowled about, tight-lipped, seeking yet more room. A deep nerve of anger throbbed in me and I prayed that she would not come. But she came. Slowly up the brick path in the heat. I watched her from the window, measuring her heavy step with my uneasy breath. Then my mother's voice greeting her in the hallway, high-pitched and over-articulated as if her listener were deaf, a standard affectation of hers with foreign visitors. 'Terrible day . . . trouble finding the house . . . Helen looking forward so much . . .' I ran to the bathroom and turned on the tap hard. I just let it run, catching sight of my face in the mirror above the basin.

Could I be called pretty? Brown hair hanging long on either side of high cheekbones, the hint of a powerful nose to come, a chin too long, cold grey eyes, wide mouth, fresh colour. No, not pretty. No heroine either. A wave of self-pity compensated me for what I saw and tears filled my eyes. Why me? Because she has to have pupils. Am I such a prize? No, but a Jew who has everything. 'Be thankful you were born in this wonderful country.' My mother's voice sounded loud in my ears. 'They're making them into lampshades over there.' I had laughed but shrank from the grotesque absurdity of the statement. Why the dramatics? All I remember is the enveloping anger directed at everything my life had been and was. I wanted to be left alone but didn't know how or where to begin. 'She has lost her whole family. Taken away and shot before her eyes . . .' So? Now she has me.

My mother and Miss Grunberg were talking about me as I stood in the doorway. My own hands were clammy as I moved forward to the outstretched unfamiliar gesture. Hers were small, fat and very white, surprisingly small for such a tall, heavily built woman, like soft snuggling grubs. She herself looked like some swollen, pale grub smiling widely and kindly, a spinster of nearly sixty. Her little eyes gleamed through thick, round spectacles. On the skin beneath her eyes tiny bluish vessels spread their nets.

'So here is *unsere liebe Helene!*'

I raised my eyebrows insolently as the girls did at school after one of my own ill-judged observations. It was essential to the code governing the treatment of victims. But this time I had the upper hand and didn't know how to handle my advantage. The cobbles of Köln and Cracow rang hollow under my boots. The light from the pink shaded lamp fell on my new teacher. The wind blew in sharp gusts outside.

'Helen, this is Miss Grunberg.' My mother with a sharp look in my direction. 'I've been telling her about the work you've done so far with Mr Grover. Miss Grunberg would like you to have another book of studies.'

'Perhaps you will play *ein Stück* for me. Liszt perhaps?' She nodded ponderously at our Bechstein grand that suddenly took on the semblance of some monstrous piece of abstract statuary, out of all proportion to the scale of the room. 'Lord no. I've never done him.' I fell into uncharacteristic breeziness. 'I'm not really in practice. Hardly anything going at the moment and I'm pretty stale on the stuff Grover had me on for the exams.' Deliberately fast, consciously idiomatic, enjoying, yes, *enjoying* the strain of comprehension on my victim's round, perpetually smiling face. 'You can *still* play those Debussy "Arabesques",' said my mother, her neck flushed. 'I put the music on the piano', and she gave me yet another warning look.

I opened the lid noisily and sat down with elaborate movements, shifting the metronome a few inches to the right, altering the position of the stand, bending to examine my feet fumbling between the pedals. The 'Arabesques' moved perfunctorily. I kept my face impassive, looked rigidly ahead at the music which I didn't see. Even during the section I liked in the second piece, a part where normally I would lean back a little and smile. I had begun to learn how not to please. But the process of self-annihilation involved the destruction of others. *Tout pardonner* did I say?

Miss Grunberg arranged with my mother to return the following week at the same time. 'Why are you behaving like this?' asked my mother, red and angry with me after she had left in a taxi. The young blond driver had tapped his foot noisily on the brick path as Miss Grunberg profusely repeated her gratitude to my mother for the privilege of teaching her talented daughter. Moving rapidly away from them I conversed with him, broadening my vowels like sharks' teeth on the subject of the noon temperature. I was desperate that the coveted outside world and its tranquil normality should recognise that I was in no way linked with the heavy foreign accent involved in demonstrative leave-taking on our front lawn.

'Behaving like what?'

'You know what I mean. You behaved abominably to that poor woman.'

'I played for her, didn't I?' She came closer to me with a vengeful mouth.

'You could call it that. I don't know what's got into you lately. You used to be such a good child. Now you know the answers to everything. A walking miracle! What terrible things have we done, your father and I, that you should behave like a pig to a woman like that? We've given you everything. *Everything!* And because I'm good to an unfortunate refugee who needs help wherever she can find it, you have to behave like that! I'm sorry for you, *really* sorry for you!'

'Spare your sympathy for the poor reffoes!' The taxi driver's word burst savagely out of my mouth. She flew at me and slapped me across the face with her outstretched hand.

'One thing I do know,' she was trembling with rage, 'the one thing I'm sure of is that I've been too good to you. We've given you too much. You're spoilt rotten! And *one* day, my girl, one day you too may be old and unwanted and . . .'

'A lampshade perhaps? So what.' I shook with guilt and fear at the enormity of what I'd said, terrified of the holocaust I'd shaken loose and my mother's twisted mouth.

But the revolution didn't get under way either that day or that year. The heroine lacked (should one say it?) courage. Sealed trains are more comforting than the unknown wastes of the steppes. The following week Miss Grunberg toiled up our front path and I sat down to the new course of Moscheles studies and a movement of a Mozart concerto. *Her* music. Scored heavily in red pencil, the loved and hated language dotted with emotional exclamation marks. Her life's work put out for my ruthless inspection. She moved her chair closer to my stool to alter the position of my right hand. 'Finger *rund*, *Kleine*, always *rund*. Hold always the wrist supple, *liebe Helene*.' I shrank from the alien endearment and her sour breath but curved my fingers, tight and deliberate. Her smell hung over me, a static haze in the dry air. Musty, pungent and stale, the last faint reminder of an airless Munich apartment house. Her dress, of cheap silky fabric, rustled when she moved her heavy body. Breathing laboriously she tried to explain to me what I should do with the Mozart. She couldn't get used to the heat of the new country and was beginning to find walking difficult. But I didn't practise between her visits and gave only spasmodic attention to her gentle directions. I was shutting myself off from words and from music, beginning a long course in alienation. I seldom looked my mother in the eye in those days. I quarrelled bitterly with my sister, ignored my brother.

About six months after my lessons with Miss Grunberg started I was not much further advanced. I spent a lot of time reading in my room or just looking out of the window at the garden which was now bare. Squalls lashed the gum-tree and drove the leaves from the weeping elm skittering across the grass. Miss Grunberg now had several pupils amongst the children of the Jewish community and even one or two gentiles from the neighbouring school. She lived in a very poorly fur-nished flat in a run-down outer suburb. She still travelled to her pupils' homes. Her breathing had become very short in the last few weeks. Inattentive and isolated as I was, I had noticed that she was even paler than usual.

My mother one day told me with some rancour how well the Lapin girl was doing with the piano. 'She never had your talent but what a worker! She's going to give a recital in the Assembly Hall next month.' I merely shrugged. The boots of the conqueror were no picnic. She was welcome to them. 'And while I'm about it, I've decided to tell Miss Grunberg not to come any more. I don't feel there's much point as you seem quite determined to do as little with music as possible. I've done all *I* can. At least she's on her feet now.' On her feet! Oh God! But I replied, 'That's all right with me' in as neutral a voice as I could summon.

But that night I ground my face into the covers of my bed, no longer a place of warmth and security but a burial trench. At the mercy of my dreams appeared Sophie Lindauer-Grunberg, pale as brick dust. Her face wasting, crumbling to ash, blasted by the force of my terrible youth. And, waking in fright, I mourned for the first time my innocent victim and our shared fate.

New Life at Kyerefaso

Efua Sutherland

Shall we say
Shall we put it this way
Shall we say that the maid of Kyerefaso, Foruwa, daughter of
the Queen Mother, was as a young deer, graceful in limb? Such
was she, with head held high, eyes soft and wide with wonder.
And she was light of foot, light in all her moving.

Stepping springily along the water path like a deer that had
strayed from the thicket, springily stepping along the water
path, she was a picture to give the eye a feast. And nobody
passed her by but turned to look at her again.

Those of her village said that her voice in speech was like the
murmur of a river quietly flowing beneath shadows of bamboo
leaves. They said her smile would sometimes blossom like a lily
on her lips and sometimes rise like sunrise.

The butterflies do not fly away from the flowers, they draw
near. Foruwa was the flower of her village.

So shall we say,

Shall we put it this way, that all the village butterflies, the
men, tried to draw near her at every turn, crossed and crossed
her path? Men said of her, 'She shall be my wife, and mine, and
mine and mine.'

But suns rose and set, moons silvered and died and as the
days passed Foruwa grew more lovesome, yet she became no
one's wife. She smiled at the butterflies and waved her hand
lightly to greet them as she went swiftly about her daily work:

'Morning, Kweku
Morning, Kwesi

Morning, Kodwo'
but that was all.

And so they said, even while their hearts thumped for her:
'Proud!

Foruwa is proud . . . and very strange'
And so the men when they gathered would say:

'There goes a strange girl. She is not just the stiff-in-the-neck proud, not just breasts-stuck-out I-am-the-only-girl-in-the-village proud. What kind of pride is hers?'

The end of the year came round again, bringing the season of festivals. For the gathering in of corn, yams and cocoa there were harvest celebrations. There were bride-meetings too. And it came to the time when the Asafo companies should hold their festival. The village was full of manly sounds, loud musketry and swelling choruses.

The pathfinding, path-clearing ceremony came to an end. The Asafo marched on toward the Queen Mother's house, the women fussing round them, prancing round them, spreading their cloths in their way.

'Osee!' rang the cry. 'Osee!' to the manly men of old. They crouched like leopards upon the branches.

Before the drums beat
Before the danger drums beat, beware!
Before the horns moaned
Before the wailing horns moaned, beware!

They were upright, they sprang. They sprang. They sprang upon the enemy. But now, blood no more! No more thundershot on thundershot.

But still we are the leopards on the branches. We are those who roar and cannot be answered back. Beware, we are they who cannot be answered back.

There was excitement outside the Queen Mother's courtyard gate.

'Gently, gently,' warned the Asafo leader. 'Here comes the Queen Mother.

Spread skins of the gentle sheep in her way.

Lightly, lightly walks our Mother Queen.
Shower her with silver,
Shower her with silver for she is peace.'

And the Queen Mother stood there, tall, beautiful, before the men and there was silence.

'What news, what news do you bring?' she quietly asked.

'We come with dusty brows from our pathfinding, Mother. We come with tired, thorn-pricked feet. We come to bathe in the coolness of your peaceful stream. We come to offer our manliness to new life.'

The Queen Mother stood there, tall and beautiful and quiet. Her fanbearers stood by her and all the women clustered near. One by one the men laid their guns at her feet and then she said:

'It is well. The gun is laid aside. The gun's rage is silenced in the stream. Let your weapons from now on be your minds and your hands' toil.

'Come maidens, women all, join the men in dance for they offer themselves to new life.'

There was one girl who did not dance.

'What, Foruwa!' urged the Queen Mother, 'Will you not dance? The men are tired of parading in the ashes of their grandfathers' glorious deeds. That should make you smile. They are tired of the empty croak: "We are men, we are men."

'They are tired of sitting like vultures upon the rubbish heaps they have piled upon the half-built walls of their grandfathers. Smile, then, Foruwa, smile.

'Their brows shall now indeed be dusty, their feet thorn-picked, and "I love my land" shall cease to be the empty croaking of a vulture upon the rubbish heap. Dance, Foruwa, dance!'

Foruwa opened her lips and this was all she said: 'Mother, I do not find him here.'

'Who? Who do you not find here?'

'He with whom this new life shall be built. He is not here, Mother. These men's faces are empty; there is nothing in them, nothing at all.'

'Alas, Foruwa, alas, alas! What will become of you, my daughter?'

'The day I find him, Mother, the day I find the man, I shall come running to you, and your worries will come to an end.'

'But, Foruwa, Foruwa,' argued the Queen Mother, although in her heart she understood her daughter, 'five years ago your rites were fulfilled. Where is the child of your womb? Your friend Maanan married. Your friend Esi married. Both had their rites with you.'

'Yes, Mother, they married and see how their steps once lively now drag in the dust. The sparkle has died out of their eyes. Their husbands drink palm wine the day long under the mango trees, drink palm wine and push counters across the draughtboards all the day, and are they not already looking for other wives? Mother, the man I say is not here.'

The conversation had been overheard by one of the men and soon others heard what Foruwa had said. That evening there was heard a new song in the village.

> There was a woman long ago,
> Tell that maid, tell that maid,
> There was a woman long ago,
> She would not marry Kwesi,
> She would not marry Kwaw,
> She would not, would not, would not.
> One day she came home with hurrying feet,
> I've found the man, the man, the man,
> Tell that maid, tell that maid,
> Her man looked like a chief,
> Tell that maid, tell that maid,
> Her man looked like a chief,
> Most splendid to see,
> But he turned into a python,
> He turned into a python
> *And swallowed her up.*

From that time onward there were some in the village who turned their backs on Foruwa when she passed.

Shall we say
Shall we put it this way

Shall we say that a day came when Foruwa with hurrying feet came running to her mother? She burst through the courtyard gate; and there she stood in the courtyard, joy all over. And a stranger walked in after her and stood in the courtyard beside her, stood tall and strong as a pillar. Foruwa said to the astonished Queen Mother:

'Here he is, Mother, here is the man.'

The Queen Mother took a slow look at the stranger standing there strong as a forest tree, and she said:

'You carry the light of wisdom on your face, my son. Greetings, you are welcome. But who are you, my son?'

'Greetings, Mother,' replied the stranger quietly, 'I am a worker. My hands are all I have to offer your daughter, for they are all my riches. I have travelled to see how men work in other lands. I have that knowledge and my strength. That is all my story.'

Shall we say,

Shall we put it this way,

strange as the story is, that Foruwa was given in marriage to the stranger.

There was a rage in the village and many openly mocked saying, 'Now the proud ones eat the dust.'

Shall we say,

Shall we put it this way

that soon, quite soon, the people of Kyerefaso began to take notice of the stranger in quite a different way.

'Who,' some said, 'is this who has come among us? He who mingles sweat and song, he for whom toil is joy and life is full and abundant?'

'See,' said others, 'what a harvest the land yields under his ceaseless care.'

'He has taken the earth and moulded it into bricks. See what a home he has built, how it graces the village where it stands.'

'Look at the craft of his fingers, baskets or kente, stool or mat, the man makes them all.'

'And our children swarm about him, gazing at him with wonder and delight.'

Then it did not satisfy them any more to sit all day at their draughtboards under the mango trees.

'See what Foruwa's husband has done,' they declared; 'shall the sons of the land not do the same?'

And soon they began to seek out the stranger to talk with him. Soon they too were toiling, their fields began to yield as never before, and the women laboured joyfully to bring in the harvest. A new spirit stirred the village. As the carelessly built houses disappeared one by one, and new homes built after the fashion of the stranger's grew up, it seemed as if the village of Kyerefaso had been born afresh.

The people themselves became more alive and a new pride possessed them. They were no longer just grabbing from the land what they desired for their stomachs' present hunger and for their present comfort. They were looking at the land with new eyes, feeling it in their blood, and thoughtfully building a permanent and beautiful place for themselves and their children.

'Osee!' It was festival-time again. 'Osee!' Blood no more. Our fathers found for us the paths. We are the roadmakers. They bought for us the land with their blood. We shall build it with our strength. We shall create it with our minds.

Following the men were the women and children. On their heads they carried every kind of produce that the land had yielded and crafts that their fingers had created. Green plantains and yellow bananas were carried by the bunch in large white wooden trays. Garden eggs, tomatoes, red oil-palm nuts warmed by the sun were piled high in black earthen vessels. Oranges, yams, maize filled shining brass trays and golden calabashes. Here and there were children proudly carrying colourful mats, baskets and toys which they themselves had made.

The Queen Mother watched the procession gathering on the new village playground now richly green from recent rains. She watched the people palpitating in a massive dance toward her where she stood with her fan bearers outside the royal house. She caught sight of Foruwa. Her load of charcoal in a large brass tray which she had adorned with red hibiscus danced with her body. Happiness filled the Queen Mother when she saw her daughter thus.

Then she caught sight of Foruwa's husband. He was carrying a white lamb in his arms, and he was singing happily with the men. She looked on him with pride. The procession had approached the royal house.

'See!' rang the cry of the Asafo leader. 'See how the best in all the land stands. See how she stands waiting, our Queen Mother. Waiting to wash the dust from our brow in the coolness of her peaceful stream. Spread skins of the gentle sheep in her way, gently. Spread the yield of the land before her. Spread the craft of your hands before her, gently, gently.

'Lightly, lightly walks our Queen Mother, for she is peace.'

Weekend

Fay Weldon

By seven-thirty they were ready to go. Martha had everything packed into the car and the three children appropriately dressed and in the back seat, complete with educational games and wholewheat biscuits. When everything was ready in the car Martin would switch off the television, come downstairs, lock up the house, front and back, and take the wheel.

Weekend! Only two hours' drive down to the cottage on Friday evenings: three hours' drive back on Sunday nights. The pleasures of greenery and guests in between. They reckoned themselves fortunate, how fortunate!

On Fridays Martha would get home on the bus at six-twelve and prepare tea and sandwiches for the family: then she would strip four beds and put the sheets and quilt covers in the washing machine for Monday: take the country bedding from the airing basket, plus the books and the games, plus the weekend food – acquired at intervals throughout the week, to lessen the load – plus her own folder of work from the office, plus Martin's drawing materials (she was a market researcher in an advertising agency, he a freelance designer) plus hairbrushes, jeans, spare T-shirts, Jolyon's antibiotics (he suffered from sore throats), Jenny's recorder, Jasper's cassette player and so on – ah, the so on! – and would pack them all, skilfully and quickly, into the boot. Very little could be left in the cottage during the week. ('An open invitation to burglars': Martin) Then Martha would run round the house tidying and wiping, doing this and that, finding the cat at one neighbour's and delivering it to another, while the others ate their tea; and would usually, proudly, have everything finished by the time they had eaten their fill. Martin would just catch the BBC 2 news, while Martha cleared away the tea table, and the children tossed up for the best positions in the car. 'Martha,' said Martin, tonight, 'you ought to get Mrs Hodder to do more. She takes advantage of you.'

Mrs Hodder came in twice a week to clean. She was over seventy. She charged two pounds an hour. Martha paid her out of her own wages: well, the running of the house was Martha's concern. If Martha chose to go out to work – as was her perfect right, Martin allowed, even though it wasn't the best thing for the children, but that must be Martha's moral responsibility – Martha must surely pay her domestic stand-in. An evident truth, heard loud and clear and frequent in Martin's mouth and Martha's heart.

'I expect you're right,' said Martha. She did not want to argue. Martin had had a long hard week, and now had to drive. Martha couldn't. Martha's licence had been suspended four months back for drunken driving. Everyone agreed that the suspension was unfair: Martha seldom drank to excess: she was for one thing usually too busy pouring drinks for other people or washing other people's glasses to get much inside herself. But Martin had taken her out to dinner on her birthday, as was his custom, and exhaustion and excitement mixed had made her imprudent, and before she knew where she was, why there she was, in the dock, with a distorted lamp-post to pay for and a new bonnet for the car and six months' suspension.

So now Martin had to drive her car down to the cottage, and he was always tired on Fridays, and hot and sleepy on Sundays, and every rattle and clank and bump in the engine she felt to be somehow her fault.

Martin had a little sports car for London and work: it could nip in and out of the traffic nicely: Martha's was an old estate car, with room for the children, picnic baskets, bedding, food, games, plants, drink, portable television and all the things required by the middle classes for weekends in the country. It lumbered rather than zipped and made Martin angry. He seldom spoke a harsh word, but Martha, after the fashion of wives, could detect his mood from what he did not say rather than what he did, and from the tilt of his head, and the way his crinkly, merry eyes seemed crinklier and merrier still – and of course from the way he addressed Martha's car.

'Come along, you old banger you! Can't you do better than that? You're too old, that's your trouble. Stop complaining. Always complaining, it's only a hill. You're too wide about the hips. You'll never get through there.'

Martha worried about her age, her tendency to complain, and the width of her hips. She took the remarks personally. Was she right to do so? The children noticed nothing: it was just funny lively laughing Daddy being witty about Mummy's car. Mummy, done for drunken driving. Mummy, with the roots of melancholy somewhere deep beneath the bustling, busy, everyday self. Busy: ah so busy!

Martin would only laugh if she said anything about the way he spoke to her car and warn her against paranoia. 'Don't get like your mother, darling.' Martha's mother had, towards the end, thought that people were plotting against her. Martha's mother had led a secluded, suspicious life, and made Martha's childhood a chilly and a lonely time. Life now, by comparison, was wonderful for Martha. People, children, houses, conversations, food, drink, theatres – even, now, a career. Martin standing between her and the hostility of the world – popular, easy, funny Martin, beckoning the rest of the world into earshot.

Ah, she was grateful: little earnest Martha, with her shy ways and her penchant for passing boring exams – how her life had blossomed out! Three children too – Jasper, Jenny and Jolyon – all with Martin's broad brow and open looks, and the confidence born of her love and care, and the work she had put into them since the dawning of their days.

Martin drives. Martha, for once, drowses.

The right food, the right words, the right play. Doctors for the tonsils: dentists for the molars. Confiscate guns: censor television: encourage creativity. Paints and paper to hand: books on the shelves: meetings with teachers. Music teachers. Dancing lessons. Parties. Friends to tea. School plays. Open days. Junior orchestra.

Martha is jolted awake. Traffic lights. Martin doesn't like Martha to sleep while he drives.

Clothes. Oh, clothes! Can't wear this: must wear that. Dress shops. Piles of clothes in corners: duly washed, but waiting to be ironed, waiting to be put away.

Get the piles off the floor, into the laundry baskets. Martin doesn't like a mess.

Creativity arises out of order, not chaos. Five years off work while the children were small: back to work with seniority lost. What, did you think something was for nothing? If you have children, mother, that is your reward. It lies not in the world.

Have you taken enough food? Always hard to judge.

Food. Oh, food! Shop in the lunch-hour. Lug it all home. Cook for the freezer on Wednesday evenings while Martin is at his car-maintenance evening class, and isn't there to notice you being unrestful. Martin likes you to sit down in the evenings. Fruit, meat, vegetables, flour for home-made bread. Well, shop bread is full of pollutants. Frozen food, even your own, loses flavour. Martin often remarks on it. Condiments. Everyone loves mango chutney. But the expense!

London Airport to the left. Look, look, children! Concorde? No, idiot, of course it isn't Concorde.

Ah, to be all things to all people: children, husband, employer, friends! It can be done: yes, it can: super woman.

Drink. Home-made wine. Why not? Elderberries grown thick and rich in London: and at least you know what's in it. Store it in high cupboards: lots of room: up and down the step-ladder. Careful! Don't slip. Don't break anything.

No such thing as an accident. Accidents are Freudian slips: they are wilful, bad-tempered things.

Martin can't bear bad temper. Martin likes slim ladies. Diet. Martin rather likes his secretary. Diet. Martin admires slim legs and big bosoms. How to achieve them both? Impossible. But try, oh try, to be what you ought to be, not what you are. Inside and out.

Martin brings back flowers and chocolates: whisks Martha off for holiday weekends. Wonderful! The best husband in the world: look into his crinkly, merry, gentle eyes; see it there. So the mouth slopes away into something of a pout. Never mind.

Gaze into the eyes. Love. It must be love. You married him. *You.* Surely *you* deserve true love?

Salisbury Plain. Stonehenge. Look, children, look! Mother, we've seen Stonehenge a hundred times. Go back to sleep.

Cook! Ah cook. People love to come to Martin and Martha's dinners. Work it out in your head in the lunch-hour. If you get in at six-twelve, you can seal the meat while you beat the egg white while you feed the cat while you lay the table while you string the beans while you set out the cheese, goat's cheese, Martin loves goat's cheese, Martha tries to like goat's cheese – oh, bed, sleep, peace, quiet.

Sex! Ah sex. Orgasm, please. Martin requires it. Well, so do you. And you don't want his secretary providing a passion you neglected to develop. Do you? Quick, quick, the cosmic bond. Love. Married love.

Secretary! Probably a vulgar suspicion: nothing more. Probably a fit of paranoics, à la mother, now dead and gone.

At peace.

R.I.P.

Chilly, lonely mother, following her suspicions where they led.

Nearly there, children. Nearly in paradise, nearly at the cottage. Have another biscuit.

Real roses round the door.

Roses. Prune, weed, spray, feed, pick. Avoid thorns. One of Martin's few harsh words.

'Martha, you can't not want roses! What kind of person am I married to? An anti-rose personality?'

Green grass. Oh, God, grass. Grass must be mown. Restful lawns, daisies bobbing, buttercups glowing. Roses and grass and books. Books.

Please, Martin, do we have to have the two hundred books, mostly twenties' first editions, bought at Christie's book sale on one of your afternoons off? Books need dusting.

Roars of laughter from Martin, Jasper, Jenny and Jolyon. Mummy says we shouldn't have the books: books need dusting!

Roses, green grass, books and peace.

Martha woke up with a start when they got to the cottage,

and gave a little shriek which made them all laugh. Mummy's waking shriek, they called it.

Then there was the car to unpack and the beds to make up, and the electricity to connect, and the supper to make, and the cobwebs to remove, while Martin made the fire. Then supper – pork chops in sweet and sour sauce ('Pork is such a *dull* meat if you don't cook it properly': Martin), green salad from the garden, or such green salad as the rabbits had left. ('Martha, did you really net them properly? Be honest, now!': Martin) and sauté potatoes. Mash is so stodgy and ordinary, and instant mash unthinkable. The children studied the night sky with the aid of their star map. Wonderful, rewarding children!

Then clear up the supper: set the dough to prove for the bread: Martin already in bed: exhausted by the drive and lighting the fire. ('Martha, we really ought to get the logs stacked properly. Get the children to do it, will you?': Martin) Sweep and tidy: get the TV aerial right. Turn up Jasper's jeans where he has trodden the hem undone. ('He can't go around like *that*, Martha. Not even Jasper': Martin)

Midnight. Good night. Weekend guests arriving in the morning. Seven for lunch and dinner on Saturday. Seven for Sunday breakfast, nine for Sunday lunch. ('Don't fuss, darling. You always make such a fuss': Martin) Oh, God, forgotten the garlic squeezer. That means ten minutes with the back of a spoon and salt. Well, who wants *lumps* of garlic? No one. Not Martin's guests. Martin said so. Sleep.

Colin and Katie. Colin is Martin's oldest friend. Katie is his new young wife. Janet, Colin's other, earlier wife, was Martha's friend. Janet was rather like Martha, quieter and duller than her husband. A nag and a drag, Martin rather thought, and said, and of course she'd let herself go, everyone agreed. No one exactly excused Colin for walking out, but you could see the temptation.

Katie versus Janet.

Katie was languid, beautiful and elegant. She drawled when she spoke. Her hands were expressive: her feet were little and female. She had no children.

Janet plodded round on very flat, rather large feet. There was something wrong with them. They turned out slightly when she walked. She had two children. She was, frankly, boring. But Martha liked her: when Janet came down to the cottage she would wash up. Not in the way that most guests washed up – washing dutifully and setting everything out on the draining board, but actually drying and putting away too. And Janet would wash the bath and get the children all sat down, with chairs for everyone, even the littlest, and keep them quiet and satisfied so the grown-ups – well, the men – could get on with their conversation and their jokes and their love of country weekends, while Janet stared into space, as if grateful for the rest, quite happy.

Janet would garden, too. Weed the strawberries, while the men went for their walk; her great feet standing firm and square and sometimes crushing a plant or so, but never mind, oh never mind. Lovely Janet; who understood.

Now Janet was gone and here was Katie.

Katie talked with the men and went for walks with the men, and moved her ashtray rather impatiently when Martha tried to clear the drinks round it.

Dishes were boring, Katie implied by her manner, and domesticity was boring, and anyone who bothered with that kind of thing was a fool. Like Martha. Ash should be allowed to stay where it was, even if it was in the butter, and conversations should never be interrupted.

Knock, knock. Katie and Colin arrived at one-fifteen on Saturday morning, just after Martha had got to bed. 'You don't mind? It was the moonlight. We couldn't resist it. You should have seen Stonehenge! We didn't disturb you? Such early birds!'

Martha rustled up a quick meal of omelettes. Saturday nights' eggs. ('Martha makes a lovely omelette': Martin) ('Honey, make one of your mushroom omelettes: cook the mushrooms separately, remember, with lemon. Otherwise the water from the mushrooms gets into the egg, and spoils everything.') Sunday supper mushrooms. But ungracious to say anything.

Martin had revived wonderfully at the sight of Colin and Katie. He brought out the whisky bottle. Glasses. Ice. Jug for water. Wait. Wash up another sinkful, when they're finished. 2 am.

'Don't do it tonight, darling.'

'It'll only take a sec.' Bright smile, not a hint of self-pity. Self-pity can spoil everyone's weekend.

Martha knows that if breakfast for seven is to be manageable the sink must be cleared of dishes. A tricky meal, breakfast. Especially if bacon, eggs, and tomatoes must all be cooked in separate pans. ('Separate pans means separate flavours!': Martin)

She is running around in her nightie. Now if that had been Katie – but there's something so *practical* about Martha. Reassuring, mind; but the skimpy nightie and the broad rump and the thirty-eight years are all rather embarrassing. Martha can see it in Colin and Katie's eyes. Martin's too. Martha wishes she did not see so much in other people's eyes. Her mother did, too. Dear, dead mother. Did I misjudge you?

This was the second weekend Katie had been down with Colin but without Janet. Colin was a photographer: Katie had been his accessoriser. First Colin and Janet: then Colin, Janet and Katie: now Colin and Katie!

Katie weeded with rubber gloves on and pulled out pansies in mistake for weeds and laughed and laughed along with everyone when her mistake was pointed out to her, but the pansies died. Well, Colin had become with the years fairly rich and fairly famous, and what does a fairly rich and famous man want with a wife like Janet when Katie is at hand?

On the first of the Colin/Janet/Katie weekends Katie had appeared out of the bathroom. 'I say,' said Katie, holding out a damp towel with evident distaste, 'I can only find this. No hope of a dry one?' And Martha had run to fetch a dry towel and amazingly found one, and handed it to Katie who flashed her a brilliant smile and said, 'I can't bear damp towels. Anything in the world but damp towels,' as if speaking to a servant in a time of shortage of staff, and took all the water so there was none left for Martha to wash up.

The trouble, of course, was drying anything at all in the cottage. There were no facilities for doing so, and Martin had a horror of clothes lines which might spoil the view. He toiled and moiled all week in the city simply to get a country view at the weekend. Ridiculous to spoil it by draping it with wet towels! But now Martha had bought more towels, so perhaps everyone could be satisfied. She would take nine damp towels back on Sunday evenings in a plastic bag and see to them in London.

On this Saturday morning, straight after breakfast, Katie went out to the car – she and Colin had a new Lamborghini; hard to imagine Katie in anything duller – and came back waving a new Yves St Laurent towel. 'See! I brought my own, darlings.'

They'd brought nothing else. No fruit, no meat, no vegetables, not even bread, certainly not a box of chocolates. They'd gone off to bed with alacrity, the night before, and the spare room rocked and heaved: well, who'd want to do washing-up when you could do that, but what about the children? Would they get confused? First Colin and Janet, now Colin and Katie?

Martha murmured something of her thoughts to Martin, who looked quite shocked. 'Colin's my best friend. I don't expect him to bring anything,' and Martha felt mean. 'And good heavens, you can't protect the kids from sex for ever, don't be so prudish,' so that Martha felt stupid as well. Mean, complaining, and stupid.

Janet had rung Martha during the week. The house had been sold over her head, and she and the children had been moved into a small flat. Katie was trying to persuade Colin to cut down on her allowance, Janet said.

'It does one no good to be materialistic,' Katie confided. 'I have nothing. No home, no family, no ties, no possessions. Look at me! Only me and a suitcase of clothes.' But Katie seemed highly satisfied with the me, and the clothes were stupendous. Katie drank a great deal and became funny. Everyone laughed, including Martha. Katie had been married twice. Martha marvelled at how someone could arrive in their mid-thirties with nothing at all to their name, neither husband, nor children, nor property and not mind.

Mind you, Martha could see the power of such helplessness. If Colin was all Katie had in the world, how could Colin abandon her? And to what? Where would she go? How would she live? Oh, clever Katie.

'My teacup's dirty,' said Katie, and Martha ran to clean it, apologising, and Martin raised his eyebrows, at Martha, not Katie.

'I wish *you'd* wear scent,' said Martin to Martha, reproachfully. Katie wore lots. Martha never seemed to have time to put any on, though Martin bought her bottle after bottle. Martha leapt out of bed each morning to meet some emergency – miaowing cat, coughing child, faulty alarm clock, postman's knock – when was Martha to put on scent? It annoyed Martin all the same. She ought to do more to charm him.

Colin looked handsome and harrowed and younger than Martin, though they were much the same age. 'Youth's catching,' said Martin in bed that night. 'It's since he found Katie.' Found, like some treasure. Discovered; something exciting and wonderful, in the dreary world of established spouses.

On Saturday morning Jasper trod on a piece of wood ('Martha, why isn't he wearing shoes? It's too bad': Martin) and Martha took him into the hospital to have a nasty splinter removed. She left the cottage at ten and arrived back at one, and they were still sitting in the sun, drinking, empty bottles glinting in the long grass. The grass hadn't been cut. Don't forget the bottles. Broken glass means more mornings at the hospital. Oh, don't fuss. Enjoy yourself. Like other people. Try.

But no potatoes peeled, no breakfast cleared, nothing. Cigarette ends still amongst old toast, bacon rind and marmalade. 'You could have done the potatoes,' Martha burst out. Oh, bad temper! Prime sin. They looked at her in amazement and dislike. Martin too.

'Goodness,' said Katie. 'Are we doing the whole Sunday lunch bit on Saturday? Potatoes! Ages since I've eaten potatoes. Wonderful!'

'The children expect it,' said Martha.

So they did. Saturday and Sunday lunch shone like reassuring beacons in their lives. Saturday lunch: family lunch: fish and chips. ('So much better cooked at home than bought': Martin) Sunday. Usually roast beef, potatoes, peas, apple pie. Oh, of

course. Yorkshire pudding. Always a problem with oven tem-
peratures. When the beef's going slowly, the Yorkshire should
be going fast. How to achieve that? Like big bosom and little
hips.

'Just relax,' said Martin. 'I'll cook dinner, all in good time.
Splinters always work their own way out: no need to have taken
him to hospital. Let life drift over you, my love. Flow with the
waves, that's the way.'

And Martin flashed Martha a distant, spiritual smile. His
hand lay on Katie's slim brown arm, with its many gold bands.

'Anyway, you do too much for the children,' said Martin. 'It
isn't good for them. Have a drink.'

So Martha perched uneasily on the step and had a glass of
cider, and wondered how, if lunch was going to be late, she
would get cleared up and the meat out of the marinade for the
rather formal dinner that would be expected that evening. The
marinaded lamb ought to cook for at least four hours in a low
oven; and the cottage oven was very small, and you couldn't
use that and the grill at the same time and Martin liked his fish
grilled, not fried. Less cholesterol.

She didn't say as much. Domestic details like this were very
boring, and any mild complaint was registered by Martin as a
scene. And to make a scene was so ungrateful.

This was the life. Well, wasn't it? Smart friends in large cars
and country living and drinks before lunch and roses and bird
song – 'Don't drink *too* much,' said Martin, and told them
about Martha's suspended driving licence.

The children were hungry so Martha opened them a can of
beans and sausages and heated that up. ('Martha, do they have
to eat that crap? Can't they wait?': Martin)

Katie was hungry: she said so, to keep the children in face.
She was lovely with children – most children. She did not
particularly like Colin and Janet's children. She said so, and he
accepted it. He only saw them once a month now, not once a
week.

'Let me make lunch,' Katie said to Martha. 'You do so much,
poor thing!'

And she pulled out of the fridge all the things Martha had

put away for the next day's picnic lunch party – Camembert cheese and salad and salami and made a wonderful tomato salad in two minutes and opened the white wine – 'Not very cold, darling. Shouldn't it be chilling?' – and had it all on the table in five amazing competent minutes. 'That's all we need, darling,' said Martin. 'You are funny with your fish-and-chip Saturdays! What could be nicer than this? Or simpler?'

Nothing, except there was Sunday's buffet lunch for nine gone, in place of Saturday's fish for six, and would the fish stretch? No. Katie had had quite a lot to drink. She pecked Martha on the forehead. 'Funny little Martha,' she said. 'She reminds me of Janet. I really do like Janet.' Colin did not want to be reminded of Janet, and said so. 'Darling, Janet's a fact of life,' said Katie. 'If you'd only think about her more, you might manage to pay her less.' And she yawned and stretched her lean, childless body and smiled at Colin with her inviting, naughty little girl eyes, and Martin watched her in admiration.

Martha got up and left them and took a paint pot and put a coat of white gloss on the bathroom wall. The white surface pleased her. She was good at painting. She produced a smooth, even surface. Her legs throbbed. She feared she might be getting varicose veins.

Outside in the garden the children played badminton. They were bad-tempered, but relieved to be able to look up and see their mother working, as usual: making their lives for ever better and nicer: organising, planning, thinking ahead, side-stepping disaster, making preparations, like a mother hen, fussing and irritating: part of the natural boring scenery of the world.

On Saturday night Katie went to bed early: she rose from her chair and stretched and yawned and poked her head into the kitchen where Martha was washing saucepans. Colin had cleared the table and Katie had folded the napkins into pretty creases, while Martin blew at the fire, to make it bright. 'Good night,' said Katie.

Katie appeared three minutes later, reproachfully holding out her Yves St Laurent towel, sopping wet. 'Oh dear,' cried Martha. 'Jenny must have washed her hair!' And Martha was obliged to rout Jenny out of bed to rebuke her, publicly, if only to demonstrate that she knew what was right and proper. That meant Jenny would sulk all weekend, and that meant a treat or an outing mid-week, or else by the following week she'd be having an asthma attack. 'You fuss the children too much,' said Martin. 'That's why Jenny has asthma.' Jenny was pleasant enough to look at, but not stunning. Perhaps she was a disappointment to her father? Martin would never say so, but Martha feared he thought so.

An egg and an orange each child, each day. Then nothing too bad would go wrong. And it hadn't. The asthma was very mild. A calm, tranquil environment, the doctor said. Ah, smile, Martha smile. Domestic happiness depends on you. 21 × 52 oranges a year. Each one to be purchased, carried, peeled and washed up after. And what about potatoes. 12 × 52 pounds a year? Martin liked his potatoes carefully peeled. He couldn't bear to find little cores of black in the mouthful. ('Well, it isn't very nice, is it?': Martin)

Martha dreamt she was eating coal, by handfuls, and liking it.

Saturday night. Martin made love to Martha three times. Three times? How virile he was, and clearly turned on by the sounds from the spare room. Martin said he loved her. Martin always did. He was a courteous lover; he knew the importance of foreplay. So did Martha. Three times.

Ah, sleep. Jolyon had a nightmare. Jenny was woken by a moth. Martin slept through everything. Martha pottered about the house in the night. There was a moon. She sat at the window and stared out into the summer night for five minutes, and was at peace, and then went back to bed because she ought to be fresh for the morning.

But she wasn't. She slept late. The others went out for a walk. They'd left a note, a considerate note: 'Didn't wake you. You looked tired. Had a cold breakfast so as not to make too much mess. Leave everything 'til we get back.' But it was ten o'clock, and guests were coming at noon, so she cleared away the bread, the butter, the crumbs, the smears, the jam, the spoons, the spilt sugar, the cereal, the milk (sour by now) and the dirty plates, and swept the floors, and tidied up quickly, and grabbed a cup of coffee, and prepared to make a rice and fish dish, and a chocolate mousse and sat down in the middle to eat a lot of bread and jam herself. Broad hips. She remembered the office work in her file and knew she wouldn't be able to do it. Martin anyway thought it was ridiculous for her to bring work back at the weekends. 'It's your holiday,' he'd say. 'Why should they impose?' Martha loved her work. She didn't have to smile at it. She just did it.

Katie came back upset and crying. She sat in the kitchen while Martha worked and drank glass after glass of gin and bitter lemon. Katie liked ice and lemon in gin. Martha paid for all the drink out of her wages. It was part of the deal between her and Martin – the contract by which she went out to work. All things to cheer the spirit, otherwise depressed by a working wife and mother, were to be paid for by Martha. Drink, holidays, petrol, outings, puddings, electricity, heating: it was quite a joke between them. It didn't really make any difference: it was their joint money, after all. Amazing how Martha's wages were creeping up, almost to the level of Martin's. One day they would overtake. Then what?

Work, honestly, was a piece of cake.

Anyway, poor Katie was crying. Colin, she'd discovered, kept a photograph of Janet and the children in his wallet. 'He's not free of her. He pretends he is, but he isn't. She has him by a stranglehold. It's the kids. His bloody kids. Moaning Mary and that little creep Joanna. It's all he thinks about. I'm nobody.'

But Katie didn't believe it. She knew she was somebody all right. Colin came in, in a fury. He took out the photograph and set fire to it, bitterly, with a match. Up in smoke they went. Mary and Joanna and Janet. The ashes fell on the floor. (Martha swept them up when Colin and Katie had gone. It hardly seemed polite to do so when they were still there.) 'Go back to her,' Katie said. 'Go back to her. I don't care. Honestly, I'd rather be on my own. You're a nice old fashioned thing. Run along then. Do your thing, I'll do mine. Who cares?'

'Christ, Katie, the fuss! She only just happens to be in the photograph. She's not there on purpose to annoy. And I do feel bad about her. She's been having a hard time.'

'And haven't you, Colin? She twists a pretty knife, I can tell you. Don't you have rights too? Not to mention me. Is a little loyalty too much to expect?'

They were reconciled before lunch, up in the spare room. Harry and Beryl Elder arrived at twelve-thirty. Harry didn't like to hurry on Sundays; Beryl was flustered with apologies for their lateness. They'd brought artichokes from their garden. 'Wonderful,' cried Martin. 'Fruits of the earth? Let's have a wonderful soup! Don't fret, Martha. I'll do it.'

'Don't fret.' Martha clearly hadn't been smiling enough. She was in danger, Martin implied, of ruining everyone's weekend. There was an emergency in the garden very shortly – an elm tree which had probably got Dutch elm disease – and Martha finished the artichokes. The lid flew off the blender and there was artichoke purée everywhere. 'Let's have lunch outside,' said Colin. 'Less work for Martha.'

Martin frowned at Martha: he thought the appearance of martyrdom in the face of guests to be an unforgivable offence.

Everyone happily joined in taking the furniture out, but it was Martha's experience that nobody ever helped to bring it in again. Jolyon was stung by a wasp. Jasper sneezed and sneezed from hay fever and couldn't find the tissues and he wouldn't use loo paper. ('Surely you remembered the tissues, darling?': Martin)

Beryl Elder was nice. 'Wonderful to eat out,' she said, fetching the cream for her pudding, while Martha fished a fly from the liquefying Brie ('You shouldn't have bought it so ripe. Martha': Martin) – 'except it's just some other woman has to do it. But at least it isn't *me*.' Beryl worked too, as a secretary, to send the boys to boarding school, where she'd rather they weren't. But her husband was from a rather grand family, and she'd been only a typist when he married her, so her life was a mass of amends, one way or another. Harry had lately opted out of the stockbroking rat race and become an artist, choosing integrity rather than money, but that choice was his alone and couldn't of course be inflicted on the boys.

Katie found the fish and rice dish rather strange, toyed at it with her fork, and talked about Italian restaurants she knew.

Martin lay back soaking in the sun: crying, 'Oh, this is the life.' He made coffee, nobly, and the lid flew off the grinder and there were coffee beans all over the kitchen especially in amongst the row of cookery books which Martin gave Martha Christmas by Christmas. At least they didn't have to be brought back every weekend. ('The burglars won't have the sense to steal those': Martin)

Beryl fell asleep and Katie watched her, quizzically. Beryl's mouth was open and she had a lot of fillings, and her ankles were thick and her waist was going, and she didn't look after herself. 'I love women,' sighed Katie. 'They look so wonderful asleep. I wish I could be an earth mother.'

Beryl woke with a start and nagged her husband into going home, which he clearly didn't want to do, so didn't. Beryl thought she had to get back because his mother was coming round later. Nonsense! Then Beryl tried to stop Harry drinking more home-made wine and was laughed at by everyone. He was driving. Beryl couldn't, and he did have a nasty scar on his temple from a previous road accident. Never mind.

'She does come on strong, poor soul,' laughed Katie when they'd finally gone. 'I'm never going to get married,' – and Colin looked at her yearningly because he wanted to marry her more than anything in the world, and Martha cleared the coffee cups.

'Oh don't *do* that,' said Katie, 'do just sit *down*, Martha, you make us all feel bad,' and Martin glared at Martha who sat down and Jenny called out for her and Martha went upstairs and Jenny had started her first period and Martha cried and cried and knew she must stop because this must be a joyous occasion for Jenny or her whole future would be blighted, but for once, Martha couldn't.

Her daughter Jenny: wife, mother, friend.

An Everyday Story

Dikken Zwilgmeyer

It was now nearly twenty-two years since little Mrs Bruvold had, as we say, secured her happiness and married *kirkesanger* Bruvold. She didn't marry out of love. She did it so that she would be provided for. She had, of course, always heard that one should not enter marriage before one had experienced, even ever so slightly, that transient feeling we call infatuation. And she had not been in love with *kirkesanger* Bruvold. So she waited and thought about it for eight days to see if love wouldn't come after all. But it didn't come; instead, the voice of reason, in the guise of an old aunt, spoke louder and louder, and so she took him.

He got married because he was tired of housekeepers who would quit at moving time just as predictably as moving time came around. He wanted to have one who couldn't quit and so he got married. Furthermore, he was struck by the fact that the sweet little thing he had cast his eyes upon possessed that quality which he considered, above all else, a wife's duty: complete relinquishment of one's own will. And on this premise they had lived together for twenty-two years. She had been given nine children, shelter, food and drink and hadn't quit, and he, well, actually he had assumed no obligations except to bring home the money that kept it all going. But that he had fulfilled this obligation and provided for the children he himself had put into the world impressed him as being the height of respectability and integrity. Not that he ever allowed these thoughts of self-esteem to reveal or even suggest themselves in the presence of the public. No, they lay well hidden in his heart under his large silver watch with the tombac case and his paramatta overcoat. But his wife knew them well enough; indeed she partook of them daily. He could never forgive her for bringing so many children into the world and with each child laying one more stone on the burden he had to haul up life's mountain. And it was also for this reason that he, with every kroner he gave to his timid little wife, seemed to spew forth oceans of honor and conscientiousness down upon her, as she stood there curtsying and thanking him. It never occurred to her that it should be any different. He was the husband, she only the wife. And men were, after all, of another ilk than women. The former shall command, the latter obey; thus has it been since the creation of the world. In silence shall woman suffer and struggle, the minister said so often – and there is something so beautiful in that thought, he added.

Little Mrs Bruvold had suffered and struggled for twenty-two years now, silent to the world. She did, on occasion, wonder where all the beauty of which the minister spoke could be found. But she had not yet discovered it. She was probably not bright enough to see it.

Still, in more recent years somewhat vague and confused thoughts sometimes entered little Mrs Bruvold's head, thoughts she seemingly breathed in with the air – she had no idea where they came from. But they were so liberating, she thought. They were thoughts about a woman's right and woman's great cause, which brightened her pitiful, repressed mind like a gleam of light. She didn't comprehend all of it; it came with messages from another, lighter world, where she didn't belong. If she found anything about this in a book or a newspaper, she would read it again and again. Humbug and drivel, from which nothing would ever come, Bruvold said.

Bruvold was a middle-aged, middle-sized man with a peculiarly flat head. His light, yellowish hair was combed down across his neck as smoothly as if it were a wall. There was, as a matter of fact, something unfinished about his entire face. It was as if nature had thrown it together in a hurry, intending to return later to finely chisel and polish it. But then the finishing touches were never added. His nose was thick and broad and his mouth was just like a crack; it served its purpose, but was ugly. Little Mrs Bruvold was a tiny woman in her forties, small-boned and quite thin, with blond hair and a high, narrow forehead. Once you saw that forehead, you could look at nothing else and the face underneath was forgotten – it all seemed so strangely empty and bare and blank.

This then is what the Bruvolds were like. The little grey house, surrounded by a high wall in back and a marshy low-growing garden underneath, was their home. Across the street on the other side was the city's poorhouse; its long yellow-brown façade with those two rows of dull, narrow windows had been Mrs Bruvold's outlook for all these years. There was something so hopelessly monotonous about those windows, never any change year out and year in, the same old faces behind the same old panes. The only change occurred when someone died; then white curtains were hung in his room until he was buried. Mrs Bruvold liked to look at the white curtains. It gave her such a feeling of peace, she thought.

For peace and quiet was something about which Mrs Bruvold knew nothing. She was always on the go. Ever since the first days of her marriage her dream had been to hire a woman to help her in the house. But that request was always rebuffed by Bruvold, who asked if she meant to ruin him. And that cut off any further discussion of the matter. And so little Mrs Bruvold toiled and slaved, sewed, darned, knit, patched, cooked and washed her way through seven days each week. Five growing boys could give a poor, exhausted little mother more than enough to do. Almost every day there were trouser seats in need of reinforcement, holes made by elbows and knees in need of mending. Not to mention shoes and boots; those she could not repair and that was her greatest sorrow. Because there was nothing that infuriated Bruvold as much as the sight of a pair of worn-out shoes. There were times when he positively went berserk up in his office and called his wife and children blood-suckers; they wouldn't give up, he claimed, till they had every drop of his blood. And then she would pick up the little worn-out shoes and descend the stairs from the office. She held the railing with her other hand, a yellow, bony little hand, and her wrist was so very thin – it shook ever so slightly on the well-worn railing.

Little Peder Even was waiting in his stocking feet at the foot of the stairs. She shook her head. 'Peder Even, you must be more careful; Father was angry that your boots have holes again.' And Peder Even solemnly promised to be careful, but in a few minutes his promise was forgotten. Little Mrs Bruvold, however, rose at four o'clock the next morning so that she could sew and earn enough money to have Peder Even's boots resoled.

One thing pierced her heart every time she saw it happen, which was often: Bruvold's drinking so much port. What did it matter that it was the corner merchant's home-brew made from blueberry juice and alcohol? To her it was something very fine indeed. How many boots couldn't be resoled and how much help couldn't she hire with that money. But not a sound crossed her lips about this touchy point. He was, after all, the husband; she only the wife. No, it was simply a matter of covering up as best she could and keeping it from the children.

When she lay awake at night, unable to sleep because she was too tired, thoughts came to her. They never came during the day, because then she was too busy. She could lie and think about everything and about what had gone wrong. For she clearly understood that something was wrong somewhere.

Was it that they had so little money? Or was it that she wasn't close enough to the Lord? It seldom occurred to Mrs Bruvold to think about love; she had met so little of it during her life that she finally began to doubt its very existence. But if there truly was a love that endured, not merely the days of one's youth, but a lifetime; survived a tight budget, children's screaming, toil and drudgery, even those hard, bitter words – then, thought little Mrs Bruvold, it must be so great and so strong that it is a joy too magnificent for this world. The mere thought brought tears to her eyes.

But recently she had hit upon a brilliant plan and on this matter she would not yield. The plan was that her daughter, Maia, now seventeen, should learn so much that she could be employed and become an independent and self-supporting woman. She sought the advice of the minister's wife one day. 'But Maia is such a pretty girl,' was the response, 'she can be married!' 'God spare her from that,' the little *klokker*'s wife blurted out. The minister's wife looked at her, but said nothing. When Mrs Bruvold was home again she regretted, for Bruvold's sake, having said that. After all, he was no worse than others and everyone had a cross to bear in this life.

Her most cherished thought was this hope for her daughter. And it therefore caused Mrs Bruvold the most heartfelt anguish that Maia didn't appear to have any particular desire for the role in life her mother had chosen for her. A young student with a shock of wavy hair had lately been walking by their house suspiciously often. And he cast such longing glances toward the window where Maia usually sat. Maia smiled and hid herself behind the curtain, though never so much that she couldn't be seen. Mrs Bruvold was beside herself. Whatever would come of this? What did he have to support a wife with? Not even as much as she and Bruvold had had. And she looked back on that long perspective of years, all those many, many burdensome, hopeless days and wakeful nights, a never-ending struggle. And should Maia start all that now? She is so frail and delicate, Mrs Bruvold often thought, just like a tiny, pink English daisy.

Bruvold had always strictly insisted that his wife go to church. Otherwise people might wonder. She was always hard put to get ready on time. But after she had managed to get through her morning chores and the entire house and all the boys were in their Sunday best, it often felt good to sit in her place behind the broad back of her better half. She loved to sing the hymns, especially those hymns about peace and rest. She was strangely moved by the tranquility; it descended upon her so softly and quietly. And she liked to sit and look at the thin, rainbow-colored rays of dust that quivered in the sunlight across the church, while the minister's voice hovered above the bowed heads of the congregation. And then, as was known to happen, sleep stole in ever so quietly; a gentle hum was all she heard and everything began to sway so peacefully; her hat slipped down across her high forehead and little Mrs Bruvold nodded and fell asleep. 'Look at the *klokker*'s wife,' said the people down in the church, nudging each other. But they didn't consider her having been up since five o'clock, or all her boys and all her toil and drudgery.

Late in the fall Mrs Bruvold's health began to fail. This wasn't something one could see from her outward appearance, for she had been so thin and shriveled for such a long time that she couldn't become any scrawnier. No, it was just that she had fainted a couple of times after climbing the steep kitchen stairs with a heavy load. She never spoke about it herself, but the children noticed that she often put her hand to her heart as if she were in pain. But that anything could be wrong with Mother, always ready to drop everything for any or all of them, was something so unheard of as to be quite beyond belief. Bruvold noticed nothing; but recently he had often had to wait for the coffee, roll, and pipe that were brought to him in bed every morning. And that put a scowl on his face. What in the world was the matter with her? What else besides his comfort and well-being did she have to think about?

But little Mrs Bruvold was tired and could go no farther. One evening she was standing, ironing Bruvold's shirts. It had been a bad day – a notice demanding payment of tax arrears had arrived. Bruvold had snarled and snapped at her like an old tomcat when she went to his office with afternoon coffee. Down in the kitchen Maia sat crying with her head in her apron. She had been promised a new dress and now that money had gone to pay taxes. Outside it was dark and rainy and there were no curtains. Mrs Bruvold stood right by the window, ironing and on the ironing board was a candle. She moved the candle and suddenly saw her image mirrored in the window and the darkness outside. She was so pale and her cheeks so hollow. She was overcome with a wild, uncontrollable desire to throw herself out into the darkness and hide herself, to run away, just get away from everything, from herself, from life. It wasn't until she smelled something burning that she came to – she had burned one of Bruvold's shirts right through the chest. She fainted again that same evening and the next day she didn't get up.

This took Bruvold by surprise; it seemed an encroachment on his own personal well-being. The whole house was upside down – no one knew where to find this or put that. But Mrs

Bruvold stayed in bed, that day and the next day as well. Most of the time she was alone in the bedchamber, but every now and then the boys came in to show her rips in their trousers or holes in their boots.

She had been in bed for two weeks now. Bruvold had been in to see her in the morning; he was rummaging around and carrying on about a candy dish which was missing and which he always used in church. Mrs Bruvold had simply turned her head toward the wall and not answered. He looked at her in astonishment: it was the first time in their marriage she had demonstrated such apathy. He turned and walked out and slammed the door behind him. Later on that afternoon Maia rushed in. Her cheeks were warm and flushed. 'Mother, Mother, Rørvig and I are engaged!' The student with the shock of wavy hair. Mrs Bruvold's cheeks turned very white. And finally, 'Maia, don't do it. You don't know what you're getting yourself into.' Maia began to cry and said that it was horrid of her mother to say such a thing today, when she was so happy – for she was really very fond of him. With great effort Mrs Bruvold raised herself up in the bed. 'If you love him, then there may be a chance after all; but love is not only kisses and loving glances of one's youth, my child, there is so much, much more that follows.' Maia wept a little and then left.

An hour later she came in again. The sun setting across the heath was so beautiful and a golden wave of sunlight illuminated the bedposts. Mrs Bruvold was lying on her side with folded hands, staring directly into the sun. She was dead.

Eight days later she was buried. It was a fall day, wet and cold, water on the ground and a chill in the air. It had rained the past seven days, a constant, grey drizzle. But now it was beginning to clear up a little. Occasional gusts of wind from the sea promised a change in the weather. But the air had turned cold and old people predicted the imminent arrival of winter. The cemetery was situated on low and swampy ground. Between the rows of gravestones the ground was wet from all the rain – a moist, earthy, decaying odor permeated the atmosphere. The grass was brown and matted against the wet earth, with a yellowed blade sticking up stiffly here and there. On the smaller trees and bushes a few leaves still hung; they were grey-brown with black splotches and one heard a strange and mournful sighing when the wind whistled through them. The large maple trees, lined up in a row all the way from the entrance, were bare; high above the enormous branches creaked and groaned.

In the uppermost corner little Mrs Bruvold's grave had been dug. Beside it the earth was heaped in a mound, black and moist and filled with small, wet stones. The funeral procession was coming up. There were only men, clothed in black and wearing top hats. The casket was small and on it were wreaths of bearberry and partially withered cowberry and artificial flowers. Interspersed were a couple of fresh wreaths, but this was no season for flowers.

The minister and Bruvold walked immediately behind the casket. The minister lifted his black gown as he walked over the grass. The top hats were removed and for a moment everyone stared into them, but a sigh of relief was heard when the hats went back on – the wind was cold and most of them either had thinning hair or were bald. And then the hymn, solemn, and ponderous, floated out over the graves and the withering world. Just as the landscape was withered and bare, so too were the hearts withered and bare; devoid of all sorrow and reflection, the strains of the hymn sounded forth. Now and then the wind carried the melody high up into the bare, creaking branches, yet the music continued to labor and lag; the notes seemed unable to reach beyond the clump of people around the grave.

Then the minister stepped forward; he belonged to the good old school and his speech was filled with lots of flowers and beautiful words. Today he dwelt on the quiet housewife's happiness in the shelter of her husband's protecting love. He returned to this frequently; a life shared together in love. He had many lovely things to say about this; in fact, it was his most eloquent theme, which was why he had chosen to speak on it again today. But the wind was cold and he hadn't put on enough clothes under his gown. He could already feel pains in his chest and he thought to himself, 'This is a fine how-do-you-do.'

The funeral sermon for little Mrs Bruvold was not long; it ended with a few flattering words about her husband, this noble, manly heart on which she had leaned during life's struggle. And he had no doubt that he could speak for the deceased and give thanks for all the warm, caring and protecting love her husband had strewn on her path. She was one of the quiet and weak ones among us, he concluded, and therefore needed it all the more. Bruvold had folded his black-gloved hands and was humbly gazing down at them. A calm confidence entered his soul and he was filled with good thoughts. Never before had he felt so pious. Later he was to look back on this as one of the best moments of his life – that half hour at his little wife's grave. He had loved her, indeed he had, and she had made a good home and been competent and able in her task. Of course most recently she hadn't amounted to much, but then the Lord had released her, and that was all for the best.

The procession walked homeward. They were glad it was over but, after all, they did owe the *klokker* that courtesy.

And once again the wind began its dance with all the withered leaves. They rustled, flew and leapt up the long boulevard like small, living creatures, but against the fence, in the lee of the wind, they gathered and lay still. During the night it began to freeze over and snow in big soft flakes. And by morning a soft snowblanket lay upon little Mrs Bruvold's grave. The wind blew across it, sighing and shrieking; each gust of wind a lament.

But little Mrs Bruvold lay snugly hidden from all the world's harsh and biting winds.

Virgin Soil

George Egerton

The bridegroom is waiting in the hall; with a trifle of impatience he is tracing the pattern of the linoleum with the point of his umbrella. He curbs it and laughs, showing his strong white teeth at a remark of his best man; then compares the time by his hunter with the clock on the stairs. He is florid, bright-eyed, loose-lipped, inclined to stoutness, but kept in good condition; his hair is crisp, curly, slightly grey; his ears peculiar, pointed at their tops like a faun's. He looks very big and well-dressed, and, when he smiles, affable enough.

Upstairs a young girl, with the suns of seventeen summers on her brown head, is lying with her face hidden on her mother's shoulder; she is sobbing with great childish sobs, regardless of reddened eyes and the tears that have splashed on the silk of her grey, going-away gown.

The mother seems scarcely less disturbed than the girl. She is a fragile-looking woman with delicate fair skin, smoothly parted thin chestnut hair, dove-like eyes, and a monotonous piping voice. She is flushing painfully, making a strenuous effort to say something to the girl, something that is opposed to the whole instincts of her life.

She tries to speak, parts her lips only to close them again, and clasp her arms tighter round the girl's shoulders; at length she manages to say with trembling, uncertain pauses:

'You are married now, darling, and you must obey' – she lays a stress upon the word – 'your husband in all things – there are – there are things you should know – but – marriage is a serious thing, a sacred thing' – with desperation – 'you must believe that what your husband tells you is right – let him guide you – tell you – '

There is such acute distress in her usually unemotional voice that the girl looks up and scans her face – her blushing, quivering, faded face. Her eyes are startled, fawn-like eyes as her mother's, her skin too is delicately fair; but her mouth is firmer, her jaw squarer, and her piquant, irregular nose is full of character. She is slightly built, scarcely fully developed in her fresh youth.

'What is it that I do not know, mother? What is it?' – with anxious impatience. 'There is something more – I have felt it all these last weeks in your and the others' looks – in his, in the very atmosphere – but why have you not told me before – I – ' Her only answer is a gush of helpless tears from the mother, and a sharp rap at the door, and the bridegroom's voice, with an imperative note that it strikes the nervous girl is new to it, that makes her cling to her mother in a close, close embrace, drop her veil and go out to him.

She shakes hands with the best man, kisses the girl friend who has acted as bridesmaid – the wedding has been a very quiet one – and steps into the carriage. The Irish cook throws an old shoe after them from the side door, but it hits the trunk of an elder-tree, and falls back on to the path, making that worthy woman cross herself and mutter of ill-omens and bad luck to follow; for did not a magpie cross the path first thing this morning when she went to open the gate, and wasn't a red-haired woman the first creature she clapped eyes on as she looked down the road?

Half an hour later the carriage pulls up at the little station and the girl jumps out first; she is flushed, and her eyes stare helplessly as the eyes of a startled child, and she trembles with quick running shudders from head to foot. She clasps and unclasps her slender, grey-gloved hands so tightly that the stitching on the back of one bursts.

He has called to the station-master, and they go into the refreshment room together; the latter appears at the door and, beckoning to a porter, gives him an order.

She takes a long look at the familiar little place. They have lived there three years, and yet she seems to see it now for the first time; the rain drips, drips monotonously off the zinc roof, the smell of the dust is fresh, and the white pinks in the borders are beaten into the gravel.

Then the train runs in; a first-class carriage, marked 'engaged', is attached, and he comes for her; his hot breath smells of champagne, and it strikes her that his eyes are fearfully big and bright, and he offers her his arm with such a curious amused proprietary air that the girl shivers as she lays her hand in it.

The bell rings, the guard locks the door, the train steams out, and as it passes the signal-box, a large well-kept hand, with a signet ring on the little finger, pulls down the blind on the window of an engaged carriage.

Five years later, one afternoon on an autumn day, when the rain is falling like splashing tears on the rails, and the smell of the dust after rain fills the mild air with freshness, and the white chrysanthemums struggle to raise their heads from the gravel path into which the sharp shower has beaten them, the same woman, for there is no trace of girlhood in her twenty-two years, slips out of a first-class carriage; she has a dressing-bag in her hand.

She walks with her head down and a droop in her shoulders; her quickness of step is due rather to nervous haste than elasticity of frame. When she reaches the turn of the road, she pauses and looks at the little villa with the white curtains and gay tiled window-boxes. She can see the window of her old room; distinguish every shade in the changing leaves of the creeper climbing up the south wall; hear the canary's shrill note from where she stands.

Never once has she set foot in the peaceful little house with its air of genteel propriety since that eventful morning when she left it with him; she has always framed an excuse.

Now as she sees it a feeling of remorse fills her heart, and she thinks of the mother living out her quiet years, each day a replica of the one gone before, and her resolve weakens; she feels inclined to go back, but the waning sun flickers over the panes in the window of the room she occupied as a girl. She can recall how she used to run to the open window on summer mornings and lean out and draw in the dewy freshness and welcome the day, how she has stood on moonlight nights and danced with her bare white feet in the strip of moonlight, and let her fancies fly out into the silver night, a young girl's dreams of the beautiful, wonderful world that lay outside.

A hard dry sob rises in her throat at the memory of it, and the fleeting expression of softness on her face changes to a bitter disillusion.

She hurries on, with her eyes down, up the neat gravelled path, through the open door into the familiar sitting-room.

The piano is open with a hymn-book on the stand; the grate is filled with fresh green ferns, a bowl of late roses perfume the room from the centre of the table. The mother is sitting in her easy chair, her hands folded across a big white Persian cat on her lap; she is fast asleep. Some futile lace work, her thimble, and bright scissors are placed on a table near her.

Her face is placid, not a day older than that day five years ago. Her glossy hair is no greyer, her skin is clear, she smiles in her sleep. The smile rouses a sort of sudden fury in the breast of the woman standing in her dusty travelling cloak at the door, noting every detail in the room. She throws back her veil and goes over and looks at herself in the mirror over the polished chiffonnier – scans herself pitilessly. Her skin is sallow with the dull sallowness of a fair skin in ill-health, and the fringe of her brown hair is so lacking in lustre that it affords no contrast. The look of fawn-like shyness has vanished from her eyes, they burn sombrefully and resentfully in their sunken orbits, there is a dragged look about the mouth; and the keynote of her face is a cynical disillusion. She looks from herself to the reflection of the mother, and then turning sharply with a suppressed exclamation goes over, and shaking the sleeping woman not too gently, says:

'Mother, wake up, I want to speak to you!'

The mother starts with frightened eyes, stares at the other woman as if doubting the evidence of her sight, smiles, then cowed by the unresponsive look in the other face, grows grave again, sits still and stares helplessly at her, finally bursting into tears with a

'Flo, my dear, Flo, is it really you?'

The girl jerks her head impatiently and says drily:

'Yes, that is self-evident. I am going on a long journey. I have something to say to you before I start! Why on earth are you crying?'

There is a note of surprised wonder in her voice mixed with impatience.

The older woman has had time to scan her face and the dormant motherhood in her is roused by its weary anguish. She is ill, she thinks, in trouble. She rises to her feet; it is characteristic of the habits of her life, with its studied regard for the observance of small proprieties, and distrust of servants as a class, that she goes over and closes the room door carefully.

This hollow-eyed, sullen woman is so unlike the fresh girl who left her five years ago that she feels afraid. With the quiet selfishness that has characterised her life she has accepted the excuses her daughter has made to avoid coming home, as she has accepted the presents her son-in-law has sent her from time to time. She has found her a husband well-off in the world's goods, and there her responsibility ended. She approaches her hesitatingly; she feels she ought to kiss her, there is something unusual in such a meeting after so long an absence; it shocks her, it is so unlike the one she has pictured; she has often looked forward to it, often; to seeing Flo's new frocks, to hearing of her town life.

'Won't you take off your things? You will like to go to your room?'

She can hear how her own voice shakes; it is really inconsiderate of Flo to treat her in this strange way.

'We will have some tea,' she adds.

Her colour is coming and going, the lace at her wrist is fluttering. The daughter observes it with a kind of dull satisfaction, she is taking out her hat-pins carefully. She notices a portrait in a velvet case upon the mantelpiece; she walks over and looks at it intently. It is her father, the father who was killed in India in a hill skirmish when she was a little lint-locked maid barely up to his knee. She studies it with new eyes, trying to read what man he was, what soul he had, what part of him is in her, tries to find herself by reading him. Something in his face touches her, strikes some underlying chord in her, and she grinds her teeth at a thought it rouses.

'She must be ill, she must be very ill,' says the mother, watching her, 'to think I daren't offer to kiss my own child!' She checks the tears that keep welling up, feeling that they may offend this woman who is so strangely unlike the girl who left her. The latter has turned from her scrutiny of the likeness and sweeps her with a cold criticising look as she turns towards the door, saying:

'I *should* like some tea. I will go upstairs and wash off the dust.'

Half an hour later the two women sit opposite one another in the pretty room. The younger one is leaning back in her chair watching the mother pour out the tea, following the graceful movements of the white, blue-veined hands amongst the tea things – she lets her wait on her; they have not spoken beyond a commonplace remark about the heat, the dust, the journey.

'How is Philip, is he well?' The mother ventures to ask with a feeling of trepidation, but it seems to her that she ought to ask about him.

'He is quite well, men of his type usually are; I may say he is particularly well just now, he has gone to Paris with a girl from the Alhambra!'

The older woman flushes painfully, and pauses with her cup half way to her lips and lets the tea run over unheeded on to her dainty silk apron.

'You are spilling your tea,' the girl adds with malicious enjoyment.

The woman gasps: 'Flo, but Flo, my dear, it is dreadful! What would your poor father have said! *No wonder* you look ill, dear, how shocking! Shall I – ask the vicar to – to remonstrate with him? –'

'My dear mother, what an extraordinary idea! These little trips have been my one solace. I assure you, I have always hailed them as lovely oases in the desert of matrimony, resting-places on the journey. My sole regret was their infrequency. That is very good tea, I suppose it is the cream.'

The older woman puts her cup on the tray and stares at her with frightened eyes and paled cheeks.

'I am afraid I don't understand you, Florence. I am old-fashioned' – with a little air of frigid propriety – 'I have always looked upon matrimony as a sacred thing. It is dreadful to hear you speak this way; you should have tried to save Philip – from – from such a shocking sin.'

The girl laughs, and the woman shivers as she hears her. She cries –

'I would never have thought it of Philip. My poor dear, I am afraid you must be very unhappy.'

'Very,' with a grim smile, 'but it is over now, I have done with it. I am not going back.'

If a bomb had exploded in the quiet, pretty room the effect could hardly have been more startling than her almost cheerful statement. A big bee buzzes in and bangs against the lace of the older woman's cap and she never heeds it, then she almost screams:

'Florence, Florence, my dear, you can't mean to desert your husband! Oh, think of the disgrace, the scandal, what people will say, the' – with an uncertain quaver – 'the sin. You took a solemn vow, you know, and you are going to break it –'

'My dear mother, the ceremony had no meaning for me, I simply did not know what I was signing my name to, or what I was vowing to do. I might as well have signed my name to a document drawn up in Choctaw. I have no remorse, no prick of conscience at the step I am taking; my life must be my own. They say sorrow chastens, I don't believe it; it hardens, embitters; joy is like the sun, it coaxes all that is loveliest and sweetest in human nature. No, I am not going back.'

The older woman cries, wringing her hands helplessly:

'I can't understand it. You must be very miserable to dream of taking such a serious step.'

'As I told you, I am. It is a defect of my temperament. How many women really take the man nearest to them as seriously as I did! I think few. They finesse and flatter and wheedle and coax, but truth there is none. I couldn't do that, you see, and so I went to the wall. I don't blame them; it must be so, as long as marriage is based on such unequal terms, as long as man demands from a wife as a right, what he must sue from a mistress as a favour; until marriage becomes for many women a legal prostitution, a nightly degradation, a hateful yoke under which they age, mere bearers of children conceived in a sense of duty, not love. They bear them, birth them, nurse them, and begin again without choice in the matter, growing old, unlovely, with all joy of living swallowed in a senseless burden of reckless maternity, until their love, granted they started with that, the mystery, the crowning glory of their lives, is turned into a duty they submit to with distaste instead of a favour granted to a husband who must become a new lover to obtain it.'

'But men are different, Florence; you can't refuse a husband, you might cause him to commit sin.'

'Bosh, mother, he is responsible for his own sins, we are not bound to dry-nurse his morality. Man is what we have made him, his very faults are of our making. No wife is bound to set aside the demands of her individual soul for the sake of imbecile obedience. I am going to have some more tea.'

The mother can only whimper:

'It is dreadful! I thought he made you such an excellent husband, his position too is so good, and he is so highly connected.'

'Yes, and it is as well to put the blame in the right quarter. Philip is as God made him, he is an animal with strong passions, and he avails himself of the latitude permitted him by the laws of society. Whatever of blame, whatever of sin, whatever of misery is in the whole matter rests *solely* and *entirely* with you, mother' – the woman sits bolt upright – 'and with no one else – that is why I came here – to tell you that – I have promised myself over and over again that I would tell you. It is with you, and you alone the fault lies.'

There is so much of cold dislike in her voice that the other woman recoils and whimpers piteously:

'You must be ill, Florence, to say such wicked things. What have I done? I am sure I devoted myself to you from the time you were little; I refused' – dabbing her eyes with her cambric handkerchief – 'ever so many good offers. There was young

Fortescue in the artillery, such a good-looking man, and such an elegant horseman, he was quite infatuated about me; and Jones, to be sure he was in business, but he was most attentive. Every one said I was a devoted mother; I can't think what you mean, I –'

A smile of cynical amusement checks her.

'Perhaps not. Sit down, and I'll tell you.'

She shakes off the trembling hand, for the mother has risen and is standing next to her, and pushes her into a chair, and paces up and down the room. She is painfully thin, and drags her limbs as she walks.

'I say it is your fault, because you reared me a fool, an idiot, ignorant of everything I ought to have known, everything that concerned me and the life I was bound to lead as a wife; my physical needs, my coming passion, the very meaning of my sex, my wifehood and motherhood to follow. You gave me not one weapon in my hand to defend myself against the possible attacks of man at his worst. You sent me out to fight the biggest battle of a woman's life, the one in which she ought to know every turn of the game, with a white gauze' – she laughs derisively – 'of maiden purity as a shield.'

Her eyes blaze, and the woman in the chair watches her as one sees a frog watch a snake when it is put into its case.

'I was fourteen when I gave up the gooseberry-bush theory as the origin of humanity; and I cried myself ill with shame when I learnt what maternity meant, instead of waking with a sense of delicious wonder at the great mystery of it. You gave me to a man, nay more, you told me to obey him, to believe that whatever he said would be right, would be my duty; knowing that the meaning of marriage was a sealed book to me, that I had no real idea of what union with a man meant. You delivered me body and soul into his hands without preparing me in any way for the ordeal I was to go through. You sold me for a home, for clothes, for food; you played upon my ignorance, I won't say innocence, that is different. You told me, you and your sister, and your friend the vicar's wife, that it would be an anxiety off your mind if I were comfortably settled –'

'It is wicked of you to say such dreadful things!' the mother

cries, 'and besides' – with a touch of asperity – 'you married
him willingly, you seemed to like his attentions –'

'How like a woman! What a thorough woman you are,
mother! The good old-fashioned kitten with a claw in her paw!
Yes, I married him willingly; I was not eighteen, I had known
no men; was pleased that you were pleased – and, as you say,
I liked his attentions. He had tact enough not to frighten me,
and I had not the faintest conception of what marriage with
him meant. I had an idea' – with a laugh – 'that the words of the
minister settled the matter. Do you think that if I had realised
how fearfully close the intimacy with him would have been that
my whole soul would not have stood up in revolt, the whole
woman in me cried out against such a degradation of myself?'
Her words tremble with passion, and the woman who bore her
feels as if she is being lashed by a whip. 'Would I not have
shuddered at the thought of *him* in such a relationship? – and
waited, waited until I found the man who would satisfy me,
body and soul – to whom I would have gone without any false
shame, of whom I would think with gladness as the father of a
little child to come, for whom the white fire of love or passion,
call it what you will, in my heart would have burned clearly
and saved me from the feeling of loathing horror that has made
my married life a nightmare to me – ay, made me a murderess
in heart over and over again. This is not exaggeration. It has
killed the sweetness in me, the pure thoughts of womanhood –
has made me hate myself and *hate you*. Cry, mother, if you
will; you don't know how much you have to cry for – I have
cried myself barren of tears. Cry over the girl you killed' – with
a gust of passion – 'why didn't you strangle me as a baby? It
would have been kinder; my life has been a hell, mother – I felt
it vaguely as I stood on the platform waiting, I remember the
mad impulse I had to jump down under the engine as it came
in, to escape from the dread that was chilling my soul. What
have these years been? One long crucifixion, one long submittal
to the desires of a man I bound myself to in ignorance of what
it meant; every caress' – with a cry – 'has only been the first
note of that. Look at me' – stretching out her arms – 'look at
this wreck of my physical self; I wouldn't dare to show you the

heart or the soul underneath. He has stood on his rights; but do you think, if I had known, that I would have given such insane obedience, from a mistaken sense of duty, as would lead to this? I have my rights too, and my duty to myself; if I had only recognised them in time.

'Sob away, mother; I don't even feel for you — I have been burnt too badly to feel sorry for what will only be a tiny scar to you; I have all the long future to face with all the world against me. Nothing will induce me to go back. Better anything than that; food and clothes are poor equivalents for what I have had to suffer — I can get them at a cheaper rate. When he comes to look for me, give him that letter. He will tell you he has only been an uxorious husband, and that you reared me a fool. You can tell him too, if you like, that I loathe him, shiver at the touch of his lips, his breath, his hands; that my whole body revolts at his touch; that when he has turned and gone to sleep, I have watched him with such growing hatred that at times the temptation to kill him has been so strong that I have crept out of bed and walked the cold passage in my bare feet until I was too benumbed to feel anything; that I have counted the hours to his going away, and cried out with delight at the sight of the retreating carriage!'

'You are very hard, Flo; the Lord soften your heart! Perhaps' — with trepidation — 'if you had had a child —'

'Of his — that indeed would have been the last straw — no, mother.'

There is such a peculiar expression of satisfaction over something — of some inner understanding, as a man has when he dwells on the successful accomplishment of a secret purpose — that the mother sobs quietly, wringing her hands.

'I did not know, Flo, I acted for the best; you are very hard on me!'

Later, when the bats are flitting across the moon, and the girl is asleep — she has thrown herself half-dressed on the narrow white bed of her girlhood, with her arms folded across her breast and her hands clenched — the mother steals into the room. She has been turning over the contents of an old desk;

her marriage certificate, faded letters on foreign paper, and a bit of Flo's hair cut off each birthday, and a sprig of orange-blossom she wore in her hair. She looks faded and grey in the silver light, and she stands and gazes at the haggard face in its weary sleep. The placid current of her life is disturbed, her heart is roused, something of her child's soul-agony has touched the sleeping depths of her nature. She feels as if scales have dropped from her eyes, as if the instincts and conventions of her life are toppling over, as if all the needs of protesting women of whom she has read with a vague displeasure have come home to her. She covers the girl tenderly, kisses her hair, and slips a little roll of notes into the dressing-bag on the table and steals out, with the tears running down her cheeks.

When the girl looks into her room as she steals by, when the morning light is slanting in, she sees her kneeling, her head, with its straggling grey hair, bowed in tired sleep. It touches her. Life is too short, she thinks, to make any one's hours bitter; she goes down and writes a few kind words in pencil and leaves them near her hand, and goes quickly out into the road.

The morning is grey and misty, with faint yellow stains in the east, and the west wind blows with a melancholy sough in it – the first whisper of the fall, the fall that turns the world of nature into a patient suffering from phthisis – delicate season of decadence, when the loveliest scenes have a note of decay in their beauty; when a poisoned arrow pierces the marrow of insect and plant, and the leaves have a hectic flush and fall, fall and shrivel and curl in the night's cool; and the chrysanthemums, the 'good-bye summers' of the Irish peasants, have a sickly tinge in their white. It affects her, and she finds herself saying: 'Wither and die, wither and die, make compost for the loves of the spring, as the old drop out and make place for the new, who forget them, to be in their turn forgotten.' She hurries on, feeling that her autumn has come to her in her spring, and a little later she stands once more on the platform where she stood in the flush of her girlhood, and takes the train in the opposite direction.

Swans

Janet Frame

They were ready to go. Mother and Fay and Totty, standing by
the gate in their next best to Sunday best, Mother with her
straw hat on with shells on it and Fay with her check dress that
Mother had made and Totty, well where was Totty a moment
ago she was here?

'Totty,' Mother called. 'If you don't hurry we'll miss the
train, it leaves in ten minutes. And we're not to forget to get off
at Beach Street. At least I think Dad said Beach Street. But hurry
Totty.'

Totty came running from the wash-house round the back.

'Mum quick I've found Gypsy and her head's down like all
the other cats and she's dying I think. She's in the wash-house.
Mum quick,' she cried urgently.

Mother looked flurried. 'Hurry up, Totty and come back Fay,
pussy will be all right. We'll give her some milk now there's
some in the pot and we'll wrap her in a piece of blanket and
she'll be all right till we get home.'

The three of them hurried back to the wash-house. It was
dark with no light except what came through the small square
window which had been cracked and pasted over with brown
paper. The cat lay on a pile of sacks in a corner near the copper.
Her head was down and her eyes were bright with a fever or
poison or something but she was alive. They found an old clean
tin lid and poured warm milk in it and from one of the shelves
they pulled a dusty piece of blanket. The folds stuck to one
another all green and hairy and a slater with hills and valleys
on his back fell to the floor and moved slowly along the cracked
concrete floor to a little secret place by the wall. Totty even
forgot to collect him. She collected things, slaters and earwigs

and spiders though you had to be careful with earwigs for when you were lying in the grass asleep they crept into your ear and built their nest there and you had to go to the doctor and have your ear lanced.

They covered Gypsy and each one patted her. Don't worry Gypsy they said. We'll be back to look after you tonight. We're going to the Beach now. Goodbye Gypsy.

And there was Mother waiting impatiently again at the gate. 'Do hurry. Pussy'll be all right now.'

Mother always said things would be all right, cats and birds and people even as if she knew and she did know too, Mother knew always.

But Fay crept back once more to look inside the wash-house. 'I promise,' she called to the cat. 'We'll be back, just you see.'

And the next moment the three Mother and Fay and Totty were outside the gate and Mother with a broom-like motion of her arms was sweeping the two little girls before her.

O the train and the coloured pictures on the station, South America and Australia, and the bottle of fizzy drink that you could only half finish because you were too full, and the ham sandwiches that curled up at the edges, because they were stale, Dad said, and he *knew*, and the rabbits and cows and bulls outside in the paddocks, and the sheep running away from the noise and the houses that came and went like a dream, clackety-clack, Kaitangata, Kaitangata, and the train stopping and panting and the man with the stick tapping the wheels and the huge rubber hose to give the engine a drink, and the voices of the people in the carriage on and on and waiting.

'Don't forget Beach Street, Mum,' Dad had said. Dad was away at work up at six o'clock early and couldn't come. It was strange without him for he always managed. He got the tea and the fizzy drinks and the sandwiches and he knew which station was which and where and why and how, but Mother didn't. Mother was often too late for the fizzy drinks and she coughed before she spoke to the children and then in a whisper in case the people in the carriage should hear and think things, and she said I'm sure I don't know kiddies when they asked about the station, but she was big and warm and knew about cats and the little ring-eyes, and Father was hard and bony and his face prickled when he kissed you.

O look the beach coming it must be coming.

The train stopped with a jerk and a cloud of smoke as if it had died and finished and would never go anywhere else just stay by the sea though you couldn't see the water from here, and the carriages would be empty and slowly rusting as if the people in them had come to an end and could never go back as if they had found what they were looking for after years and years of travelling on and on. But they were disturbed and peeved at being forced to move. The taste of smoke lingered in their mouths, they had to reach up for hat and coat and case, and comb their hair and make up their face again, certainly they had arrived but you have to be neat arriving with your shoes brushed and your hair in place and the shine off your nose. Fay and Totty watched the little cases being snipped open and shut and the two little girls knew for sure that never would they grow up and be people in bulgy dresses, people knitting purl and plain with the ball of wool hanging safe and clean from a neat brown bag with hollyhocks and poppies on it. Hollyhocks and poppies and a big red initial, to show that you were you and not the somebody else you feared you might be, but Fay and Totty didn't worry they were going to the Beach.

The Beach. Why wasn't everyone going to the Beach? It seemed they were the only ones for when they set off down the fir-bordered road that led to the sound the sea kept making forever now in their ears, there was no one else going. Where had the others gone? Why weren't there other people?

'Why Mum?'

'It's a week-day chicken,' said Mum smiling and fat now the rushing was over. 'The others have gone to work I suppose. I don't know. But here we are. Tired?' She looked at them both in the way they loved, the way she looked at them at night at other people's places when they were weary of cousins and hide the thimble and wanted to go home to bed. Tired? she would say. And Fay and Totty would yawn as if nothing in the world would keep them awake and Mother would say knowingly and fondly: The dustman's coming to someone. But no they weren't tired now for it was day and the sun though a watery sad sun was up and the birds, the day was for waking in and the night was for sleeping in.

They raced on ahead of Mother eager to turn the desolate crying sound of sea to the more comforting and near sight of long green and white waves coming and going forever on the sand. They had never been here before, not to this sea. They had been to other seas, near merry-go-rounds and swings and slides, among people, other girls and boys and mothers, mine are so fond of the water the mothers would say, talking about mine and yours and he, that meant father, or the old man if they did not much care but Mother cared always.

The road was stony and the little girls carrying the basket had skiffed toes by the time they came to the end, but it was all fun and yet strange for they were by themselves no other families and Fay thought for a moment what if there is no sea either and no nothing?

But the sea roared in their ears it was true sea, look it was breaking white on the sand and the seagulls crying and skimming and the bits of white flying and look at all of the coloured shells, look a little pink one like a fan, and a cat's eye. Gypsy. And look at the seaweed look I've found a round piece that plops, you tread on it and it plops, you plop this one, see it plops, and the little girls running up and down plopping and plopping and picking and prying and touching and listening, and Mother plopping the seaweed too, look Mum's doing it and Mum's got a crab.

But it cannot go on for ever.

'Where is the place to put our things and the merry-go-rounds and the place to undress and that, and the place to get ice-creams?'

There's no place, only a little shed with forms that have bird-dirt on them and old pieces of newspapers stuffed in the corner and writing on the walls, rude writing.

'Mum, have we come to the wrong sea?'

Mother looked bewildered. 'I don't know kiddies, I'm sure.'

'Is it the wrong sea?' Totty took up the cry.

It was the wrong sea. 'Yes kiddies,' Mother said, 'now that's strange I'm sure I remembered what your Father told me but I couldn't have but I'm sure I remembered. Isn't it funny. I didn't know it would be like this. Oh things are never like you think they're different and sad. I don't know.'

'Look, I've found the biggest plop of all,' cried Fay who had wandered away intent on plopping. 'The biggest plop of all,' she repeated, justifying things. 'Come on.'

So it was all right really it was a good sea, you could pick up the foam before it turned yellow and take off your shoes and sink your feet down in the wet sand almost until you might disappear and come up in Spain, that was where you came up if you sank. And there was the little shed to eat in and behind the rushes to undress but you couldn't go in swimming.

'Not in this sea,' Mother said firmly.

They felt proud. It was a distinguished sea oh and a lovely one noisy in your ears and green and blue and brown where the seaweed floated. Whales? Sharks? Seals? It was the right kind of sea.

All day on the sand, racing and jumping and turning head over heels and finding shells galore and making castles and getting buried and unburied, going dead and coming alive like the people in the Bible. And eating in the little shed for the sky had clouded over and a cold wind had come shaking the heads of the fir-trees as if to say I'll teach you, springing them backwards and forwards in a devilish exercise.

Tomatoes, and a fire blowing in your face. The smoke burst out and you wished. Aladdin and the genie. What did you wish?

I wish today is always but Father too jumping us up and down on his knee. This is the maiden all forlorn that milked the cow.

'Totty, it's my turn, isn't it Dad?'

'It's both of your turns. Come on, sacks on the mill and *more on still.*' Not Father away at work but Father here making the fire and breaking sticks, quickly and surely, and Father showing this and that and telling why. Why? Did anyone in the world ever know why? Or did they just pretend to know because they didn't like anyone else to know that they didn't know? Why?

They were going home when they saw the swans. 'We'll go

this quicker way,' said Mother, who had been exploring. 'We'll walk across the lagoon over this strip of land and soon we'll be at the station and then home to bed.' She smiled and put her arms round them both. Everything was warm and secure and near, and the darker the world outside got the safer you felt for there were Mother and Father always, for ever.

They began to walk across the lagoon. It was growing dark now quickly and dark sneaks in. Oh home in the train with the guard lighting the lamps and the shiny slippery seat growing hard and your eyes scarcely able to keep open, the sea in your ears, and your little bagful of shells dropped somewhere down the back of the seat, crushed and sandy and wet, and your baby crab dead and salty and stiff fallen on the floor.

'We'll soon be home,' Mother said, and was silent.

It was dark black water, secret, and the air was filled with murmurings and rustlings, it was as if they were walking into another world that had been kept secret from everyone and now they had found it. The darkness lay massed across the water and over to the east, thick as if you could touch it, soon it would swell and fill the earth.

The children didn't speak now, they were tired with the dustman really coming, and Mother was sad and quiet, the wrong sea troubled her, what had she done, she had been sure she would find things different, as she had said they would be, merry-go-rounds and swings and slides for the kiddies, and other mothers to show the kiddies off too, they were quite bright for their age, what had she done?

They looked across the lagoon then and saw the swans, black and shining, as if the visiting dark tiring of its form, had changed to birds, hundreds of them resting and moving softly about on the water. Why, the lagoon was filled with swans, like secret sad ships, secret and quiet. Hush-sh the water said; rush-hush, the wind passed over the top of the water; no other sound but the shaking of rushes and far away now it seemed the roar of the sea like a secret sea that had crept inside your head for ever. And the swans, they were there too, inside you, peaceful and quiet watching and sleeping and watching, there was nothing but peace and warmth and calm, everything found, train and sea and Mother and Father and earwig and slater and spider.

And Gypsy?

But when they got home Gypsy was dead.

Princess Ida

Alice Munro

Now my mother was selling encyclopedias. Aunt Elspeth and
Auntie Grace called it 'going on the road!'

'Is your mother going on the road much these days?' they
would ask me, and I would say no, oh no, she isn't going out
much any more, but I knew they knew I lied. 'Not much time
for ironing,' they might continue compassionately, examining
the sleeve of my blouse. 'Not much time for ironing when she
has to go out on the road.'

I felt the weight of my mother's eccentricities, of something
absurd and embarrassing about her – the aunts would just show
me a little at a time – land on my own coward's shoulders. I
did want to repudiate her, crawl into favor, orphaned, abandoned, in my wrinkled sleeves. At the same time I wanted to
shield her. She would never have understood how she needed
shielding, from two old ladies with their mild bewildering
humor, their tender proprieties. They wore dark cotton dresses
with fresh, perfectly starched and ironed, white lawn collars,
china flower brooches. Their house had a chiming clock, which
delicately marked the quarter hours; also watered ferns, African
violets, crocheted runners, fringed blinds, and over everything
the clean, reproachful smell of wax and lemons.

'She was in here yesterday to pick up the scones we made for
you. Were they all right, we wondered about them, were they
light? She told us she had got stuck away out on the Jericho
Road. All by herself, stuck on the Jericho Road! Poor Ada! But
the mud on her, we had to laugh!'

'We had to scrub the hall linoleum,' said Auntie Grace, with
a note of apology, as if it was a thing she did not like to tell
me.

From such a vantage point, my mother did seem a wild-woman.

She drove our thirty-seven Chevy over all of the highways and back roads of Wawanash County, drove it over gravel roads, dirt roads, cow tracks, if she thought they might lead her to customers. She carried a jack and a shovel in the trunk, and a couple of short planks for easing her way out of mudholes. She drove all the time as if she would not be surprised to see the ground crack open ten feet in front of her wheels; she honked her horn despairingly at blind country corners; she was continually worried that the wooden bridges would not hold, and she would never let anything force her onto the treacherous crumbling shoulders of the road.

The war was still on then. Farmers were making money at last, making it out of pigs or sugar beets or corn. Possibly they did not mean to spend it on encyclopedias. They had their minds set on refrigerators, cars. But these things were not to be had, and in the meantime there was my mother, gamely lugging her case of books, gaining entry to their kitchens, their cold funeral-smelling front rooms, cautiously but optimistically opening fire on behalf of Knowledge. A chilly commodity that most people, grown up, can agree to do without. But nobody will deny that it is a fine thing for children. My mother was banking on that.

And if happiness in this world is believing in what you sell, why, then my mother was happy. Knowledge was not chilly to her, no; it was warm and lovely. Pure comfort even at this stage of her life to know the location of the Celebes Sea and the Pitti Palace, to get the wives of Henry VIII in order, and be informed about the social system of ants, the methods of sacrificial butchery used by the Aztecs, the plumbing in Knossos. She could get carried away, telling about such things; she would tell anybody. 'Your mother knows such a lot of things, my,' said Aunt Elspeth and Auntie Grace lightly, unenviously, and I saw that to some people, maybe to most people, knowledge was just oddity; it stuck out like warts.

But I shared my mother's appetite myself, I could not help it. I loved the volumes of the encyclopedia, their weight (of mystery, of beautiful information) as they fell open in my lap; I loved their sedate dark-green binding, the spidery, reticent-looking gold letters on their spines. They might open to show me a steel engraving of a battle, taking place on the moors, say, with a castle in the background, or in the harbor of Constantinople. All bloodshed, drowning, hacking off of heads, agony of horses, was depicted with a kind of operatic flourish, a superb unreality. And I had the impression that in historical times the weather was always theatrical, ominous; landscape frowned, sea glimmered in various dull or metallic shades of gray. Here was Charlotte Corday on her way to the guillotine, Mary Queen of Scots on her way to the scaffold, Archbishop Laud extending his blessing to Stafford through the bars of his prison window – nobody could doubt this was just the way they looked, robes black, lifted hands and faces white, composed, heroic. The encyclopedia did of course provide other sorts of things to look at: beetles, varieties of coal, diagrammed insides of engines, photographs of Amsterdam or Bucharest taken on smudgy dim days in the nineteen-twenties (you could tell by the little high square cars). I preferred history.

Accidentally at first and then quite deliberately I learned things from the encyclopedia. I had a freak memory. Learning a list of facts was an irresistible test to me, like trying to hop a block on one foot.

My mother got the idea that I might be useful in her work.

'My own daughter has been reading these books and I am just amazed at what she has picked up. Children's minds are just like flypaper, you know, whatever you give them will stick. Del, name the presidents of the United States from George Washington down to the present day, can you do that?' Or: name the countries and capitals of South America. The major explorers, tell where they came from and where they went. Dates too please. I would sit in a strange house rattling things off. I put on a shrewd, serious, competitive look, but that was mostly for effect. Underneath I felt a bounding complacency. I knew I knew it. And who could fail to love me, for knowing where Quito was?

Quite a few could, as a matter of fact. But where did I get

the first hint in that direction? It might have been from looking up and seeing Owen, without two dates or capitals or dead presidents to string together, as far as anybody knew, tenderly, privately, wrapping a long chewed-out piece of gum around his finger. It might have been from the averted faces of country children, with their subtle, complicated embarrassment. One day I did not want to do it any more. The decision was physical; humiliation prickled my nerve ends and the lining of my stomach. I started to say, 'I don't know them –' but was too miserable, too ashamed, to tell this lie.

'George Washington, John Adams, Thomas Jefferson –'

My mother said sharply, 'Are you going to be sick?'

She was afraid I might be about to throw up. Both Owen and I were totally committed, on-the-spot throwers-up. I nodded and slid off the chair and went and hid in the car, holding my stomach. My mother when she came had figured out that it was more than that.

'You're getting self-conscious,' she said in a practical tone. 'I thought you enjoyed it.' The prickling started again. That was just it, I had enjoyed it, and it was not decent of her to say so. 'Shyness and self-consciousness,' said my mother rather grandly, 'those are the luxuries I could never afford.' She started the car. 'Though I can tell you, there are members of your father's family who would not open their mouths in public to say their house was burning down.'

Thereafter when asked – lightly asked – 'Do you want to do some questions today?' I would slump away down in the seat and shake my head and clutch my stomach, indicating the possible quick return of my malady. My mother had to resign herself, and now when I rode out with her on Saturdays I rode like Owen, free and useless cargo, no longer a sharer in her enterprises. 'You want to hide your brains under a bushel out of pure perversity but that's not my lookout,' she said. 'You just do as you please.'

I still had vague hopes of adventure, which Owen shared, at least on the more material level. We both hoped to buy bags of a certain golden-brown candy, broken in chunks like cement and melting almost immediately on the tongue, sold in one special harness-draped, horsy-smelling country store. We hoped at least to stop for gas at a place that sold cold pop. I hoped to travel as far as Porterfield or Blue River, towns which derived their magic simply from being places we did not know and were not known in, by not being Jubilee. Walking in the streets of one of these towns I felt my anonymity like a decoration, like a peacock's train. But by some time in the afternoon these hopes would ebb, or some of them would have been satisfied, which always leaves a gap. In my mother too there would be some ebbing, of those bright ruthless forces which pushed her out here in the first place. Approaching dark, and cold air coming up through the hole in the floor of the car, the tired noise of the engine, the indifference of the countryside, would reconcile us to each other and make us long for home. We drove through country we did not know we loved – not rolling or flat, but broken, no recognisable rhythm to it; low hills, hollows full of brush, swamp and bush and fields. Tall elm trees, separate, each plainly showing its shape, doomed but we did not know that either. They were shaped like slightly opened fans, sometimes like harps.

Jubilee was visible from a rise about three miles away, on the No. 4 Highway. Between us and it lay the river flats, flooded every spring, and the hidden curve of the Wawanash River, and the bridge over it, painted silver, hanging in the dusk like a cage. The No. 4 Highway was also the main street of Jubilee. We could see the towers of the post office and the Town Hall facing each other, the Town Hall with its exotic cupola hiding the legendary bell (rung for wars starting and ending, ready to ring in case of earthquake, or final flood) and the post office with its clock tower, square, useful, matter-of-fact. The town lay spread almost equidistantly on either side of the main street. Its shape, which at the time of our return would usually be defined in lights, was seen to be more or less that of a bat, one wing lifted slightly, bearing the water tower, unlighted, indistinct, on its tip.

My mother would never let this sighting go by without saying something. 'There's Jublilee,' she might say simply, or, 'Well, yonder lies the metropolis,' or she might even quote, fuzzily, a poem about going in the same door as out she went. And by these words, whether weary, ironic, or truly grateful, Jubilee seemed to me to take its being. As if without her connivance, her acceptance, these streetlights and sidewalks, the fort in the wilderness, the open and secret pattern of the town – a shelter and a mystery – would not be there.

Over all our expeditions, and homecomings, and the world at large, she exerted this mysterious, appalling authority, and nothing could be done about it, not yet.

My mother rented a house in town, and we lived there from September to June, going out to the house at the end of the Flats Road only for the summers. My father came in for supper, and stayed overnight, until the snow came; then he came in, if he could, for Saturday night and part of Sunday.

The house we rented was down at the end of River Street not far from the CNR station. It was the sort of house that looks bigger than it is; it had a high but sloping roof – the second story, wood, and the first story brick – and a bulging bay window in the dining room and verandas front and back; the front veranda had a useless and in fact inaccessible little balcony stuck into its roof. All the wooden parts of the house were painted gray, probably because gray does not need to be re-painted so often as white. In the warm weather the downstairs windows had awnings, striped and very faded; then the house with its bleached gray paint and sloping verandas made me think of a beach – the sun, the tough windy grass.

Yet it was a house that belonged to a town; things about it suggested leisure and formality, of a sort that were not possible out on the Flats Road. I would sometimes think of our old house, its flat pale face, the cement slab outside the kitchen door, with a forlorn, faintly guilty, tender pain, as you might think of a simple old grandparent whose entertainments you have outgrown. I missed the nearness of the river and the swamp, also the real anarchy of winter, blizzards that shut us up tight in our house as if it were the Ark. But I loved the order, the wholeness, the intricate arrangement of town life, that only an outsider could see. Going home from school, winter afternoons, I had a sense of the whole town around me, all the streets which were named River Street, Mason Street, John Street, Victoria Street, Huron Street, and strangely, Khartoum Street; the evening dresses gauzy and pale as crocuses in Krall's Ladies' Wear window; the Baptist Mission Band in the basement of their church, singing 'There's a New Name Written Down in Glory, And it's Mine, Mine, Mine!' Canaries in their cages in the Selrite store and books in the library and mail in the post office and pictures of Olivia de Havilland and Errol Flynn in pirate and lady costumes outside the Lyceum Theatre – all these things, rituals and diversions, frail and bright, woven together – town! In town there were soldiers on leave, in their khaki uniforms which had an aura of anonymous brutality, like the smell of burning; there were beautiful, shining girls, whose names everybody knew – Margaret Bond, Dorothy Guest, Pat Mundy – and who in turn knew nobody's name, except if they chose; I watched them coming downhill from the high school, in their fur-trimmed velvet boots. They traveled in a little cluster, casting a radiance like a night lantern, blinding them to the rest of the world. Though one day one of them – Pat Mundy – had smiled at me in passing, and I made up daydreams about her – that she saved me from drowning, that she became a nurse and nursed me, risking her life rocking me in her velvet arms, when I nearly died of diphtheria.

If it was a Wednesday afternoon my mother's boarder, Fern Dogherty, would be at home, drinking tea, smoking, talking with my mother in the dining room. Fern's talk was low, she would ramble and groan and laugh against my mother's sharper, more economical commentary. They told stories about people in the town, about themselves; their talk was a river that never dried up. It was the drama, the ferment of life just beyond my reach. I would go to the deep mirror in the built-in sideboard and look at the reflection of the room – all dark wainscoting, dark beams, the brass lighting fixture like a little formal tree growing the wrong way, with five branches stiffly curved, ending in glass flowers. By getting them into a certain spot in the mirror I could make my mother and Fern Dogherty pull out like rubber bands, all wavering and hysterical, and I could make my own face droop disastrously down one side, as if I had had a stroke.

I said to my mother, 'Why didn't you bring that picture in?'
'What picture? *What picture?*'
'The one over the couch.'
Because I had been thinking – every so often I had to think – of our kitchen out on the farm, where my father and Uncle Benny were at that moment probably frying potatoes for their supper, in an unwashed pan (why wash away good grease?), with mitts and scarves steaming dry on top of the stove. Major our dog – not allowed into the house during my mother's reign – asleep on the dirty linoleum in front of the door. Newspapers spread on the table in place of a cloth, dog-haired blankets on the couch, guns and snowshoes and washtubs hung along the walls. Smelly bachelor comfort. Over the couch there was a picture actually painted by my mother, in the far-off early days – the possibly leisured, sunny, loving days – of her marriage. It showed a stony road and a river between mountains, and sheep driven along the road by a little girl in a red shawl. The mountains and the sheep looked alike, lumpy, woolly, purplish-gray. Long ago I had believed that the little girl was really my mother and that this was the desolate country of her early life. Then I learned that she had copied the scene from the *National Geographic*.
'That one? Do you want that in here?'
I didn't really. As often in our conversations I was trying to lead her on, to get the answer, or the revelation, I particularly wanted. I wanted her to say she had left it for my father. I remembered she had said once that she had painted it for him, he was the one who had liked that scene.
'I don't want it hanging where people would see,' she said. 'I'm no artist. I only painted it because I had nothing to do.'
She gave a ladies' party, to which she asked Mrs Coutts, sometimes called Mrs Lawyer Coutts, Mrs Best whose husband was the manager of the Bank of Commerce, various other ladies she only knew to speak to on the street, as well as neighbors, Fern Dogherty's co-workers from the post office, and of course Aunt Elspeth and Auntie Grace. (She asked them to make creamed-chicken tarts and lemon tarts and matrimonial cake, which they did.) The party was all planned in advance. As soon

as the ladies came into the front hall they had to guess how many beans in a jar, writing their guess on a slip of paper. The evening proceeded with guessing games, quizzes made up with the help of the encyclopedia, charades which never got going properly because many ladies could not be made to understand how to play, and were too shy anyway, and a pencil and paper game where you write a man's name, fold it down, and pass it on, write a verb, fold it down, write a lady's name, and so on, and at the end all the papers are unfolded and read out. In a pink wool skirt and bolero, I joyfully passed peanuts.

Aunt Elspeth and Auntie Grace kept busy in the kitchen, smiling and affronted. My mother was wearing a red dress, semitransparent, covered with little black and blue pansies, like embroidery. 'We thought it was beetles she had on that dress,' whispered Aunt Elspeth to me. 'It gave us a start!' After that it did seem to me the party was less beautiful than I had supposed; I noticed some ladies were not playing any games, that my mother's face was feverish with excitement and her voice full of organising fervor, that when she played the piano, and Fern Dogherty – who had studied to be a singer – sang 'What Is Life without My Lover?' ladies contained themselves, and clapped from some kind distance, as if this might be showing off.

Auntie Grace and Aunt Elspeth would in fact say to me, off and on for the next year. 'How is that lady boarder of yours? How is she finding life without her lover?' I would explain to them that it was a song from an opera, a translation, and they would cry, 'Oh, is *that* it? And we were all the time feeling so sorry for her!'

My mother had hoped that her party would encourage other ladies to give parties of this sort, but it did not, or if it did we never heard of them; they continued giving bridge parties, which my mother said were silly and snobbish. She gave up on social life, gradually. She said that Mrs Coutts was a stupid woman who in one of the quizzes had been uncertain who Julius Caesar was – she thought he was Greek – and who also made mistakes in grammar, saying things like 'he told her and I' instead of 'her and me' – a common mistake of people who thought they were being genteel.

She joined the Great Books discussion group which was meeting every second Thursday during the winter in the Council Chambers in the Town Hall. There were five other people in the group, including a retired doctor, Dr Comber, who was very frail, courteous, and as it turned out, dictatorial. He had pure white, silky hair and wore an ascot scarf. His wife had lived in Jubilee over thirty years and still knew hardly anybody's name, or where the streets were. She was Hungarian. She had a magnificent name she would serve up to people sometimes, like a fish on a platter, all its silvery, scaly syllables intact, but it was no use, nobody in Jubilee could pronounce or remember it. At first my mother was delighted with this couple, whom she had always wanted to know. She was overjoyed to be invited to their house where she looked at photographs of their honeymoon in Greece and drank red wine so as not to offend them – though she did not drink – and listened to funny and dreadful stories of things that had happened to them in Jubilee because they were atheists and intellectuals. Her admiration persisted through *Antigone*, dampened a bit in *Hamlet*, grew dimmer and dimmer through *The Republic* and *Das Kapital*. Nobody could have any opinions, it appeared, but the Combers; the Combers knew more, they had seen Greece, they had attended lectures by H. G. Wells, they were always right. Mrs Comber and my mother had a disagreement and Mrs Comber brought up the fact that my mother had not gone to university and only to a – my mother imitated her accent – *backwoods* high school. My mother reviewed some of the stories they had told her and decided they had a persecution complex ('What is that?' said Fern, for such terms were just coming into fashion at the time) and that they were even possibly a little crazy. Also there had been an unpleasant smell in their house which she had not mentioned to us at the time, and the toilet, which she had to use after drinking that red wine, was hideous, scummy yellow. What good is it if you read Plato and never clean your toilet? asked my mother, reverting to the values of Jubilee.

She did not go back to Great Books the second year. She signed up for a correspondence course called 'Great Thinkers of History,' from the University of Western Ontario, and she wrote letters to the newspapers.

My mother had not let anything go. Inside that self we knew, which might at times appear blurred a bit, or sidetracked, she kept her younger selves strenuous and hopeful; scenes from the past were liable to pop up any time, like lantern slides, against the cluttered fabric of the present.

In the beginning, the very beginning of everything, there was that house. It stood at the end of a long lane, with wire fences, sagging windowpanes of wire on either side, in the middle of fields where the rocks – part of the pre-Cambrian Shield – were poking through the soil like bones through flesh. The house which I had never seen in a photograph – perhaps none had ever been taken – and which I had never heard my mother describe except in an impatient, matter-of-fact way ('It was just an old frame house – it never had been painted'), nevertheless appeared in my mind as plainly as if I had seen it in a newspaper – the barest, darkest, tallest of all old frame houses, simple and familiar yet with something terrible about it, enclosing evil, like a house where a murder has been committed.

And my mother, just a little girl then named Addie Morrison, spindly I should think, with cropped hair because her mother guarded her against vanity, would walk home from school up the long anxious lane, banging against her legs the lard pail that had held her lunch. Wasn't it always November, the ground hard, ice splintered on the puddles, dead grass floating from the wires? Yes, and the bush near and spooky, with the curious unconnected winds that lift the branches one by one. She would go into the house and find the fire out, the stove cold, the grease from the men's dinner thickened on the plates and pans.

No sign of her father, or her brothers who were older and through with school. They did not linger around the house. She would go through the front room into her parents' bedroom and there, more often than not, she would find her mother on her knees, bent down on the bed, praying. Far more clearly than her mother's face she could picture now that bent back, narrow shouldered in some gray or tan sweater over a dirty kimono or housedress, the back of the head with the thin hair pulled tight from the middle parting, the scalp unhealthily white. It was white as marble, white as soap.

'She was a religious fanatic,' says my mother of this kneeling woman, who at other times is discovered flat on her back and weeping – for reasons my mother does not go into – with a damp cloth pressed to her forehead. Once in the last demented stages of Christianity she wandered down to the barn and tried to hide a little bull calf in the hay, when the butcher's men were coming. My mother's voice, telling these things, is hard with her certainty of having been cheated, her undiminished feelings of anger and loss.

'Do you know what she did? I told you what she did? I told you about the money?' She draws a breath to steady herself. 'Yes. Well. She inherited some money. Some of her people had money, they lived in New York State. She came into two hundred and fifty dollars, not a lot of money, but more then than now and you know we were poor. You think this is poor. This is *nothing* to how we were poor. The oilcloth on our table, I remember it, it was worn through so you could see the bare boards. It was hanging in shreds. It was a rag, not an oilcloth. If I ever wore shoes I wore boys' shoes, hand-downs of my brothers. It was the kind of farm you couldn't raise chickweed on. For Christmas I got a pair of navy blue bloomers. And let me tell you, I was *glad*. I knew what it was to be cold.

'Well. My mother took her money and she ordered a great box of Bibles. They came by express. They were the most expensive kind, maps of the Holy Land and gilt-edged pages and the words of Christ were all marked in red. *Blessed are the poor in spirit.* What is so remarkable about being poor in spirit? She spent every cent.

'So then, we had to go out and give them away. She had bought them for distribution to the heathen. I think my brothers hid some in the granary. I know they did. But I was too much of a fool to think of that. I was tramping all over the country at the age of eight, in boys' shoes and not owning a pair of mittens, giving away Bibles.

'One thing, it cured me of religion for life.'

Once she ate cucumbers and drank milk because she had heard that this combination was poisonous and she wished to die. She was more curious than depressed. She lay down and hoped to wake in heaven, which she had heard so much about, but opened her eyes instead on another morning. That too had its effect on her faith. She told nobody at the time.

The older brother sometimes brought her candy, from town. He shaved at the kitchen table, a mirror propped against the lamp. He was vain, she thought, he had a moustache, and he got letters from girls which he never answered, but left lying around where anybody could read them. My mother appeared to hold this against him. 'I have no illusions about him,' she said, 'though I guess he was no different from most.' He lived in New Westminster now, and worked on a ferryboat. The other brother lived in the States. At Christmas they sent cards, and she sent cards to them. They never wrote letters, nor did she.

It was the younger brother she hated. What did he do? Her answers were not wholly satisfactory. He was evil, bloated, cruel. A cruel fat boy. He fed firecrackers to cats. He tied up a toad and chopped it to pieces. He drowned my mother's kitten, named Misty, in the cow trough, though he afterwards denied it. Also he caught my mother and tied her up in the barn and tormented her. Tormented her? He *tortured* her.

What with? But my mother would never go beyond that – that word, *tortured*, which she spat out like blood. So I was left to imagine her tied up in the barn, as at a stake, while her brother, a fat Indian, yelped and pranced about her. But she had escaped, after all, unscalped, unburnt. Nothing really accounted for her darkened face at this point in the story, for her way of saying *tortured*. I had not yet learned to recognise the gloom that overcame her in the vicinity of sex.

Her mother died. She went away for an operation but she had large lumps in both breasts and she died, my mother always said, on the table. On the *operating* table. When I was younger I used to imagine her stretched out dead on an ordinary table among the teacups and ketchup and jam.

'Were you sad?' I said hopefully and my mother said yes, of

course she was sad. But she did not linger round this scene. Important things were coming. Soon she was through school, she had passed her entrance exams and she wanted to go to high school, in town. But her father said no, she was to stay home and keep house until she got married. ('Who would I marry in God's name?' cried my mother angrily every time at this point in the story, 'out there at the end of the world with everybody cross-eyed from inbreeding?') After two years at home, miserable, learning some things on her own from old high-school textbooks that had belonged to her mother (a schoolteacher herself before marriage and religion overtook her), she defied her father, she walked a distance of nine miles to town, hiding in the bushes by the road every time she heard a horse coming, for fear it would be them, with the old wagon, come to take her back home. She knocked on the door of a boarding house she knew from the egg business and asked if she could have her room and board in return for kitchen work and waiting on table. And the woman who ran the house took her in – she was a rough-talking, decent old woman that everybody called Grandma Seeley – and kept her from her father till time had passed, even gave her a plaid dress, scratchy wool, too long, which she wore to school that first morning when she stood up in front of a class all two years younger than she was and read Latin, pronouncing it just the way she had taught herself, at home. Naturally, they all laughed.

And my mother could not help, could never help, being thrilled and tender, recalling this; she was full of wonder at her old, young self. Oh, if there could be a moment out of time, a moment when we could choose to be judged, naked as can be, beleaguered, triumphant, then that would have to be the moment for her. Later on comes compromise and error, perhaps; there, she is absurd and unassailable.

Then, in the boarding house, begins a whole new chapter in life. Up in the morning dark to peel the vegetables, leave them in cold water for dinner at noon. Clean out the chamber pots, sprinkle them with talcum. No flush toilets in that town. 'I have cleaned chamber pots to get my education!' she would say, and not mind who was listening. But a nice class of people used them. Bank clerks. The CNR telegraph operator. The teacher, Miss Rush. Miss Rush taught my mother to sew, gave her some beautiful merino wool for a dress, gave her a yellow fringed scarf, ('What *became* of it?' asked my mother in exasperated grief), gave her some eau de cologne. My mother loved Miss Rush; she cleaned Miss Rush's room and saved the hair from her tray, cleanings from her comb, and when she had enough she made a little twist of hair which she looped from a string, to wear around her neck. That was how she loved her. Miss Rush taught her how to read music and play on Miss Rush's own piano, kept in Grandma Seeley's front room, those songs she could play yet, though she hardly ever did. 'Drink to Me Only with Thine Eyes' and 'The Harp that Once through Tara's Halls' and 'Bonny Mary of Argyle'.

What had happened to Miss Rush, then, with her beauty and her embroidery and her piano playing? She had married, rather late, and died having a baby. The baby died too and lay in her arm like a wax doll, in a long dress; my mother had seen it.

Stories of the past could go like this, round and round and down to death; I expected it.

Grandma Seeley, for instance, was found dead in bed one summer morning just after my mother had completed four years of high school and Grandma Seeley had promised to let her have the money to go to Normal School, a loan to be paid back when she became a teacher. There was somewhere a piece of paper with writing on it to this effect, but it was never found. Or rather, my mother believed, it was found, by Grandma Seeley's nephew and his wife, who got her house and her money; they must have destroyed it. The world is full of such people.

So my mother had to go to work; she worked in a large store in Owen Sound where she was soon in charge of dry goods and notions. She became engaged to a young man who remained a shadow – no clear-cut villain, certainly, like her brother, or Grandma Seeley's nephew, but not luminous and loved, either, not like Miss Rush. For mysterious reasons she was compelled to break her engagement. ('He did not turn out to be the sort of person I had thought he was.') Later, an indefinite time later, she met my father, who must have turned out to be the sort of person she thought he was, because she married him, though she had always sworn to herself she would never marry a farmer (he was a fox farmer, and at one time had thought he might get rich by it; was that any different?), and his family had already begun to make remarks to her that were not well-meant.

'But you fell in love with him,' I would remind her sternly, anxiously, wanting to get it settled for good. 'You fell in love.'

'Well yes of course I did.'

'Why did you fall in love?'

'Your father was always a gentleman.'

Was that all? I was troubled here by a lack of proportion, though it was hard to say what was missing, what was wrong. In the beginning of her story was dark captivity, suffering, then daring and defiance and escape. Struggle, disappointment, more struggle, godmothers and villains. Now I expected as in all momentous satisfying stories – the burst of Glory, the Reward. Marriage to my father? I hoped this was it. I wished she would leave me in no doubt about it.

When I was younger, out at the end of the Flats Road, I would watch her walk across the yard to empty the dishwater, carrying the dishpan high, like a priestess, walking in an unhurried, stately way, and flinging the dishwater with a grand gesture over the fence. Then, I had supposed her powerful, a ruler, also content. She had power still, but not so much as perhaps she thought. And she was in no way content. Nor a priestess. She had a loudly growling stomach, whose messages she laughed at or ignored, but which embarrassed me unbearably. Her hair grew out in little wild gray-brown tufts and thickets; every permanent she got turned to frizz. Had all her stories, after all, to end up with just her, the way she was now, just my mother in Jubilee?

One day she came to the school, representing the encyclopedia company, to present a prize for the best essay on why we should buy Victory Bonds. She had to go to Porterfield, Blue River, Stirling schools and do the same thing; that week was a proud one for her. She wore a terrible mannish navy blue suit, with a single button at the waist, and a maroon-colored felt hat, her best, on which I agonisingly believed I could see a fine dust. She gave a little speech. I fixed my eyes on the sweater of the girl ahead of me – pale blue, little nubby bits of wool sticking out – as if hanging on to such indifferent straws of fact would keep me from drowning in humiliation. She was so different, that was all, so brisk and hopeful and guileless in her maroon hat, making little jokes, thinking herself a success. For two cents she would have launched into her own educational history, nine miles to town and the chamber pots. Who else had a mother like that? People gave me sly and gloating and pitying looks. Suddenly I could not bear anything about her – the tone of her voice, the reckless, hurrying way she moved, her lively absurd gestures (any minute now she might knock the ink bottle off the principal's desk), and most of all her innocence, her way of not knowing when people were laughing, of thinking she could get away with this.

I hated her selling encyclopedias and making speeches and wearing that hat. I hated her writing letters to the newspapers. Her letters about local problems or those in which she promoted education and the rights of women and opposed compulsory religious education in the school, would be published in the Jubilee *Herald-Advance* over her own name. Others appeared on a page in the city paper given over to lady correspondents, and for them she used the nom de plume *Princess Ida*, taken from a character in Tennyson whom she admired. They were full of long decorative descriptions of the countryside from which she had fled (*This morning a marvelous silver frost enraptures the eye on every twig and telephone wire and makes the world a veritable fairyland –*) and even contained references to Owen and me (*my daughter, soon-to-be-no-longer-a-child, forgets her new-found dignity to frolic in the snow*) that made the roots of my teeth ache with shame. Other people than Aunt Elspeth and Auntie Grace would say to me, 'I seen that letter of your mother's in the paper,' and I would feel how contemptuous, how superior and silent and enviable they were, those people who all their lives could stay still, with no need to do or say anything remarkable.

I myself was not so different from my mother, but concealed it, knowing what dangers there were.

That second winter we lived in Jubilee we had visitors. It was a Saturday afternoon and I was shoveling our sidewalk. I saw a big car come nosing along between the snowbanks almost silently, like an impudent fish. American license plates. I thought it was somebody lost. People did drive out to the end of River Street – which nowhere bothered to have a sign warning that it was a dead end – and by the time they reached our house would have begun to wonder.

A stranger got out. He wore an overcoat, gray felt hat, silk scarf in winter. He was tall and heavy; his face was mournful, proud, sagging. He held out his arms to me alarmingly.

'Come on out here and say hello to me! I know your name but I bet you don't know mine!'

He came right up to me – standing stock-still with the shovel in my hand – and kissed me on the cheek. A sweetish-sour masculine smell; shaving lotion, uneasy stomach, clean starched shirt, and some secret hairy foulness. 'Was your momma's name Addie Morrison? Was it, eh?'

No one ever called my mother Addie any more. It made her sound different – rounder, dowdier, simpler.

'Your momma's Addie and you're Della and I'm your Uncle Bill Morrison. That's who I am. Hey, I gave you a kiss and you never gave me one. Is that what you call fair up here?'

By this time my mother with a fresh, haphazard streak of lipstick on her mouth was coming out of the house.

'Well, Bill. You don't believe in advance notice, do you? Never mind, we're happy to see you.' She said this with some severity, as if arguing a point.

It really was her brother then, the American, my blood uncle.

He turned and waved at the car. 'You can get out now. Nothing here going to bite you.'

The door opened on the other side of the car and a tall lady got out, slowly, with difficulty over her hat. This hat went high on one side of the head and low on the other; green feathers sticking up made it even higher. She wore a three-quarter-length silver fox coat and a green dress and green high-heeled shoes, no rubbers.

'That's your Aunt Nile,' said Uncle Bill to me as if she couldn't hear, or understand English, as if she was some awesome feature of the landscape, that needed identifying. 'You never have seen her before. You have seen me but you were too young to remember. You never have seen her. I never saw her myself before last summer. I was married to your Aunt Callie when I saw you before and now I'm married to your Aunt Nile. I met her in August, I married her in September.'

The sidewalk was not shoveled clear. Aunt Nile stumbled in her high heels and moaned, feeling snow in her shoe. She moaned miserably like a child, she said to Uncle Bill, 'I nearly twisted my ankle,' as if there was nobody else around.

'Not far to go,' he said encouragingly, and took her arm, and supported her the rest of the way up the sidewalk and up the steps and across the veranda as if she was a Chinese lady (I had just been reading *The Good Earth*, from the town library) for whom walking is a rare and unnatural activity. My mother and I, who had exchanged no greetings with Nile, followed, and in the dark hall mother said, 'Well now, welcome!' and Uncle Bill helped Nile off with her coat and said to me. 'Here now, you take this and hang it up. Hang it up someplace by itself. Don't hang it up next to any barn jackets!' Touching the fur, my mother said to Nile, 'You ought to go out to our farm, you could see some of these on the hoof.' Her tone was jocose and unnatural.

'She means foxes,' Uncle Bill told Nile. 'Like your coat is made from.' He said to us, 'I don't think she even knew that fur come off a creature's back. She thought they manufactured them right in the store!' Nile meanwhile looked amazed and unhappy as someone who had never even heard of foreign countries, and who is suddenly whisked away and deposited in one, with everybody around speaking an undreamt-of language. Adaptability could not be one of her strong points. Why should it be? It would put in question her own perfection. She was perfect, and younger than I had thought at first, maybe only twenty-two or -three. Her skin was without a mark, like a pink teacup; her mouth could have been cut out of burgundy-colored velvet, and pasted on. Her smell was inhumanly sweet and her fingernails – I saw this with shock, delight, and some slight misgiving, as if she might have gone too far – were painted *green*, to match her clothes.

'It's a very handsome coat,' said my mother, with more dignity.

Uncle Bill looked at her regretfully. 'Your husband'll never make any money this end of the business, Addie, it's all controlled by Jews. Now, have you got such a thing as a cup of coffee in the house? Get me and my little wife warmed up?'

The trouble was, we didn't have such a thing. My mother and Fern Dogherty drank tea, which was cheaper, and Postum in the mornings. My mother led everybody into the dining room and Nile sat down and my mother said, 'Wouldn't you like a hot cup of tea? I am absolutely out of coffee.'

Uncle Bill took this in stride. No tea, he said, but if she was out of coffee he would get some coffee. 'Have you got any grocery stores in this town?' he said to me. 'You must have one or two grocery stores in this town. Big town like this, it's got street lights even, I saw them. You and me'll get in the car and go and buy some groceries, leave these two sister-in-laws to get acquainted.'

I floated beside him, in this big cream-and-chocolate, clean-smelling car, down River Street, down Mason Street, down the main street of Jubilee. We parked in front of the Red Front Grocery behind a team and sleigh.

'This a grocery store?'

I did not commit myself. Suppose I said it was, and then it had none of the things he wanted?

'Your momma shop here?'

'Sometimes.'

'Then I guess it has to be good enough for us.'

From the car I saw the team and sleigh, with sacks of feed on it, and the Red Front Grocery, and the whole street, differently. Jubilee seemed not unique and permanent as I had thought, but almost makeshift, and shabby; it would barely do.

The store had just been turned into a self-serve, the first in town. The aisles were too narrow for carts but there were baskets you carried over your arm. Uncle Bill wanted a cart.

He asked if there were any other stores in town where carts were available, and was told there were none. When this was settled he went up and down the aisles calling out the names of things. He behaved as if nobody else was in the store at all, as if they only came to life when he called to ask them something, as if the store itself was not real but had been thrown together the moment he said he needed one.

He bought coffee and canned fruit and vegetables and cheese and dates and figs and pudding mixes and macaroni dinners and hot-chocolate powders and tinned oysters and sardines. 'Do you like this?' he kept saying. 'Do you like these here? You like raisins? You like cornflakes? You like ice cream? Where do they keep the ice cream? What flavor do you like? Chocolate? You like chocolate the best?' Finally I was afraid to look at anything, or he would buy it.

He stopped in front of the Selrite window where there were bins of bulk candy. 'You like candy, I bet. What do you want? Licorice? Fruit jellies? Candy peanuts? Let's get a mixture, let's get all three. That going to make you thirsty, all those candy peanuts? We better find some pop.'

That was not all. 'Have you got a bakeshop in this town?' he said, and I took him to McArter's Bakery where he bought two dozen butter tarts and two dozen buns with glazed sugar and nuts on top, and a coconut cake half a foot high. This was exactly like a childish story I had at home in which a little girl manages to get her wishes granted, one a day for a week and they all turn out, of course, to make her miserable. One wish was to have everything she had ever wanted to eat. I used to get that out and read the description of the food over again for pure pleasure, ignoring the punishments which soon followed, inflicted by supernatural powers always on the lookout for greed. But I saw now that too much really might be too much. Even Owen might in the end have been depressed by this idiot largesse, which threw the whole known system of rewards and delights out of kilter.

'You're like a fairy godfather,' I said to Uncle Bill. I meant this to sound unchildish, slightly ironic; also in this exaggerated way I meant to express the gratitude I was afraid I did not sufficiently feel. But he took it as the simplest childishness, repeating it to my mother when we got home.

'She says I'm a fairy godfather, but I had to pay cash!'

'Well I don't know what I'm supposed to do with all this, Bill. You'll have to take some home.'

'We never drove up here from Ohio to buy our groceries. You put them away. We don't need them. As long as I got my chocolate ice cream for dessert I don't care what else I've got or haven't got. My sweet tooth has never gone sour on me. But I lost some weight, you know. I lost thirty pounds since last summer.'

'You are not a case for war relief yet.'

My mother removed the tablecloth with its day-old tea and ketchup stains, and spread a fresh one, the one she called the Madeira cloth, her wedding-present best.

'You know I was a runt at one time. I was a skinny baby. When I was two years old I nearly died of pneumonia. Momma pulled me through and she started feeding me. I never got any exercise for a long time and I got fat.

'Momma,' he said with a gloomy kind of luxuriance. 'Wasn't she some sort of a saint on earth? I tell Nile she ought to have known her.'

My mother gave Nile a startled look (had these two sisters-in-law been getting acquainted?) but did not say whether she thought this would have been a good idea.

I said to Nile, 'Do you want a plate with birds on it or the one with flowers?' I just wanted to make her speak.

'I don't care,' she said faintly, looking down at her green nails as if they were talismans to keep her in this place.

My mother cared. 'Put plates on the table that match, we're not so impoverished that we don't own a set of dishes!'

'Do you wear Nile green because your name is Nile?' I said, still prodding. 'Is that color Nile green?' I thought she was an idiot, and yet I frantically admired her, was grateful for every little colorless pebble of a word she dropped. She reached some extreme of feminine decorativeness, perfect artificiality, that I had not even known existed; seeing her, I understood that I would never be beautiful.

'It's just a coincidence my name is Nile.' (She might even have said *cocinidence*.) 'It was my favorite color long before I even heard there was a color Nile green.'

'I didn't know you could get green nail polish.'

'You have to order it in.'

'Momma hoped we would stay on the farm the way we were raised,' said Uncle Bill, following his own thoughts.

'I wouldn't wish it on anybody to live on a farm like that. You couldn't raise chickweed on it.'

'The financial aspect isn't always the only thing, Addie. There's the being closer to Nature. Without all this – you know, running around, doing what isn't good for you, living high. Forgetting about Christianity. Momma felt it was a good life.'

'What is so good about Nature? Nature is just one thing preying on another all the way down the line. Nature is just a lot of waste and cruelty, maybe not from Nature's point of view but from a human point of view. Cruelty is the law of Nature.'

'Well I don't mean like that, Addie. I don't mean wild animals and all like that. I mean like our life we had at home, where we didn't have too many of the comforts, I'll grant you that, but we had a simple life and hard work and fresh air and a good spiritual example in our momma. She died young, Addie. She died in pain.'

'Under anesthetic,' my mother said. 'So strictly speaking I hope she did not die in pain.'

During supper she told Uncle Bill about her encyclopedia selling.

'I sold three sets last fall,' was what she said, though actually she had sold one and was still working on two fairly promising cases. 'There is money in the country now, you know. It is due to the war.'

'You won't make no money peddling to farmers,' said Uncle Bill, hanging low over his plate and eating steadily, as old people do. He looked old. 'What did you say you're selling?'

'Encyclopedias. Books. They are a very fine set. I would have given my right arm to have had a set of books like these around the house when I was a child.' This was perhaps the fiftieth time I had heard her make that statement.

'You got your education. I did without. That didn't stop me.
You won't sell books to farmers. They got too much sense.
They are tight with their money. Money is not in things like
that. It is in property. Money is in property and investments if
you know what you are doing.' He began a long story, with
complicated backtracking and correcting himself on details,
about buying and selling houses. Buying, selling, buying, building, rumors, threats, perils, safety. Nile did not listen at all but
pushed the canned corn around on her plate, spearing the
kernels one at a time with her fork – a childish game not even
Owen could have got away with. Owen himself said not one
word but ate with his gum on his thumbnail; my mother had
not noticed. Fern Dogherty was not there; she had gone to see
her mother in the County Hospital. My mother listened to her
brother with a look that was a mixture of disapproval and
participatory cunning.

Her brother! This was the thing, the indigestible fact. This
Uncle Bill was my mother's brother, the terrible fat boy, so
gifted in cruelty, so cunning, quick, fiendish, so much to be
feared. I kept looking at him, trying to pull that boy out of the
yellowish man. But I could not find him there. He was gone,
smothered, like a little spotted snake, once venomous and
sportive, buried in a bag of meal.

'Remember the caterpillars, how they used to get on the
milkweed?'

'Caterpillars?' said my mother disbelievingly. She got up and
brought a little brass-handled brush and pan, also a wedding
present. She began to sweep the crumbs from the cloth.

'They come on the milkweed in the fall. They're after the
milk, you know – the juice in it. They drink it all up and get
fat and sleepy and go into their cocoon. Well, she found one
was on the milkweed and she brought it into the house –'

'Who did?'

'*Momma* did, Addie. Who else would take the trouble? It
was away before your time. She found this one and brought it
in and she set it up above the door where I couldn't get at it. I
wouldn't have meant any harm but I was like boys are. It went
into its cocoon and it stayed in all winter. I forgot about it was

there. Then we were all sitting after our dinner on Easter Sunday
– Easter Sunday but it was a blizzard out – and Momma says,
"Look!" *Look*, she says, so we looked and up above the door
was that thing beginning to stir. Just thinning out the cocoon,
just pulling and working it from the inside, getting tired and
letting up and going to work again. It took it half an hour, forty
minutes maybe, and we never quit watching. Then we saw the
butterfly come out. It was like the cocoon just finally weakened,
fell off like an old rag. It was a yellow butterfly, little spotty
thing. Its wings all waxed down. It had to work some to get
them loosed up. Works away on one, works away, flutters it
up. Works away on the other. Gets that up, takes a little fly.
Momma says, "Look at that. Never forget. That's what you
saw on Easter." Never forget. I never did, either.'

'What became of it?' said my mother neutrally.

'I don't remember that. Wouldn't last long, weather like it
was. It was a funny thing to see, though – works away on one
wing, works away on the other. Takes a little fly. First time it
ever used its wings.' He laughed, with a note of apology, the
first and last we were to hear from him. But then he appeared
tired, vaguely disappointed, and folded his hands over his
stomach from which came dignified, necessary digestive noises.

That was in the same house. The same house where my
mother used to find the fire out and her mother at prayer and
where she took milk and cucumbers in the hope of getting to
heaven.

Uncle Bill and Nile stayed all night, sleeping on the front-room
couch which could be pulled out and made into a bed. Those
long, perfumed, enameled limbs of Nile's lay down so close to
my uncle's dragging flesh, his smell. I did not imagine anything
more they might have to do, because I thought the itchy hot
play of sex belonged to childhood, and was outgrown by decent
adults, who made their unlikely connection only for the purpose
of creating a child.

Sunday morning, as soon as they had eaten breakfast, they
went away, and we never saw either of them again.

Some days later my mother burst out to me, 'Your Uncle Bill
is a dying man.'

It was nearly suppertime; she was cooking sausages. Fern was not home from work yet. Owen had just come in from hockey practice and was dumping his skates and stick in the back hall. My mother cooked sausages until they were hard and shiny and very dark on the outside; I had never eaten them any other way.

'He is a dying man. He was sitting here Sunday morning when I came down to put the kettle on and he told me. He has a cancer.'

She continued rolling the sausages around with a fork and she had the crossword puzzle from the newspaper torn out, half done, on the counter beside the stove. I thought of Uncle Bill going downtown and buying butter tarts and chocolate ice cream and cake, and coming home and eating. How could he do it?

'He always had a big appetite,' said my mother, as if her thoughts ran along the same lines, 'and the prospect of death doesn't seem to have diminished it. Who knows? Maybe with less eating he would have lived to be old.'

'Does Nile know?'

'What does it matter what she knows. She only married him for a meal ticket. She'll be well off.'

'Do you still hate him?'

'Of course I don't hate him,' said my mother quickly and with reserve. I looked at the chair where he had sat. I had a fear of contamination, not of cancer but of death itself.

'He told me he had left me three hundred dollars in his will.'

After that, what was there to do but get down to realities?

'What are you going to spend it on?'

'No doubt something will occur to me when the time comes.'

The front door opened, Fern coming in.

'I could always send away for a box of Bibles.'

Just before Fern came in one door and Owen came in the other, there was something in the room like the downflash of a wing or knife, a sense of hurt so strong, but quick and isolated, vanishing.

'There is an Egyptian god with four letters,' said my mother, frowning at the crossword, 'that I know I know, and I cannot think of it to save my soul.'

'Isis.'

'Isis is a goddess, I'm surprised at *you*.'

Soon after this the snow began to melt; the Wawanash River overflowed its banks, and carried away road signs and fence posts and henhouses, and receded; the roads became more or less navigable, and my mother was out again in the afternoons. One of my father's aunts – it never matters which – said, 'Now she will miss her writing to the newspapers.'

Honor Thy Father and Thy Mother

Judith Chernaik

They fell from the back of the large scrapbook into which my parents had pasted a complete pictorial survey of my infancy, half a dozen photographs of college boys standing with arms about one another's shoulders, or sprawling in blazers and knickers on the great lawns in springtime, or in meditative pose, pipe in hand, gazing out over Cayuga's blue waters.

'The playing fields of America,' Mother said. 'Why, you must have clung to one another for dear life.'

'That's the Library Tower,' Father said. 'Three hundred and twenty-four steps to the top. Did I ever tell you that I tried out for Chimesmaster?'

'That must have been a long climb,' Mother said.

'Well, it was strictly for Anglo-Saxons. But it's not true that we clung together. Even Herb learned how to order a cup of coffee. It was a broadening experience.'

'Let me see the pictures, Esther.' Mother looked at one curiously, then another. 'How young you looked!'

I leaned over her shoulder, my cheek grazing her thick hair. My father was the handsome boy on the end, his dark hair pasted down over clear, childlike eyes, his mustache trim and neat over a sensitive mouth. You would have said he breathed self-confidence.

Mother shut the scrapbook abruptly. 'Where did you find this, anyway? Look how dusty it is! Look at your hands!'

I dutifully scrubbed my hands, but I was unwilling to give up the photographs, and hid the album in my bottom drawer, under sweaters packed away for the winter. It was a familiar pattern, I knew; the boy from a poor immigrant family was expected to break all the records. But it was one thing to be ambitious and hardworking, another to embrace gaiety, comradeship, and winter sports. As a child, my father had boarded at a day-care center while Grandmother Sophie organised her fellow garment-workers, then he passed through the New York public schools and Stuyvesant High; how had he managed to look so elegant as a college junior? I thought of that cavernous apartment on Second Avenue, with its sudden corners and vanishing horizons, its hospitality open to every destitute fourth cousin from Pereyaslev. Grandfather Isadore might be patiently clipping Yiddish newspapers in the back bedroom, while Sophie cut patterns on the living-room table, surrounded by yards of flowered cotton, faded rayon prints, crimson ribbon, boxes of sequins, glass beads, gilt tape; in the rocking chair by the radiator the boarder sipped a glass of tea, and nodded over the *Daily Forward*. How remote the green hills of Ithaca must have seemed as soon as he walked through that door! Or, more likely, it was the other way around, and the smells of Second Avenue vanished into thin air when he set foot on the shaded quadrangles of the University. What more could a man need? The world lay open to him.

They must have been proud of their son when he brought home his roommates Herb and Maxie, and his pretty girlfriend Flo (my mother conceded that Flo was pretty), and Sophie could feed them and question them minutely about college life. Dances and football, bridge, even tennis; Sophie must have thought she had finally triumphed over the new world. Hard work and politics were for the old; why shouldn't the young have fun? Florence held a skein of yellow wool for a magnificent cable-knit sweater which figured in the photographs; my father picked at a mandolin, and Herb and Maxie sang:

> There's a long, long trail a-winding
> Into the land of my dreams!
> Where the nightingale is singing
> And the bright moon beams!

(Once, I dreamed that I went up to the apartment on Second Avenue; at the far end of the hall I saw Grandfather Isadore bent over a sewing machine, working in the circle of light from the naked bulb overhead. He was thin and exhausted; I knew he was dying. He slowly raised his head and turned toward me; the hollows that were his eyes stared at me without recognition, though I gestured frantically. The door shut suddenly, but the marble face was fixed on my mind, an image of terrible authority. Were Sophie's embraces, her pie and strudel, a careful plot to seduce me from looking into that other room? Or did the room exist anywhere but in my mind? I had invented the sewing machine; my grandfather in real life was a diamond-setter, with his own shop in the downtown jewelry center. I pushed the dream aside; it was better to leave the comfortable surface of life as it was, untarnished by my morbid fears.)

As I brooded over the photographs, it occurred to me that what my mother resented most about my father's college days was simply that he liked to have a good time. I knew without asking that she had never played tennis, or bridge, or sat around campfires in the moonlight. She was intense and fiercely intellectual, and suffered easily; I knew too well who the young girl inside her was. But my father's youth had the unreality of time halted and framed in photographs. I loved to imagine its archaic splendor, investing it with the charm of the Ford Model A and the silent movies. As we drove down the curving expanse of the Harlem River Drive at night, Father sang old college songs in a cheerful baritone. I watched the lights stream by, and drowsed to the strains of youth departed, golden-haired boys drinking to all they loved best, vowing eternal loyalty to school and schoolmates, defying time and change and fortune.

We picked my mother up at Harlem Evening High School, where she taught English and Civics four nights a week; when she came home she sometimes cried from exhaustion and ill temper. She lay down in the dark bedroom and called me to wet a linen napkin for her throbbing head. I stood in the shadow of the doorway, within call, to soak it again as it grew warm, until she fell into a restless sleep. Meanwhile my father, shirt-sleeves rolled to his elbow, worked at the secretary, his eyeshade softening the bright circle of light on the green felt. The heavy desk drawers held the records of our lives, neatly filed in manila envelopes, tied and labeled; birth certificates, insurance policies, paid bills, check stubs held for fifteen years against that day when my father might be called for an accounting. The day's bills sorted, Father removed from a bottom drawer an unfinished monograph from law school days, marked in sober black lettering, 'Volens non fit injuria.' I sat near him and did my homework or read, sometimes coming close to peer over his shoulder at the marked-up page. He showed me a passage; what did I think?

'Why don't you show it to Mama?'

He patted the stack of typed sheets carefully into line. 'No . . . she has enough to think about. Besides, women aren't interested in legal questions. They like things to be right or wrong in a clear-cut way.'

'I'll bet it was fascinating, practicing law,' I offered, to make up for my mother's lack of interest.

'I wish I could say it was. But things were very tight. I used to walk to the office to save carfare. Most days I could just as well have saved the walk.'

I thought of my father striding along in the morning rush, a young man trying to make his way. 'It would have been better for you and Mama if I hadn't been born just then.'

He put his arm about my shoulders. 'Why, you were the best thing that could have happened to us!'

He hadn't answered my half-question, though. And I wondered uneasily if my parents spent bitter hours going back over their mistakes, blaming themselves or each other for errors of judgment, poor planning, insufficient daring. Father had practiced law, I knew, only for two or three years, when the depression had forced him to other expedients. He had been, since the beginning of the war, assistant manager of a small tool and die company. I was dimly, reluctantly, aware that he was not a success by other people's standards. He had gone to college on scholarship, worked his way through law school; he should eventually have become rich and respected. Others less talented, like Herb and Maxie, had prospered; why not my father? I never dared to ask him point-blank about his career; the question was so hedged around with mystery, the possible answers so dangerously suggestive of failure and incapacity.

The war made ordinary ambitions irrelevant, in any case; it was clearly the wrong time to worry about dreams abandoned, chances missed. Our neighbors grumbled about rationing and hoarded sugar and coffee; I religiously saved newspapers and collected scrap metal, scouring the gutters for rusty cans, nails, the staples in used matchbooks. I dreamed about the concentration camps, hunger marches, sealed trains. I was escaping across the border, carrying my sister Jennie in my arms; my brother Paul clutched my hand. We came to a stream; which child must I save, which must I sacrifice? How could I manage the two of them? Could Paul hang on to my back, perhaps? I turned indecisively from Jennie to Paul, while precious time slipped by; whom did I love best? I woke into living nightmare, orphaned, bereft, screams echoing in my ears. Where were my mother and father? In panic I listened for sounds of life in the house, trying to bolster my shaky conviction that they were all safe in their beds. In the saner daylight hours the children on the block played Gestapo or War, passionate exercises in cunning; we collaborated in postponing until suppertime the inevitable capture of Nazis and Japs.

When my father turned thirty-eight it seemed to me that everyone we knew, our neighbors, the shopkeepers on Kings Highway, must rejoice at our narrow escape from the war. I labored over a birthday card:

> A great event to celebrate!
> Today at last you're 38!
> And for the draft you're just too late!

But after I presented it to Father, with a bottle of after-shave lotion, I was suddenly ashamed of my selfishness. He could have volunteered. I would have volunteered in his place; I would have been fighting with the French Resistance, spiriting away refugees, meeting death in the cause of freedom.

'Did you ever think of volunteering?' I asked casually.

'I think we've given enough,' Mother said. Her brothers were overseas, Bernard in India, Emanuel in North Africa.

'Your mother would never let me be a hero,' Father said. A

look crossed between my parents, private, amused. I was puzzled but relieved; not everyone, it seemed, need aspire to a heroic life.

That year Mother had decided not to return to work; Jennie was a baby; my brother Paul must have been four. We spent most afternoons at the large iron tubs in our basement, scrubbing diapers on large tin washboards; then we hung them out in the backyard, where old Mr Ehrenstein, who lived downstairs, coaxed into life a fine victory-garden of tomatoes, string beans, squash, and carrots. For a while I liked the image of myself as a fresh country girl from a child's storybook, skirts blowing, hair tossing in the wind, but I was perplexed by my mother's increasing irritability, and her late afternoon spells of headache, when she would lie in her darkened room, unable to sleep or read.

'You ought to go back to work,' I told her. 'It's bad for you, staying home like this.' I sat down carefully on the far edge of the bed.

'Don't do that, Esther,' she said. 'You're shaking the bed.'

I stood up, suddenly tearful. 'I was only thinking about your headaches. It might be a change for you. You seem so sad.'

'Do I? I don't mean to.'

'You don't seem happy,' I said boldly.

'Oh my dear, you shouldn't worry about me. These are hard years. Nobody's very happy.'

'Not everybody spends all day doing housework and laundry and chasing after children,' I said. 'You're not even good at it.'

She passed her hand wearily across her forehead, then unexpectedly smiled at me. 'I'll think about it. But it's hard to plan ahead. I'd have to find someone to take care of Paul and Jennie. It isn't as if I have to work, now that your father's making enough money, for a change.' Her eyes moved restlessly among the objects in the room, from the novels on the dresser, the clock and baby photographs, to the girdle and stockings on the chair, and the pyramid of unironed clothes in the corner. It seems to me now that those four walls and all they contained must have hemmed her in, oppressed her with a physical constriction.

Father was thirty-eight; Mother, then, would have been thirty-four, my age as I write. I project myself inside her skin with ease; I look out on the world through the same darkened windows, the senses alert to disaster, suspicious of offered gifts. Beyond her adult defensiveness I see the child with a pinched wan face, pale eyes, thick corkscrew curls, secretly nursing, cherishing, mistrusting her fine intelligence, forced to learn again and again that she was not of particular use to anyone. She must have felt that what she valued in my father was not going to be an asset to him in the same world that had been so irritated by her childish precocity.

On Sundays, while Paul and Jennie napped and Mother withdrew to some far haven with the *Times* crossword puzzle, my father and I pursued healthful outdoor activities. On bright winter Sunday mornings we went ice-skating in Prospect Park, gliding around the pond until fence, skaters, and the rocks and trees beyond disappeared in a blur. I tried to lure my father into another spin, and then another, until he shook himself free with a laugh. 'Let's go, princess!' We walked the two miles home, skates slung over our shoulders, exalted by the numbing cold and the glare of sun and sky. We walked past the hardened brown-capped mounds of city snow, the rows of red brick houses with small bare trees in front, the forlorn little corner groceries and drugstores, until our own house loomed around a turning, and I was flooded with love for its familiar streaked stucco. My father made us each a thick sandwich of corned beef and a pot of rich chocolate, we turned the radio to the Philharmonic broadcast, and spread the Sunday papers on the living room floor, happy until nighttime.

But in between these islands of content, I suffered from a growing restlessness as the days of perfect freedom and comradeship with my father became fewer, receded, merged with the ordinary succession of days. I was bewildered by the limitless range of possibilities which time seemed to offer, and which isolated events merely interrupted. What to do? what to be? what to make of oneself? My restlessness widened until it included my parents; it seemed to me that our lives had no solidity, and that my uncertainties were echoes of theirs. I had always assumed the sharpest distinction between my parents, whom I loved, and everyone else; the circle of love, as if in proof of its value, was very small, consisting of parents, grandparents, brother and sister. Beyond that magic circle stretched arid wildernesses, requiring of anyone foolhardy enough to explore them great independence of heart. Suddenly I began to wonder about the wilderness; it might not be unthinkable that I should try to find out what life was like. Were we as different as I thought from others, as remarkably and self-evidently privileged?

On the long summer weekends, our sway-backed yellow Studebaker sat in front of the house, a silent reproach to my parents' lack of imagination. My mother sat curled up, abstracted, with a novel or the newspaper, through the sticky afternoons. I paced the floor in new squeaking shoes, popping bubble gum, cracking my knuckles; in despair I practiced the opening phrase of the Chopin 'Butterfly' étude.

'Why don't we ever go for a drive like other people?' I swung around from the piano, letting the unresolved chord hang in the air.

Father was studying the stock market quotations; Mother was half-lying on the faded green couch, in a loose housecoat, absorbed in the crossword puzzle. She looked up vaguely and adjusted her glasses so she could see me.

'Are you out of your mind?' she said. 'In that Sunday traffic?'

'We could take Paul and Jennie to a state park.' There had been a polio outbreak at Coney Island; I knew better than to suggest the beach. 'We could have a picnic.'

'Don't you remember our last picnic, with the bees? We had to eat in the car with the windows shut!'

'I suppose you're also going to bring up the time you almost died of poison ivy, a hundred years ago.'

'Don't get excited, Esther. I like the country as much as you do.'

The country was a special place set aside for weekend visits. Did people live in the country? 'How about driving to Connecticut?' I said hopefully.

'What on earth would we do in Connecticut?'

'Just go. See it.'

'Darling' (to my father), 'you don't happen to know what the capital of Afghanistan is, do you?'

'You never want to do anything. I could suggest twenty places and you would find a good reason not to go to any of them.'

Mother looked at me severely. 'I do precisely what I want to do. Most people do, you'll find.'

'In that case I think I'll leave. It's like a prison in here, it smells of death.'

I slammed out, leaving, I hoped, a stunned silence behind me. Our street was busy with children, old ladies sunned themselves on the front porches, boys played softball in the street, dodging an occasional car. Three or four blocks further down it was suddenly still, the houses were larger, widely spaced, the maple trees taller, the people rich, out of sight. Houses, lawns, sleek black cars basked in the thin sunlight as if the day were to last forever. I stopped to stare over thick shrubbery at a rambling stone house; I could see a dim interior suggestive of a fireplace, dark oil paintings (perhaps family portraits), a grand piano, heavy furniture. A large German shepherd came leaping out from the back and barked rhythmically, the palace guard. He pointed, ears alert, as if he had just sighted a prey somewhere behind my left shoulder, then began to dig fiercely in the lawn.

Oppressed by my solitude, I turned back; I wished passionately that I had somewhere to go other than home, or that home were somewhere other than an undistinguished corner of Flatbush. Why did my mother insist that we live like hermits, knowing nobody, seeing nobody, going nowhere? We were like the three monkeys, blind, deaf, and dumb to the world, locked into our proud, sensitive selves. Our only link with the outside world was our monthly expedition to S. Klein's, when Mother firmly maneuvered me through the steaming aisles, and we tried on wrinkled jersey dresses, sweater seconds, last year's coats, slacks, slips, nightgowns, adding layer upon layer as if for a bizarre costume party. I had only recently begun to suspect that our shopping trips might be not only a function of economy but my mother's way of deliberately refusing to admit the possibility of grace or beauty in her life.

That night I listened to the earnest subdued voices from the living room, certain that my parents must be discussing me, and remorseful for my implied criticism of their lives. I comforted myself with the thought that I was, as their child, unable to hurt them, while they could want only to do everything possible for me. Dozing off in spite of myself, I caught a phrase repeated, something about a thousand dollars; with sudden joy I thought they must have decided to save enough money to send me to an out-of-town college, in the country.

The following Saturday, Father signaled quietly to me. 'How would you like to go into partnership for a few weeks?' My mother was in a rage of housecleaning; the beds were stripped, pillows airing in the windows. I was chasing cobwebs with a dustmop; Mother swept the carpets, pointedly ignoring all signs of a mystery. 'I'll tell you about it in the car.'

'Hey, Ma, I'm done,' I called; Father cheerily kissed her, and we left for the city.

'Is it the pinochle book?' I asked. For several weeks, Father had been recording his Wednesday night pinochle hands, with some notion of putting them together as a book.

He sighed. 'I'll tell you what the problem is. The public library has a dozen books on bridge, not one on pinochle. So I decide there's no market for another book on bridge; why don't I write a guide to pinochle? What do you think the publisher says when I send him an outline? Now, there's a market for anything on bridge, but who's going to buy a book about pinochle?'

'That's too bad.' I thought it probably wasn't supply and demand at all; Father just didn't know the right people.

We crossed into Manhattan, moving in slow traffic past a large neon sign flashing LOVE THY NEIGHBOR through the smoky haze, then down Third Avenue under the blackened girders of the elevated, to Tenth Street and my grandparents' apartment. Sophie embraced us and promised that we could work undisturbed.

'It's not too drafty?' she asked anxiously. 'The window don't close right, maybe you could call them?'

'Don't worry about us, Mama, just forget we're here,' Father said firmly, following her into the warm kitchen and taking a knish.

I saw Grandfather Isadore at the far end of the hall, sitting by the window reading the *Freiheit*. He gave us a weary 'gut morgen.'

'How's your back, Papa?'

'Ech, you shouldn't ask. All night I'm lying awake with the pain. I couldn't go into the shop this morning, I'm all alone there, anything happens.'

Sophie shook her fist at him. 'They didn't come here to listen to you complain.'

'He asked me, Sasha. My own son asks me how I'm getting along, it's not allowed to tell him?'

'Shut up and drink your tea. I'm up all night too and I don't go around making everyone miserable. Sit down and eat something, darling,' she urged me. 'Aren't you drinking milk? Look, she's getting so tall, if I pinch her there's nothing there. A skinny beanstalk! Cream I used to give your papa, he should grow nice.'

In Sophie's eyes, Father was a prince, a brilliant student, a paragon of sons. If only he had married a rich girl whose father could have set him up in business! She saved him the best pieces of chicken, the last of the strudel, worried about his sinus infections, was convinced that my mother served a cup of lukewarm coffee for breakfast. Secretly she thought he had been trapped into marriage. Such a baby!

'Can I help you make the knishes?' I asked cannily.

'Next week, maybe, if you're early enough. Now go and help your papa, and take him a bit of strudel for later.'

My father had replaced Grandfather Isadore's newspaper files with drafting materials, laid out on the sagging bedstead against the wall; stacks of papers and cardboard were arranged neatly on the bridge table. He explained the project to me, patient, good-humored about its chances. What was the source of the high percentage of error in most bookkeeping? The human factor, in particular, the tendency of the eye to skip from one column to the next. If parallel columns were distinguished by color, the percentage of error could be cut close to zero. As my father said, it was just an idea. Our 'partnership' consisted of making up some sample charts and marketing them. My job was to paste graph paper onto 5" × 12" cardboard charts, which Father filled in with the tables of the W-2 income tax form.

'You're not a neat worker, Esther,' Father said. 'You're like your mother.'

I had barely started, and my fingers were already gritty with paste. 'I hate arts and crafts,' I said. My hands would be stained with india ink as well; I regretted the light gray skirt I was wearing, which I needed for school.

After the ink dried Father went over the columns carefully with pale transparent blocks of yellow, red and blue. The finished charts were lovely; we admired them together.

'It looks so simple,' I said.

'You have to remember that it's the simple mistakes which cost the most.'

It was a delightful child's game that might, like the fabled golden egg, make our fortune one day. I imagined our lives transformed, my mother in mink and jewels, Father turned philanthropist, perhaps, an honorary advisor to the New York Stock Exchange. We could move from Flatbush to an elegant apartment on Riverside Drive, like Father's rich cousin Abe; my mother's melancholy would dissolve in the luxury of her new life, and her pride in my father's success.

By the fourth weekend we had a handsome stack of one hundred charts, enough to test the market. Father was very confident, I thought; as for me I loved being part of the real world of business, inventions, and trade. It would be a grand dream to contribute to the sum of human knowledge, but it would be almost as satisfying to have one's original idea, however modest, put to use in the world. Besides, Father needed me as a sounding board. We were in a happy alliance against my grandparents, quarreling and cooking and eating in the front rooms, and my mother, who never asked about our progress or showed the slightest curiosity about our weekly disappearances.

One Friday night, as we were finishing dinner, Father leaned back in his chair and announced that he had something to tell us. He looked the image of the traditional head of the family, presiding over the festive dinner table, the white tablecloth set with good dishes and brightened by tall silver candlesticks. He reached into his vest pocket and extracted a long brown envelope. 'Well, children,' he nodded benevolently in turn to Paul and Jennie and me. 'How would you like to have a new name?'

Our family name was Rosavitsky, transliterated from the Russian. As I write it now it has a slightly absurd air about it, like the name of a minor comic character in a Russian novel, a junior subaltern or an aged clerk. When I was a child it was always a stumbling block, a name teachers asked to have spelled aloud, pronounced again, and which they still remained doubtful about afterwards; a name to which a precarious dignity attached only when I walked down Second Avenue with my grandparents, and they were greeted by acquaintances from the Workmen's Circle. 'How are you, Mrs Rosavitsky. How do you do, Mr Rosavitsky, and so this is the *kleine enekele*!'

'A new name?' How I longed to change my name from Esther to Rosamund, or Arabella, Louisa, or Marianne! Where was the romance in Esther? If I could only change my name to Catherine!

'A new name, a new character, a new life, with the blessing of the Office of Records. What do you think?'

'How about Roosevelt?' I said. I was trembling.

'Esther, what's gotten into you?' Mother said.

My tongue seemed to be out of control. 'I'd like to know what was wrong with the old name. Our name. Yours and mine and Grandpa's.'

'I never said there was anything wrong with the old name,' Father said mildly.

'Why, there's nothing wrong with a name,' Mother said. 'I

suppose there's nothing wrong with firms which don't hire people with the wrong name, and government agencies which hire a man only if his name is Smith or Brown. Ask your father!'

'Now, what's the point of going into that. What's done is done.'

'Well, then let's change our name to Smith! Or Roosevelt! Or Rothschild! Except that if we changed our name to Rothschild everyone would know we were Jewish!'

Mother's face tightened. 'Don't be childish,' she said sharply.

'Isn't that the reason? You don't want people to know we're Jewish.'

'It's not that simple,' Father said. He was still holding the brown envelope. I wanted to seize it and set it ablaze in the dying Sabbath candles.

'Well, what is the new name, anyway?'

The surprise was gone from it. Mother must have known already; the surprise had been for me. 'Ross,' Father said flatly. It was his cousin Abe's name.

'It's not too bad,' Mother said placatingly. 'It's like marrying into the family.'

I turned on her. 'What do you care? It's not your name. You would never let him change it if it were.'

'What are you talking about, you foolish girl? My family name was picked out of a hat by an immigration officer. It's a matter of convenience, that's all. I'm afraid you have delusions of grandeur.'

'It's more than convenience,' Father said. He pushed his hair back. 'I cannot market the color charts under the name Rosavitsky. There are still parts of this country where people are likely to think that someone named Rosavitsky has horns.'

'Excuse me,' I said coldly. 'I simply forgot the color charts. I just never happened to think of them as a nationwide enterprise.'

'What's an enterprise?' said Paul.

'Well, you and Mama call yourselves Ross, and I'll call myself Rosavitsky, and anyone who thinks I have horns can look and see that I don't.'

'You'd look funny with horns,' Paul said. He and Jennie giggled, egging each other on.

'Shut up, you two,' I screamed.

'You can't call yourself Rosavitsky,' Father said quietly. 'It's not your legal name now.'

I pounded on the table. 'I won't have any name. I'll be the Jewess Nobody. I'll never be Ross, no matter how many stupid forms you fill out. I'll leave home! I'll run away!'

Paul shrieked 'Hooray!' He pounded rhythmically with both fists.

'Esther! Paul!' Mother swung at Paul furiously, knocking over a glass of grape juice.

'You spilled it!' he shouted. 'It's your fault!'

I ran to my room and slammed the door. I rocked myself back and forth on the bed, arms hugging my knees, my head buried, my ears ringing. They would never call me Ross. It wasn't my name.

Father marketed his charts without my help. The tool and die company he had been working for converted from war parts to cigarette lighters; they went bankrupt a few months after the war ended. Father spent all his time in the little back room of Sophie's apartment; what precisely he was doing neither Mother nor I inquired into.

Mother returned to night teaching; I was pleased that she was following my advice until she pointed out that we needed the money to live on.

'Still,' I said, 'it's important for you to have a job, isn't it? I mean, it would be terrible not to do anything. You hate housework, and Paul and Jennie are in school, and I certainly don't need you at home.'

'Well, if I'm not needed . . .' she said. We were sitting on the big double bed sorting and folding a pile of clean laundry.

I pursued my own thought. 'At least you have some impact on other people. You don't have to feel that you're hiding that one talent which is death to hide.' I hesitated. 'That's Milton's sonnet on his blindness.'

'I know,' Mother said, smiling. She had had her hair cut short, and it curled softly behind her ears; she looked very pretty. 'One talent is right. I'm afraid talent is very cheap these days. Now, do you really think that I'm going to be valued as a teacher by complete strangers when my own child tells me I'm not needed?'

'It's different. You're not as involved personally.'

'That's true enough,' she said ruefully. 'Look, Esther, the socks came out even. Don't you think that's a good sign?'

'Of what?'

'Oh, I don't know, better things to come. Better management generally.'

'If it's a matter of counting socks!' I exclaimed.

'Well, my dear, you're so impatient. There's not much I can do for you. There's been so little I could do for your father. Sometimes I think every decision we've made has been wrong. If I were more confident I could make it a rule of thumb. I suppose I am more help to people I don't love. It's so easy to be sympathetic, to give sensible advice when it doesn't matter one way or the other.'

'They're lucky, anyway,' I said.

'I don't mean to exaggerate. You ought to be thankful for your intelligence.'

'But you said talent was cheap.'

'I meant a useful talent. Intelligence isn't cheap, it's very rare. But it's not always useful; in fact it rather gets in people's way, and it's not going to endear you to anyone.'

I dismissed her advice as typical of Mother's fatalism; it was obviously necessary for her to rationalise my father's inability to get on in the world. But while my parents might accept defeat cheerfully, I meant to fight, and I put a ferocious energy into my studies, determined to win top grades on the statewide examinations.

By the end of the year, my father, unable to market the charts, had sold his patent for considerably less than the thousand dollars he had invested. Late into the night I heard my parents talking in low voices, night after night, as my father, just turned forty, the world all before him, pondered his future.

We seldom spent Sundays together now. I had worked out a reading schedule for weekends, aiming to read every Great Book before I was eighteen, the date I had set for my entry into adult life. When we were together we quarreled, a sad, pointless bickering that flared up out of nowhere, and usually ended when I stormed furiously away, only to apologise guiltily a few hours later. But one bright, warm Sunday, when Father proposed to Paul and Jennie that they take a ride on the Staten Island ferry, I couldn't resist the lure of the soft air and the transparent blue sky, and thinking it would please my father, offered to go along. So, leaving Mother to the *Saturday Review* double-crostic, we drove down to the Sixty-ninth Street pier.

The ferry pushed slowly off with a great churning of waters. 'Imagine this still costing a nickel! Your mother and I used to come down here when we were courting.'

The deck was crowded with families, elderly ladies, a Boy Scout troop. 'There aren't any courting couples now,' I said. 'There's probably not enough privacy.'

'You'd be surprised. We managed to find a few dark corners. Times haven't changed as much as you think.'

My father didn't look very much like the lover he had been, the dashing young man with a trim mustache. He was heavy now, though still muscular, and his forehead was permanently furrowed. He looked preoccupied, absent, worn, and yet he seemed possessed by a flickering hopefulness, as if a light touch might startle him into a return to the promise of his youth, an unexpected break in the clouds, relief streaming through, lighten the burden which pressed on him perpetually. Or did I project my own uneasiness onto him, dramatising his distress, investing it with my own rebelliousness?

I gave Paul and Jennie sandwiches, and we sat watching the foaming wake of the boat, shuddering and rumbling beneath us.

'Why aren't we going faster?' Paul asked. 'I like to go fast.'

Father drew Paul down to the bench beside him. 'How do you think the boat moves?'

'By an engine, of course.'

'It's moved by propellers, under the boat. The engine moves the propellers. The propellers push the water aside in a circular motion, and the boat moves forward. That's why it goes slowly, even though there's a lot of noise and action.'

'You ought to be a teacher,' I said. 'You're wonderful at explaining things.'

'I did teach for a while, oh, years ago, during the depression. It's funny, I never thought much about it. It was a way of making some money.'

As opposed to what, I wondered. I was assaulted by a vision of my father twenty years ago, with the best intentions, and the worst possible instincts about his future, permanently mistaking his vocation. He was so patient, scrupulously exact, willing to go over the same ground again and again; why had he thrown himself into the money game? Nobody else obeyed the archaic rules he had set for himself.

'Why don't you teach now? It's not too late, is it?'

'No, it's never too late,' he said thoughtfully, looking into the waters, gray beneath the oil slick visible on the surface. 'It's the wrong time, though. The veterans have priority now.'

'But that's terrible,' I said. 'That means you don't have a chance.'

'It looks that way. For the next few years, anyway.'

I was horrified. In a few years he would be old, he might be ill, his life would be over. Why wasn't he angrier? 'It's a vicious system!' I cried.

'How can you say that, Esther? I'm surprised at you. How could it be fair otherwise? The system happens to be unfortunate for me, that's all. It's just the way it worked out. I can't blame the system for my own mistakes.'

I couldn't understand his detachment. It was the market theory again; either there was no market at all or it was flooded with those talents he had to offer. If anything were at fault, it was his own unremarkable inability to foretell which way the needle was pointing. Oh, how I hated the market, the buying and selling of human energy, of life itself! It was so obvious that the highest price went to those who were aggressive, unscrupulous, and clever at reading the signs; it was so clear that nobody valued a man for being honorable or good. I couldn't help it if my fury spilled over onto my father, for his passive submissiveness to the system which had defeated him, and his reverence for its mysterious operations.

'What are you going to do?' I asked. We were drawing toward the long wooden piers beyond which lay the pastoral fastnesses of Staten Island. Surely my father must see that I understood the urgency of the question, that I suffered for his desperation!

He peered up into the sun, shading his eyes with one hand, like a hardened sailor testing for rain. 'Well, right now I think we'll go back by way of Manhattan.'

'I don't want to go on another stupid old boat,' Paul said, loud and clear.

'I want to go home,' Jennie whimpered. 'I feel sick.'

On the way to Manhattan I held her on my lap while she vomited into newspaper, cheese sandwich, tomato, orange juice, fig newtons. The afternoon had grown warm and sticky, the sky clouded over, and the Manhattan shore was screened by a gray haze. Father paced the deck with Paul, examined the caulking, tested the lifeboats, resolutely exploring the small ferry for whatever navigational secrets it might yield, and ignoring the woeful picture we made. I slipped the soiled newspapers over the side before we landed. As we painfully inched back to Brooklyn in heavy Sunday traffic, I decided not to ask any more questions; the time for a frank adult talk as between equals had passed. As I had been forced to realise before, my father, being fully grown, had to make his own decisions.

In early fall I applied for admission to college. Where should I go but to fabled Ithaca? My mother fought bitterly against it, and when she saw me studying a photograph of my father grinning quizzically at the world from the lap of Ezra Cornell, she tore it up angrily.

'You can't say it's not a great university, just because Papa went there.'

'That's not it at all.' She was still holding the pieces in her hand. 'We can't afford to send you away to college, not as things are now.'

'I wouldn't dream of asking you for money. Do you want me to get a job to help support you and Papa? Things aren't that bad, are they?'

'No,' she said icily. 'I do not expect you to contribute to our support.'

Father had apprenticed himself for some months to Grandfather Isadore, and was now installed in the small jewelry shop on the Bowery. His chief customers were his old college friends, Herb and Maxie, and his rich cousin Abe. My mother exerted herself to move out of her cocoon; she picked up a long-lapsed membership in local chapters of Planned Parenthood and the League of Women Voters, so that when Father sent out his new cards, together they were able to draw up a respectable list of names. Whether the names would turn into customers was another question, and I knew that my parents were resigned to a long period of waiting before their modest investment could begin to show returns.

Analysing my parents' failures, I decided that they had not wanted enough to be rich and successful; otherwise they could not possibly have mismanaged their lives so badly. I was torn between the desire to help them, to change their lives, to present them with some extraordinary gift, and the determination not to repeat their mistakes. I had a superstitious belief in my power to get what I wanted, which events seemed to confirm; after months of dogged studying I won a full college scholarship. My father could barely contain his pride in me, and my mother reluctantly yielded before my triumph and his.

'You'll have to come up to Ithaca and go to football games with us, Mama.' We were having a celebration dinner.

'I'll try my best,' she said generously. 'I might be the right age now.'

'My twenty-fifth reunion should be coming up in a couple of years. They probably have a father-and-daughter dance.'

'Or potato races,' I said.

'I wouldn't mind seeing some of the fellows again. Remember O'Brien, the big *macher* in that bond swindle? He was in my class.'

Mother laughed. 'That's some recommendation.'

'The funny thing is, we were in an ethics course together. Of course, we were more keen on theory than practice. Balaam's ass, Solomon and the two mothers. Dilemmas. I'll give you the classic example. You're climbing a mountain, and the rope slips; you've got your favorite aunt on one side, and Rembrandt on the other; you can only save one. Whom do you sacrifice? The one you love best, or the one whose life is most valuable?'

'That's why I never go mountain climbing,' Mother said.

'You've just never had the sporting instinct.'

We drank to the future. Father poured two fingers of whiskey for himself and a wineglass of sherry for Mother. As he turned away I recklessly poured some whiskey for myself.

'You're not drinking whiskey,' Father said.

'I don't see why not.' I quickly swallowed half a shot.

'I just said you're not to drink whiskey.'

'I heard you.' The glass was still in my hand; I took another swallow. 'Everyone drinks in college.'

'You're not in college, you're in your home.'

'Leave her alone,' Mother warned.

'I'm old enough to do as I like,' I said.

'I don't care how old you are. While you're under this roof you'll do as I say.'

'You've got no right to order me around. I'm paying for my own college education.' I held the glass to the light, then drank the last of it.

'Esther, that's enough!' Mother said.

'I'll pay you room and board if you like. I'll work nights.'

'Get out of here!' Father shouted.

'That's what I'm planning to do,' I said calmly. I felt on fire and my legs were shaking. I'm free, I thought exultantly, I'm on my own.

I woke up late the next morning, after my father had left for the shop. Mother was washing breakfast dishes, up to her elbows in soapy water, on which small pools of coffee grounds floated. 'You put on a fine performance last night,' she said.

'Why can't he leave me alone?' I said bitterly.

'You're very hard. You probably don't realise it yourself. You have a hard core.'

'That's a nice thing to say to me.'

She hesitated, and waited while the water ran out. 'He cried last night. After you left.' She looked me full in the face then, greatly troubled. 'You might talk to him.'

'I don't see why I should. Why should I be the one to apologise?'

'Oh, Esther, it's not you that's worrying him. Can't you see how he's changed?'

'I haven't noticed that he's any different.'

'He's so irritable. Every little thing . . . It's an effort for him not to snap at the children. He can't sleep at night. Haven't you heard him? He goes through the drawers, I don't know what he's looking for, papers, old checks, policies. He sits at the desk adding figures, subtracting, figuring, and checking, starting all over again. I'd like to burn everything in those drawers.'

'But what can I do? It's not my fault.'

Mother sat down wearily at the kitchen table. She rested her head in her hands. 'That's the hardest part, not being able to do anything,' she said. I could hardly hear her. She roused herself with an effort. 'You can try to make it easier for him. You know how he loves you. He would do anything for you.'

I considered this in silence. I really couldn't see what my mother wanted of me. 'I'm going to the library,' I said finally. 'I have work to do.'

I was unable to concentrate on my books, and late that afternoon I found myself on Canal Street and Third Avenue, across the street from the diamond center. Derelicts lounged in the shadows of the elevated, or slept curled up, empty pint bottles cradled between their knees. A gaunt figure weaved in between cars stopped for the red light, offering to wipe the windows. As I passed he held his hand out to me. I shook my head and crossed quickly, but stopped again outside my father's building, postponing the moment when I should go in. The windows on the main floor were glittering with diamonds and platinum and gold on display, heavy diamond circlets luxuriating against black velvet, ornate rings, twisted into wreaths of tiny jewels, pins in the shape of flowers, with ruby centers, diamond petals, gold stem and leaves. I stared at the precious gems, pure living drops of color, enticing, luring the eye with their beauty through the double thickness of glass.

There weren't many customers inside but those I could see through the window looked prosperous, absorbed in examining the diamonds offered by the white-shirted jewelers. Their edges blurred as I watched; they swam past in slow motion, magnified – fabulous creatures, poised, elegant predators. I hated them, hated my own weakness. Why should life be so easy for some, so difficult for others?

My grandfather's shop was up two flights of the narrow old building, at the end of a long corridor hung with steam and water pipes; the dark green walls were cracked and flaking. I could see the dim lettering, 'I. Rosavitsky, Diamond Setting'; the door was partly open, but nobody seemed to be there. Then I saw that my father was down on the floor on his hands and knees, groping about with his fingers, a jeweler's glass strapped to his eye. I stood transfixed in the doorway, watching him.

'What is it?' I said.

He straightened up painfully and unfastened the glass. His face was haggard; he looked like an old man, his muscles gone slack, his eyes unfocused.

'I dropped a diamond,' he said. 'I can't seem to find it.'

'Can I help you look for it?'

'No, I don't think so. It must be here somewhere. It should turn up.'

'Maybe it dropped into your clothes,' I suggested.

'I turned my pockets inside out already.' He turned them out again to demonstrate. I had never seen him look so worried.

'When did you drop it?'

'This morning, when I came in. About nine o'clock, it must have been.'

I still stood in the doorway, unable to move toward him. 'And you've been looking for it since then?'

He nodded. 'It can't just disappear like that. I'll stay here until I find it.'

'Where's Grandpa?'

'His back is bad today, he's staying home. It's just as well.'

'Have you had lunch?'

'No.'

'I'll bring you a sandwich and some coffee.'

'I'm not hungry.'

I saw that he was anxious for me to leave so that he could return to searching the floor. I was afraid to ask how much the diamond was worth. It might be less than a thousand dollars; to judge by my father's concern, it might be more. I was sure he wouldn't find it.

Children's Liberation

Jan Clausen

You know it is summer because she is wearing a tube top the color of those violent pink artificially flavored ices you buy in pizza stores and a pair of navy blue shorts that probably fit last year. She has dark hair and brown eyes and skinny, scarred brown legs, and in this context you might reasonably assume her to be Puerto Rican, though in fact she is half Italian and half something else she can never remember, not having seen her father since she was four years old. She is sitting on a rubber tire in the middle of a rubble-strewn lot.

Before her stretches a desert vista of half-cleared blocks, interrupted in the distance by a residential street. To her left are some fire-gutted apartment buildings which their owner, the city, has neglected either to tear down or board up; to her right is the mural project. Behind her is Brooklyn, a habit, a tropical nightmare she takes for reality, a street of heat and heroin, ailanthus, open hydrants, and women in advanced stages of pregnancy pushing strollers. The sun is a yellowish stain soaking through the smog; the air tastes of metal. She takes for granted her clogged nose, the hair lying wet and heavy on her neck. Adults may squint up at the sky and talk about rain. Children endure.

> Been on a train
> And I'm never gonna be the same

she sings to herself. She is going to be a musician someday, which is even more exciting than being a painter.

She's been visiting the mural site ever since the scaffolding went up. It has taken several weeks for the panorama of faces, fists and bright flags to transfigure what had been an ordinary brick wall. Today they are painting the apex of the design, the World Trade Center with a banner reading, 'Viva Puerto Rico Libre!' unfurling from the top. It is not the mural itself, however, but the purposefulness and camaraderie of the painters, most of them high school Youth Corps workers, which really attracts her. She is enchanted by their casual horseplay on the scaffold, their skill in transferring an image from a four-by-seven color sketch to a four-story wall. She has made no effort to talk to any of them.

But now for the first time someone approaches her, no high school student but a grown man with paint-stained jeans and tufts of paint in his afro. His salutation startles her. She had counted on not being noticed.

'You live around here?'

She nods a reluctant 'uh-huh', concentrating on a pattern she is making in the dirt with the toe of her sandal.

'Here on the block?'

'No.'

'Where, then?'

'Up near the Park.'

'Oh, up near the Park. The Park,' he repeats. 'It's real nice up there. Clean streets.'

She looks up at him now, having almost anticipated but still not quite understanding the sarcasm of his voice. She is in a hurry to figure out what he wants so she can give it to him and make him go away.

'What street, up near the Park?'

'Twelfth Street.'

'Twelfth Street? And you come all the way down here every day to watch some people paint pictures on a wall?'

Actually he is impressed, now, but she misinterprets the remark as a further reproach. 'It's not so far,' she says defensively.

'Your mother work?'

'She goes to school. Welfare sends her.'

'But she knows you come down here?'

'Sure. She doesn't care.' She still doesn't know what he wants.

'I've been watching you sitting there every day. I thought maybe you'd like to help us paint.'

'Maybe,' she says reluctantly, playing for time. Nervously she twists the keys strung around her neck.

'Maybe? You can't give me any better than a maybe? I was going to say, if you come tomorrow you could help paint down there in the left-hand corner. That woman's face. We can't let you up on the scaffold, but there's plenty to finish on the ground.' He waits.

'That would be okay,' she answers, understanding finally what he wants. 'Thank you.'

'Fine, that's great, it's a deal then, see you tomorrow.' Smiling as if he'd just given her a present, he goes back to work.

Angry and depressed, she gets up to leave. The vacant lot with its bustle of legitimate activity from the street and the mural was perfect, and he has ruined it for her. She will never be able to come back now, at least not until the mural is finished. And she can't go to the Park anymore. She used to hang out there at the beginning of the summer. But then she began hearing stories, getting nervous, thinking creepy people might be hiding in the woods. Finally one morning a woman's body was found dumped in the lake.

It's only three-fifteen according to the clock on the Williamsburgh Savings Bank tower. Not time to go home yet. More than any other time of day she hates midafternoon, hates returning then to the stuffy empty apartment where bored, lethargic cats greet you in the hall, not understanding that you too are bored, lonely and hot. She hates the posters shouting slogans from the walls everywhere except in her own room, which is not really even hers because you have to walk through it to get to Chris's room. No, she would rather loiter along Fifth Avenue as though on an errand for her mother, peering into the dark cluttered windows of bodegas, daring herself to snatch an apple from the display outside the Korean vegetable store. In fact, she now recalls, she is supposed to pick up a quart of milk; she has a whole dollar in her pocket and could stop for something.

Now she is comfortably inconspicuous again because she has nothing anybody wants, though in a few years walking the same street wearing the same shorts and brief top she will occasion innumerable murmured propositions, hissed obscenities.

> You've got more tracks on you mister
> Than the tracks on this train

she begins humming again, prompted by the sight of the knots of idle men jamming each sidewalk corner and spilling over into the intersection. The street is famous for dope traffic; in fact, she has heard that a baby carriage parked in front of a certain laundromat means they're selling stuff there that day.

She passes a laundromat. Outside the women stand, waiting for their washing to get done, for clothes get dirty and have to be washed even in the middle of a heat wave. Sure enough, there's a baby carriage with a baby asleep in it. She wonders if this is *the* laundromat, *the* baby carriage. Would whoever it is really use a carriage with a real live baby? It seems wrong somehow. She wonders how a needle stuck into your arm can feel good, and which of the men she passes, averting her eyes slightly because already she knows better than to look directly at them, is a junkie. Her father was a junkie too, or she thinks so; Chris has hinted at this in certain unguarded moments, mainly during fights.

> I saw a man
> Take a needle full of hard drugs
> And die slow

she sings, feeling better now, in love with the energy of despair behind that song, in love with the life of the street, the rotten city's vitality, the women clustered on stoops. She envies them their rootedness, language, the Puerto Rican Spanish and Haitian French they speak with authority and fantastic speed, the babies they rock in carriages.

'Comidas Latinas y Chinas': this is the sign by which she recognises the restaurant she's been looking for. She used to be taken here regularly in the years before she was old enough to stay alone. It would be very late at night following some meeting or other; she would be sleepy and irritable and fed up with the haphazard system of rotating childcare to which she'd invariably been relegated. Chris and the others would just keep talking, clicking off the familiar phrases like rosary beads: contradiction, exploitation, struggle. But they would eat chicken fried rice, and that she liked.

The restaurant is cool, empty except for a few people sitting up at the counter. She has hardly ever been in a restaurant alone before, and feels nervous ordering. But the Chinese waiter doesn't even blink when she says 'cafe con leche' a little quickly, a little loudly, afraid perhaps he'll ask to see her money or tell her little girls shouldn't drink coffee. And in fact she has always hated coffee, beverage of grownups, but now she sits there comfortably drinking it. For a few minutes she is happy, wrapped in childhood like a cloak of invisibility, free, not accountable to anyone.

> Tell me why love is like
> Just like a baaaaaalll
> And chain

Hearing the music all the way out in the street, Chris knows it's coming from her apartment. Lisa's on this music kick lately, says she wants to be a singer when she grows up. She has resurrected all of Chris's least favorite records – these include, for example, the Stones, Cream and the Grateful Dead – from a box in the back of a closet. She has begged for piano lessons, hoping someday to accompany herself like Laura Nyro. But Chris remembers hours of enforced piano practice, her own mother working at a luncheonette to pay for the hated lessons; she is not about to sacrifice to what she calls Lisa's bourgeois aspirations.

The apartment, three flights up, is hotter than the street. 'Turn that fucking masochistic heterosexual noise down,' Chris hollers on her way into the kitchen, where she discovers the carton of milk, purchased two hours ago and warm now, sitting out on the counter in a paper bag.

Lisa appears, lounges in the kitchen doorway, long-limbed and dirty-faced. The record's still blasting away.

'What's for dinner?'

'Cold bean salad.'

'Yuk.'

'Lisa, I asked you to turn the record down. And I told you day before yesterday and last week and a million times before that, put the milk in the refrigerator. It goes bad. It's not like we have money to throw away.'

'I want a grilled cheese sandwich.'

'Make it yourself, then. Take care of the record first.'

'You don't have to start yelling the minute you walk in the door.'

Glaring, they sit down at the table. They might be ill-matched roommates, siblings rubbing each other the wrong way. It had been different when Lisa was little; they were closer then.

'When's school going to be over? It's boring when you're always gone,' Lisa says finally.

'I'm sorry, babe. You know I'd be working if I wasn't in school.'

'Eileen's mother stays home.'

'Eileen's father works.'

'You could get married.'

There it is again, Lisa's solution to every human ill: get married. Stubbornly she continues to trot it out, though she's perfectly aware of Chris's position. When, several years ago, Chris announced she was a lesbian, Lisa's instant comeback was, 'I'm not.' Chris's friends were amused by the story and sure Lisa would outgrow it, but so far the kid remains passionately supportive of everything heterosexual: rock music, romantic movies, her grandmother's tales of church weddings and babies being born. And yet she's tough as nails; as Marcie says, there's not a femme bone in her body.

Of course this is all Lisa's business; 'her karma,' Chris once would have put it. Lisa may do as she pleases, at least so long as her actions affect only Lisa. Among the many posters which Lisa does not like because they symbolise Chris's violent, unreasonable opposition to the status quo, one on the kitchen wall proclaims: 'Children's Liberation!'

'Christ, Lisa, you sound like my mother. Do we have to go over this again? You know I'm not getting married,' Chris remonstrates now.

'Oh for god's sake. Other people's mothers aren't lesbians. Why do I have to have a fucking lesbian for a mother,' Lisa bursts out.

'Wanting kids has nothing to do with being lesbian or not.'

'But you didn't want me, Chris. You even said.' At times like this Lisa seizes any weapon.

'You know I never said I didn't want you. I always wanted a baby. I just didn't plan to get pregnant so soon, that's all. I was young, I was eighteen.'

'Well, people ought to think before they do a thing like that,' Lisa insists. 'It's not like playing with dolls. It's serious.'

'Most people who have babies don't have the faintest idea what they're doing. Don't feel so sorry for yourself.'

'And if you had to have me, you should have stayed with my father.' Lisa is inexorable. And has now gone too far.

'Oh, your father. Your father and beans and rice and food stamps and no money for the doctor and roaches hatching in the stove and him doing up in the bathroom and me sitting on a bench in Washington Square Park with you in a stroller and so fucked up on acid I couldn't figure out how to get home – no, I don't think I should have stayed with your father.'

'Grownups should think what the hell they're doing,' Lisa reiterates, starting to cry now but unsoftened by tears.

'Hey, I'm not putting up with this shit. You can stay here and cry and carry on and talk to yourself all night if you want. I'm going over to Marcie's.'

'You promised you weren't. You promised.'

'I did not promise. I said probably. That was before you started in.'

'You're always going over there.'

'Oh quit guilt-tripping me. You're big now. You don't need me every minute.'

Chris goes into the bedroom, starts stuffing a change of clothes into her knapsack. Lisa follows, wailing, 'Chris, you promised.'

'I did not promise.'

'You did so.'

'Look, you can ask Eileen up if you want. Just don't play the

music too loud. You can call me if there's anything important.
I'll be back in the morning on my way to school.'

'Mother!' Lisa screams; it is the ultimate appeal. 'Mother, I'll
kill myself, I'll kill you, Mother.'

Chris, who refuses to be manipulated by such references to
their ancient relationship, reflects on the stairs that the one
advantage in living in an apartment full of wife- and child-
beaters is that a scene like this is not going to startle the
neighbors. But she is not entirely unmoved by what she calls
'Lisa's theatrics,' for later she sits at Marcie's kitchen table,
talking about it to Marcie and her two roommates.

'Sometimes I get this awful vision,' she says. 'Little apartments
all over the city, single mothers trapped in there with their kids,
like some torture where people are shut up with rats. Except in
this case it's mutual.'

'Isn't there any place Lisa could stay, even for just a little
while, to give you a vacation?' one of the roommates sensibly
suggests.

'Oh, my mother would love to get her hands on Lisa. But I
wouldn't do that. I've lived with the woman myself.'

Alone in the apartment, Lisa tries to think, finds she cannot.
Nor can she hang onto her fear, her desperate sense of having
been abandoned. Instead, she is flooded with a tremendous
energy, a confidence which she does not quite know how to
use. She is possessed by a few large, simple emotions: anger,
the urge to flee.

Still, she is practical enough to remember she'll need money.
In the kitchen cupboard is a sugar bowl in which Chris keeps
cash for food and household supplies. Lisa has been pinching
change from there for years, though Chris always says, 'Ask,
honey, and if I have the money I'll give it to you.' Now she
takes what she finds, a ten and several ones. There are subway
slugs on top of Chris's bureau. Hot as it is, she snatches up a
sweater on her way out.

She closes but does not lock the door, hurries the three and
a half blocks to the subway. She can hardly believe that this
could be so simple, yet once there her luck holds: the slug drops

smoothly into the slot, the heavy revolving door turns without incident. Arbitrarily she picks the Manhattan-bound platform.

Lisa has never before been alone at night in a train station. The cavernous place, hospitable as a bomb shelter, seems even darker than usual; they've unscrewed half the light bulbs to save the city's money. The platform is nearly empty. She hunches against a pillar, hoping not to be noticed.

Finally the train comes. It is one of those new ones, air-conditioned, with orange, yellow and red seats. She is reassured by the familiar ads with their pictures of streams, forests and cigarette-smoking couples; by Miss Subways with her processed hair. Prudently she looks around for crazy people and teenage boys and, finding none, selects an outside seat in the middle of the car. Now she really must think.

She thinks all the way to Jamaica, Queens; all the way back down through Manhattan and Brooklyn to Coney Island; all the way back to Jamaica again. She imagines all the cities she could run away to if she had more money. She could even hitchhike to the west coast and find her father. If she were only a little taller, had breasts, she could hustle in Times Square.

By the second trip to Queens she has admitted to herself that these are not practical solutions. By the time they hit Coney Island again, she has made up her mind, resigned herself, draped her sweater over her shoulders to ward off the chill of the air conditioning, and curled up on the seat.

About three o'clock in the morning it occurs to a transit cop that this is a bad hour for a small white female child to be asleep in an otherwise empty car. He shakes her, rather gently for a cop.

'You lost, little girl?'

'No,' she says immediately. Then, opening her eyes and seeing the uniform, she understands that he can make it easy. 'Yes, I mean,' she says without emotion.

'How'd you manage that?'

'I don't know.'

The transit cop, though irritated by her self-possession, abides by his duty.

'Do you know where you live?'

'Of course. I live with Grandma.'

They are in Brooklyn again. She gives him the phone number, and at Jay Street they get out and he makes the call.

'Something funny going on here,' he mentions, handing her over to the regular cop in the squad car. 'This grandmother didn't sound like the kid was expected. Check it out when you get there.'

Lisa's grandmother, who lives in an old brick apartment building in Flatbush, is a tough woman. She has reared five children, outlived a difficult husband, managed to attain some small degree of economic security. Her hair is not even gray yet. Now she stands behind the glass coldly watching the two of them mount the steps: her granddaughter, accompanied by an officer of the law. Grudgingly, at last, she opens the door.

'Grandma, I want to stay with you,' Lisa hurriedly announces.

'It's four o'clock in the morning. Where is your mother?'

'She's not home. I said I want to live here with you.'

'Look, lady, make up your mind. Does this kid live here or not?' the cop starts in.

'You'd better leave her here,' Lisa's grandmother replies, having sense enough at least to recognise the common enemy. 'If you take her home I guarantee you won't find her mother. She goes out at all hours and leaves this girl totally unsupervised.'

'Yeah, how'm I supposed to make sense of all this,' the cop grumbles. But leaves.

Lisa waits now, confidently, to be admitted. But her grand-mother still bars the door. She is accustomed to driving hard bargains, and has waited a long time for her chance at this one.

'You understand that if you live with me it won't be anything like it is at your mother's? You'll behave. You'll go to mass with me. You'll quit your swearing and lying and disobedience. I'll send you to Sacred Heart when school opens.'

Lisa sighs, appearing for the sake of form to hesitate. In fact, she has thought it out already; without exactly knowing, she's been thinking it out for weeks. There is no stereo in her grand-mother's apartment. On the other hand, there is a piano. Per-haps there will be money for music lessons. After all, it's a matter of endurance, and Lisa knows all about that. She's ten going on eleven now, already more than halfway to her eighteenth birthday.

The Young Girl

Katherine Mansfield

In her blue dress, with her cheeks lightly flushed, her blue, blue eyes, and her gold curls pinned up as though for the first time – pinned up to be out of the way for her flight – Mrs Raddick's daughter might have just dropped from this radiant heaven. Mrs Raddick's timid, faintly astonished, but deeply admiring glance looked as if she believed it, too; but the daughter didn't appear any too pleased – why should she? – to have alighted on the steps of the Casino. Indeed, she was bored – bored as though Heaven had been full of casinos with snuffy old saints for *croupiers* and crowns to play with.

'You don't mind taking Hennie?' said Mrs Raddick. 'Sure you don't? There's the car, and you'll have tea and we'll be back here on this step – right here – in an hour. You see, I want her to go in. She's not been before, and it's worth seeing. I feel it wouldn't be fair to her.'

'Oh, shut up, mother,' said she wearily. 'Come along. Don't talk so much. And your bag's open; you'll be losing all your money again.'

'I'm sorry, darling,' said Mrs Raddick.

'Oh, *do* come in! I want to make money,' said the impatient voice. 'It's all jolly well for you – but I'm broke!'

'Here – take fifty francs, darling, take a hundred!' I saw Mrs Raddick pressing notes into her hand as they passed through the swing doors.

Hennie and I stood on the steps a minute, watching the people. He had a very broad, delighted smile.

'I say,' he cried, 'there's an English bulldog. Are they allowed to take dogs in there?'

'No, they're not.'

'He's a ripping chap, isn't he? I wish I had one. They're such fun. They frighten people so, and they're never fierce with their – the people they belong to.' Suddenly he squeezed my arm. 'I say, *do* look at that old woman. Who is she? Why does she look like that? Is she a gambler?'

The ancient, withered creature, wearing a green satin dress, a black velvet cloak and a white hat with purple feathers, jerked slowly, slowly up the steps as though she were being drawn up on wires. She stared in front of her, she was laughing and nodding and cackling to herself; her claws clutched round what looked like a dirty boot-bag.

But just at that moment there was Mrs Raddick again with – *her* – and another lady hovering in the background. Mrs Raddick rushed at me. She was brightly flushed, gay, a different creature. She was like a woman who is saying 'goodbye' to her friends on the station platform, with not a minute to spare before the train starts.

'Oh, you're here, still. Isn't that lucky! You've not gone. Isn't that fine! I've had the most dreadful time with – her,' and she waved to her daughter, who stood absolutely still, disdainful, looking down, twiddling her foot on the step, miles away. 'They won't let her in. I swore she was twenty-one. But they won't believe me. I showed the man my purse; I didn't dare to do more. But it was no use. He simply scoffed . . . And now I've just met Mrs MacEwen from New York, and she just won thirteen thousand in the *Salle Privée* – and she wants me to go back with her while the luck lasts. Of course I can't leave – her. But if you'd –'

At that 'she' looked up; she simply withered her mother. 'Why can't you leave me?' she said furiously. 'What utter rot! How dare you make a scene like this? This is the last time I'll come out with you. You really are too awful for words.' She looked her mother up and down. 'Calm yourself,' she said superbly.

Mrs Raddick was desperate, just desperate. She was 'wild' to go back with Mrs MacEwen, but at the same time . . .

I seized my courage. 'Would you – do you care to come to tea with – us?'

'Yes, yes, she'll be delighted. That's just what I wanted, isn't it darling? Mrs MacEwen . . . I'll be back here in an hour . . . or less . . . I'll –'

Mrs R. dashed up the steps. I saw her bag was open again.

So we three were left. But really it wasn't my fault. Hennie looked crushed to the earth, too. When the car was there she wrapped her dark coat round her – to escape contamination. Even her little feet looked as though they scorned to carry her down the steps to us.

'I am so awfully sorry,' I murmured as the car started.

'Oh, I don't *mind*,' said she. 'I don't *want* to look twenty-one. Who would – if they were seventeen! It's' – and she gave a faint shudder – 'the stupidity I loathe, and being stared at by fat old men. Beasts!'

Hennie gave her a quick look and then peered out of the window.

We drew up before an immense palace of pink-and-white marble with orange-trees outside the doors in gold-and-black tubs.

'Would you care to go in?' I suggested.

She hesitated, glanced, bit her lip, and resigned herself. 'Oh well, there seems nowhere else,' said she. 'Get out, Hennie.'

I went first – to find the table, of course – she followed. But the worst of it was having her little brother, who was only twelve, with us. That was the last, final straw – having that child, trailing at her heels.

There was one table. It had pink carnations and pink plates with little blue tea-napkins for sails.

'Shall we sit here?'

She put her hand wearily on the back of a white wicker chair.

'We may as well. Why not?' said she.

Hennie squeezed past her and wriggled on to a stool at the end. He felt awfully out of it. She didn't even take her gloves off. She lowered her eyes and drummed on the table. When a faint violin sounded she winced and bit her lip again. Silence.

The waitress appeared. I hardly dared to ask her. 'Tea – coffee? China tea – or iced tea with lemon?'

Really she didn't mind. It was all the same to her. She didn't really want anything. Hennie whispered, 'Chocolate!'

But just as the waitress turned away she cried out carelessly, 'Oh, you may as well bring me a chocolate, too.'

While we waited she took out a little, gold powder-box with a mirror in the lid, shook the poor little puff as though she loathed it, and dabbed her lovely nose.

'Hennie,' she said, 'take those flowers away.' She pointed with her puff to the carnations, and I heard her murmur, 'I can't bear flowers on a table.' They had evidently been giving her intense pain, for she positively closed her eyes as I moved them away.

The waitress came back with the chocolate and the tea. She put the big, frothing cups before them and pushed across my clear glass. Hennie buried his nose, emerged, with, for one dreadful moment, a little trembling blob of cream on the tip. But he hastily wiped it off like a little gentleman. I wondered if I should dare draw her attention to her cup. She didn't notice it – didn't see it – until suddenly, quite by chance, she took a sip. I watched anxiously; she faintly shuddered.

'Dreadfully sweet!' said she.

A tiny boy with a head like a raisin and a chocolate body came round with a tray of pastries – row upon row of little freaks, little inspirations, little melting dreams. He offered them to her. 'Oh, I'm not at all hungry. Take them away.'

He offered them to Hennie. Hennie gave me a swift look – it must have been satisfactory – for he took a chocolate cream, a coffee éclair, a meringue stuffed with chestnut and a tiny horn filled with fresh strawberries. She could hardly bear to watch him. But just as the boy swerved away she held up her plate.

'Oh well, give me *one*,' said she.

The silver tongs dropped one, two, three – and a cherry tartlet. 'I don't know why you're giving me all these,' she said, and nearly smiled. 'I shan't eat them; I couldn't!'

I felt much more comfortable. I sipped my tea, leaned back, and even asked if I might smoke. At that she paused, the fork in her hand, opened her eyes and really did smile. 'Of course,' said she. 'I always expect people to.'

But at that moment a tragedy happened to Hennie. He speared his pastry horn too hard, and it flew in two, and one half spilled on the table. Ghastly affair! He turned crimson. Even his ears flared, and one ashamed hand crept across the table to take what was left of the body away.

'You *utter* little beast!' said she.

Good heavens! I had to fly to the rescue. I cried hastily, 'Will you be abroad long?'

But she had already forgotten Hennie. I was forgotten, too. She was trying to remember something . . . She was miles away.

'I – don't – know,' she said slowly, from that far place.

'I suppose you prefer it to London. It's more – more –'

When I didn't go on she came back and looked at me, very puzzled. 'More –?'

'*Enfin* – gayer,' I cried, waving my cigarette.

But that took a whole cake to consider. Even then, 'Oh well, that depends!' was all she could safely say.

Hennie had finished. He was still very warm.

I seized the butterfly list off the table. 'I say – what about an ice, Hennie? What about tangerine and ginger? No, something cooler. What about a fresh pineapple cream?'

Hennie strongly approved. The waitress had her eye on us. The order was taken when she looked up from her crumbs.

'Did you say tangerine and ginger? I like ginger. You can bring me one.' And then quickly, 'I wish that orchestra wouldn't play things from the year One. We were dancing to that all last Christmas. It's too sickening!'

But it was a charming air. Now that I noticed it, it warmed me.

'I think this is rather a nice place, don't you, Hennie?' I said.

Hennie said: 'Ripping!' He meant to say it very low, but it came out very high in a kind of squeak.

Nice? This place? Nice? For the first time she stared about her, trying to see what there was . . . She blinked; her lovely eyes wondered. A very good-looking elderly man stared back at her through a monocle on a black ribbon. But him she simply couldn't see. There was a hole in the air where he was. She looked through and through him.

Finally the little flat spoons lay still on the glass plates. Hennie looked rather exhausted, but she pulled on her white gloves again. She had some trouble with her diamond wrist-watch; it got in her way. She tugged at it – tried to break the stupid little thing – it wouldn't break. Finally, she had to drag her glove over. I saw, after that, she couldn't stand this place a moment longer, and, indeed, she jumped up and turned away while I went through the vulgar act of paying for the tea.

And then we were outside again. It had grown dusky. The sky was sprinkled with small stars; the big lamps glowed. While we waited for the car to come up she stood on the step, just as before, twiddling her foot, looking down.

Hennie bounded forward to open the door and she got in and sank back with – oh – such a sigh!

'Tell him,' she gasped, 'to drive as fast as he can.'

Hennie grinned at his friend the chauffeur. '*Allie veet!*' said he. Then he composed himself and sat on the small seat facing us.

The gold powder-box came out again. Again the poor little puff was shaken; again there was that swift, deadly-secret glance between her and the mirror.

We tore through the black-and-gold town like a pair of scissors tearing through brocade. Hennie had great difficulty not to look as though he were hanging on to something.

And when we reached the Casino, of course Mrs Raddick wasn't there. There wasn't a sign of her on the steps – not a sign.

'Will you stay in the car while I go and look?'

But no – she wouldn't do that. Good heavens, no! Hennie could stay. She couldn't bear sitting in a car. She'd wait on the steps.

'But I scarcely like to leave you,' I murmured. 'I'd very much rather not leave you here.'

At that she threw back her coat; she turned and faced me; her lips parted. 'Good heavens – why! I – I don't mind it a bit. I – I like waiting.' And suddenly her cheeks crimsoned, her eyes grew dark – for a moment I thought she was going to cry. 'L – let me, please,' she stammered, in a warm, eager voice. 'I like it. I love waiting! Really – really I do! I'm always waiting – in all kinds of places . . .'

Her dark coat fell open, and her white throat – all her soft young body in the blue dress – was like a flower that is just emerging from its dark bud.

Love Must Not Be Forgotten

Zhang Jie

I am thirty, the same age as our People's Republic. For a republic thirty is still young. But a girl of thirty is virtually on the shelf.

Actually, I have a bonafide suitor. Have you seen the Greek sculptor Myron's Discobolus? Qiao Lin is the image of that discus thrower. Even the padded clothes he wears in winter fail to hide his fine physique. Bronzed, with clear-cut features, a broad forehead and large eyes, his appearance alone attracts most girls to him.

But I can't make up my mind to marry him. I'm not clear what attracts me to him, or him to me.

I know people are gossiping behind my back, 'Who does she think she is, to be so choosy?'

To them, I'm a nobody playing hard to get. They take offence at such preposterous behaviour.

Of course, I shouldn't be captious. In a society where commercial production still exists, marriage like most other transactions is still a form of barter.

I have known Qiao Lin for nearly two years, yet still cannot fathom whether he keeps so quiet from aversion to talking or from having nothing to say. When, by way of a small intelligence test, I demand his opinion of this or that, he says 'good' or 'bad' like a child in kindergarten.

Once I asked, 'Qiao Lin, why do you love me?' He thought the question over seriously for what seemed an age. I could see from his normally smooth but now wrinkled forehead that the little grey cells in his handsome head were hard at work cogitating. I felt ashamed to have put him on the spot.

Finally he raised his clear childlike eyes to tell me, 'Because you're good!'

Loneliness flooded my heart. 'Thank you, Qiao Lin!' I couldn't help wondering, if we were to marry, whether we could discharge our duties to each other as husband and wife. Maybe, because law and morality would have bound us together. But how tragic simply to comply with law and morality! Was there no stronger bond to link us?

When such thoughts cross my mind I have the strange sensation that instead of being a girl contemplating marriage I am an elderly social scientist.

Perhaps I worry too much. We can live like most married couples, bringing up children together, strictly true to each other according to the law . . . Although living in the seventies of the twentieth century, people still consider marriage the way they did millennia ago, as a means of continuing the race, a form of barter or a business transaction in which love and marriage can be separated. As this is the common practice, why shouldn't we follow suit?

But I still can't make up my mind. As a child, I remember, I often cried all night for no rhyme or reason, unable to sleep and disturbing the whole household. My old nurse, a shrewd though uneducated woman, said an ill wind had blown through my ear. I think this judgement showed prescience, because I still have that old weakness. I upset myself over things which really present no problem, upsetting other people at the same time. One's nature is hard to change.

I think of my mother too. If she were alive, what would she say about my attitude to Qiao Lin and my uncertainty about marrying him?

My thoughts constantly turn to her, not because she was such a strict mother that her ghost is still watching over me since her death. No, she was not just my mother but my closest friend. I loved her so much that the thought of her leaving me makes my heart ache.

She never lectured me, just told me quietly in her deep, unwomanly voice about her successes and failures, so that I could learn from her experience. She had evidently not had many successes – her life was full of failures.

During her last days she followed me with her fine, expressive eyes, as if wondering how I would manage on my own and as if she had some important advice for me but hesitated to give it. She must have been worried by my naiveté and sloppy ways. She suddenly blurted out, 'Shanshan, if you aren't sure what you want, don't rush into marriage – better live on your own!'

Other people might think this strange advice from a mother to her daughter, but to me it embodied her bitter experience. I don't think she underestimated me or my knowledge of life. She loved me and didn't want me to be unhappy.

'I don't want to marry, mum!' I said, not out of bashfulness or a show of coyness. I can't think why a girl should pretend to be coy. She had long since taught me about things not generally mentioned to girls.

'If you meet the right man, then marry him. Only if he's right for you!'

'I'm afraid no such man exists!'

'That's not true. But it's hard. The world is so vast, I'm afraid you may never meet him.' Whether I married or not was not what concerned her, but the quality of the marriage.

'Haven't you managed fine without a husband?'

'Who says so?'

'I think you've done fine.'

'I had no choice . . .' She broke off, lost in thought, her face wistful. Her wistful lined face reminded me of a withered flower I had pressed in a book.

'Why did you have no choice?'

'You ask too many questions,' she parried, not ashamed to confide in me but afraid that I might reach the wrong conclusion. Besides, everyone treasures a secret to carry to the grave. Feeling a bit put out, I demanded bluntly, 'Didn't you love my dad?'

'No, I never loved him.'

'Did he love you?'

'No, he didn't.'

'Then why get married?'

She paused, searching for the right words to explain this

mystery, then answered bitterly, 'When you're young you don't always know what you're looking for, what you need, and people may talk you into getting married. As you grow older and more experienced you find out your true needs. By then, though, you've done many foolish things for which you could kick yourself. You'd give anything to be able to make a fresh start and live more wisely. Those content with their lot will always be happy, they say, but I shall never enjoy that happiness.' She added self-mockingly, 'A wretched idealist, that's all I am.'

Did I take after her? Did we both have genes which attracted ill winds?

'Why don't you marry again?'

'I'm afraid I'm still not sure what I really want.' She was obviously unwilling to tell me the truth.

I cannot remember my father. He and Mother split up when I was very small. I just recall her telling me sheepishly that he was a fine handsome fellow. I could see she was ashamed of having judged by appearances and made a futile choice. She told me, 'When I can't sleep at night, I force myself to sober up by recalling all those stupid blunders I made. Of course it's so distasteful that I often hide my face in the sheet for shame, as if there were eyes watching me in the dark. But distasteful as it is, I take some pleasure in this form of atonement.'

I was really sorry that she hadn't remarried. She was such a fascinating character, if she'd married a man she loved, what a happy household ours would surely have been. Though not beautiful, she had the simple charm of an ink landscape. She was a fine writer too. Another author who knew her well used to say teasingly, 'Just reading your works is enough to make anyone love you!'

She would retort, 'If he knew that the object of his affection was a white-haired old crone, that would frighten him away.'

At her age, she must have known what she really wanted, so this was obviously an evasion. I say this because she had quirks which puzzled me.

For instance, whenever she left Beijing on a trip, she always took with her one of the twenty-seven volumes of Chekov's stories published between 1950 and 1955. She also warned me, 'Don't touch these books. If you want to read Chekov, read that set I bought you.' There was no need to caution me. Having a set of my own why should I touch hers? Besides, she'd told me this over and over again. Still she was on her guard. She seemed bewitched by those books.

So we had two sets of Chekov's stories at home. Not just because we loved Chekov, but to parry other people like me who loved Chekov. Whenever anyone asked to borrow a volume, she would lend one of mine. Once, in her absence, a close friend took a volume from her set. When she found out she was frantic, and at once took a volume of mine to exchange for it.

Ever since I can remember, those books were on her bookcase. Although I admire Chekov as a great writer, I was puzzled by the way she never tired of reading him. Why, for over twenty years, had she had to read him every single day?

Sometimes, when tired of writing, she poured herself a cup of strong tea and sat down in front of the bookcase, staring raptly at that set of books. If I went into her room then it flustered her, and she either spilt her tea or blushed like a girl discovered with her lover.

I wondered: Has she fallen in love with Chekov? She might have if he'd still been alive.

When her mind was wandering just before her death, her last words to me were: 'That set . . .' She hadn't the strength to give it its complete title. But I knew what she meant. 'And my diary . . . "Love Must Not Be Forgotten" . . . Cremate them with me.'

I carried out her last instruction regarding the works of Chekov, but couldn't bring myself to destroy her diary. I thought, if it could be published, it would surely prove the most moving thing she had written. But naturally publication was out of the question.

At first I imagined the entries were raw material she had jotted down. They read neither like stories, essays, a diary or letters. But after reading the whole I formed a hazy impression, helped out by my imperfect memory. Thinking it over, I finally realised that this was no lifeless manuscript I was holding, but an anguished, loving heart. For over twenty years one man had occupied her heart, but he was not for her. She used these diaries as a substitute for him, a means of pouring out her feelings to him, day after day, year after year.

No wonder she had never considered any eligible proposals, had turned a deaf ear to idle talk whether well-meant or malicious. Her heart was already full, to the exclusion of anybody else. 'No lake can compare with the ocean, no cloud with those on Mount Wu.' Remembering those lines I often reflected sadly that few people in real life could love like this. No one would love me like this.

I learned that towards the end of the thirties, when this man was doing underground work for the Party in Shanghai, an old worker had given his life to cover him, leaving behind a helpless wife and daughter. Out of a sense of duty, of gratitude to the dead and deep class feeling, he had unhesitatingly married the girl. When he saw the endless troubles caused by 'love' of couples who had married for 'love', he may have thought, 'Thank Heaven, though I didn't marry for love, we get on well, able to help each other.' For years, as man and wife they lived through hard times.

He must have been my mother's colleague. Had I ever met him? He couldn't have visited our home. Who was he?

In the spring of 1962, Mother took me to a concert. We went on foot, the theatre being quite near.

A black limousine pulled up silently by the pavement. Out stepped an elderly man with white hair in a black serge tunic-suit. What a striking shock of white hair! Strict, scrupulous, distinguished, transparently honest — that was my impression of him. The cold glint of his flashing eyes reminded me of lightning or swordplay. Only ardent love for a woman really deserving his love could fill cold eyes like those with tenderness.

He walked up to Mother and said, 'How are you, Comrade Zhong Yu? It's been a long time.'

'How are you!' Mother's hand holding mine suddenly turned icy cold and trembled a little.

They stood face to face without looking at each other, each appearing upset, even stern. Mother fixed her eyes on the trees by the roadside, not yet in leaf. He looked at me. 'Such a big girl already. Good, fine – you take after your mother.'

Instead of shaking hands with Mother he shook hands with me. His hand was as icy as hers and trembling a little. As if transmitting an electric current, I felt a sudden shock. Snatching my hand away I cried, 'There's nothing good about that!'

'Why not?' he asked with the surprised expression grown-ups always have when children speak out frankly.

I glanced at Mother's face. I did take after her, to my disappointment. 'Because she's not beautiful!'

He laughed, then said teasingly, 'Too bad that there should be a child who doesn't find her own mother beautiful. Do you remember in '53, when your mum was transferred to Beijing, she came to our ministry to report for duty? She left you outside on the verandah, but like a monkey you climbed all the stairs, peeped through the cracks in doors, and caught your finger in the door of my office. You sobbed so bitterly that I carried you off to find her.'

'I don't remember that.' I was annoyed at his harking back to a time when I was still in open-seat pants.

'Ah, we old people have better memories.' He turned abruptly and remarked to Mother, 'I've read that last story of yours. Frankly speaking, there's something not quite right about it. You shouldn't have condemned the heroine . . . There's nothing wrong with falling in love, as long as you don't spoil someone else's life . . . In fact, the hero might have loved her too. Only for the sake of a third person's happiness, they had to renounce their love . . .'

A policeman came over to where the car was parked and ordered the driver to move on. When the driver made some excuse, the old man looked round. After a hasty 'Goodbye' he strode to the car and told the policeman, 'Sorry. It's not his fault, it's mine . . .'

I found it amusing watching this old cadre listening respectfully to the policeman's strictures. When I turned to Mother with a mischievous smile, she looked as upset as a first-form primary schoolchild standing forlornly in front of the stern headmistress. Anyone would have thought she was the one being lectured by the policeman.

The car drove off, leaving a puff of smoke. Very soon even this smoke vanished with the wind, as if nothing at all had happened. But the incident stuck in my mind.

Analysing it now, he must have been the man whose strength of character won Mother's heart. That strength came from his firm political convictions, his narrow escapes from death in the revolution, his active brain, his drive at work, his well-cultivated mind. Besides, strange to say, he and Mother both liked the oboe. Yes, she must have worshipped him. She once told me that unless she worshipped a man, she couldn't love him even for one day.

But I could not tell whether he loved her or not. If not, why was there this entry in her diary?

'This is far too fine a present. But how did you know
  that Chekov's my favourite writer?'
'You said so.'
'I don't remember that.'
'I remember. I heard you mention it when you were chatting
  with someone.'

So he was the one who had given her the *Selected Stories of Chekov*. For her that was tantamount to a love letter.

Maybe this man, who didn't believe in love, realised by the time his hair was white that in his heart was something which could be called love. By the time he no longer had the right to love, he made the tragic discovery of this love for which he would have given his life. Or did it go deeper than that?

This is all I remember about him.

How wretched Mother must have been, deprived of the man to whom she was devoted! To catch a glimpse of his car or the back of his head through its rear window, she carefully figured out which roads he would take to work and back. Whenever he made a speech, she sat at the back of the hall watching his face rendered hazy by cigarette smoke and poor lighting. Her eyes would brim with tears, but she swallowed them back. If a fit of coughing made him break off, she wondered anxiously why no one persuaded him to give up smoking. She was afraid he would get bronchitis again. Why was he so near yet so far?

He, to catch a glimpse of her, looked out of the car window every day, straining his eyes to watch the streams of cyclists, afraid that she might have an accident. On the rare evenings on which he had no meetings, he would walk by a roundabout way to our neighbourhood, to pass our compound gate. However busy, he would always make time to look in papers and journals for her work.

His duty had always been clear to him, even in the most difficult times. But now confronted by this love he became a weakling, quite helpless. At his age it was laughable. Why should life play this trick on him?

Yet when they happened to meet at work, each tried to avoid the other, hurrying off with a nod. Even so, this would make Mother blind and deaf to everything around her. If she met a colleague named Wang she would call him Guo and mutter something unintelligible.

It was a cruel ordeal for her. She wrote:

We agreed to forget each other. But I deceived you, I have never forgotten. I don't think you've forgotten either. We're just deceiving each other, hiding our misery. I haven't deceived you deliberately, though; I did my best to carry out our agreement. I often stay far away from Beijing, hoping time and distance will help me to forget you. But on my return, as the train pulls into the station, my head reels. I stand on the platform looking round intently, as if someone were waiting for me. Of course there is no one. I realise then that I have forgotten nothing. Everything is unchanged. My love is like a tree the roots of which strike deeper year after year – I have no way to uproot it.

At the end of every day, I feel as if I've forgotten something important. I may wake with a start from my dreams wondering what has happened. But nothing has happened. Nothing. Then it comes home to me that you are missing! So everything seems lacking, incomplete, and there is nothing to fill up the blank. We are nearing the ends of our lives, why should we be carried away by emotion like children? Why should life submit people to such ordeals, then unfold before you your lifelong dream? Because I started off blindly I took the wrong turning, and now there are insuperable obstacles between me and my dream.

Yes, Mother never let me go to the station to meet her when she came back from a trip, preferring to stand alone on the platform and imagine that he had met her. Poor mother with her greying hair was as infatuated as a girl.

Not much space in the diary was devoted to their romance. Most entries dealt with trivia: Why one of her articles had not come off; her fear that she had no real talent; the excellent play she missed by mistaking the time on the ticket; the drenching she got by going out for a stroll without her umbrella. In spirit they were together day and night, like a devoted married couple. In fact, they spent no more than twenty-four hours together in all. Yet in that time they experienced deeper happiness than some people in a whole lifetime. Shakespeare makes Juliet say, 'I cannot sum up half my sum of wealth.' And probably that is how Mother felt.

He must have been killed in the 'cultural revolution'. Perhaps because of the conditions then, that section of the diary is ambiguous and obscure. Mother had been so fiercely attacked for her writing, it amazed me that she went on keeping a diary. From some veiled allusions I gathered that he had queried the theories advanced by that 'theoretician' then at the height of favour, and had told someone, 'This is sheer Rightist talk'. It was clear from the tear-stained pages of Mother's diary that he had been harshly denounced; but the steadfast old man never knuckled under to the authorities. His last words were, 'When I go to meet Marx, I shall go on fighting my case!'

That must have been in the winter of 1969, because that was when Mother's hair turned white overnight, though she was not yet fifty. And she put on a black arm-band. Her position then was extremely difficult. She was criticised for wearing this old-style mourning, and ordered to say for whom she was in mourning.

'For whom are you wearing that, mum?' I asked anxiously.

'For my lover.' Not to frighten me she explained, 'Someone you never knew.'

'Shall I put one on too?' She patted my cheeks, as she had when I was a child. It was years since she had shown me such affection. I often felt that as she aged, especially during these last years of persecution, all tenderness had left her, or was concealed in her heart, so that she seemed like a man.

She smiled sadly and said, 'No, you needn't wear one.'

Her eyes were as dry as if she had no more tears to shed. I longed to comfort her or do something to please her. But she said, 'Off you go.'

I felt an inexplicable dread, as if dear Mother had already half left me. I blurted out, 'Mum!'

Quick to sense my desolation, she said gently, 'Don't be afraid. Off you go. Leave me alone for a little.'

I was right. She wrote:

You have gone. Half my soul seems to have taken flight with you.

I had no means of knowing what had become of you, much less of seeing you for the last time. I had no right to ask either, not being your wife or friend . . . So we are torn apart. If only I could have borne that inhuman treatment for you, so that you could have lived on! You should have lived to see your name cleared and take up your work again, for the sake of those who loved you. I knew you could not be a counter-revolutionary. You were one of the finest men killed. That's why I love you – I am not afraid now to avow it.

Snow is whirling down. Heavens, even God is such a hypocrite, he is using this whiteness to cover up your blood and the scandal of your murder.

I have never set store by my life. But now I keep wondering whether anything I say or do would make you contract your shaggy eyebrows in a frown. I must live a worthwhile life like you, and do some honest work for our country. Things can't go on like this – those criminals will get what's coming to them.

I used to walk alone along that small asphalt road, the only place where we once walked together, hearing my footsteps in the silent night . . . I always paced to and fro and lingered there, but never as wretchedly as now. Then though you were not beside me, I knew you were still in this world and felt that you were keeping me company. Now I can hardly believe that you have gone.

At the end of the road I would retrace my steps, then walk along it again.

Rounding the fence I always looked back, as if you were still standing there waving goodbye. We smiled faintly, like casual acquaintances, to conceal our undying love. That ordinary evening in early spring, a chilly wind was blowing as we walked silently away from each other. You were wheezing a little because of your chronic bronchitis. That upset me. I wanted to beg you to slow down, but somehow I couldn't. We both walked very fast, as if some important business were waiting for us. How we prized that single stroll we had together, but we were afraid we might lose control of ourselves and burst out with 'I love you' – those three words which had tormented us for years. Probably no one else could believe that we never once even clasped hands!

No, Mother, I believe it. I am the only one able to see into your locked heart.

Ah, that little asphalt road, so haunted by bitter memories. We shouldn't overlook the most insignificant spots on earth. For who knows how much secret grief and joy they may hide.

No wonder that when tired of writing, she would pace slowly along that little road behind our window. Sometimes at dawn after a sleepless night, sometimes on a moonless, windy evening. Even in winter during howling gales which hurled sand and pebbles against the window pane . . . I thought this was one of her eccentricities, not knowing that she had gone to meet him in spirit.

She liked to stand by the window too, staring at the small asphalt road. Once I thought from her expression that one of our closest friends must be coming to call. I hurried to the window. It was a late autumn evening. The cold wind was stripping dead leaves from the trees and blowing them down the small empty road.

She went on pouring out her heart to him in her diary as she had when he was alive. Right up to the day when the pen slipped from her fingers. Her last message was:

> I am a materialist, yet I wish there were a Heaven. For then, I know, I would find you there waiting for me. I am going there to join you, to be together for eternity. We need never be parted again or keep at a distance for fear of spoiling someone else's life. Wait for me, dearest, I am coming —

I do not know how Mother, on her death bed, could still love so ardently with all her heart. To me it seemed not love but a form of madness, a passion stronger than death. If undying love really exists, she reached its extreme. She obviously died happy, because she had known true love. She had no regrets.

Now these old people's ashes have mingled with the elements. But I know that, no matter what form they may take, they still love each other. Though not bound together by earthly laws or morality, though they never once clasped hands, each possessed the other completely. Nothing could part them. Centuries to come, if one white cloud trails another, two grasses grow side by side, one wave splashes another, a breeze follows another . . . believe me, that will be them.

Each time I read that diary 'Love Must Not Be Forgotten' I cannot hold back my tears. I often weep bitterly, as if I myself experienced their ill-fated love. If not a tragedy it was too laughable. No matter how beautiful or moving I find it, I have no wish to follow suit!

Thomas Hardy wrote that 'the call seldom produces the comer, the man to love rarely coincides with the hour for loving'. I cannot censure them from conventional moral standards. What I deplore is that they did not wait for a 'missing counterpart' to call them.

If everyone could wait, instead of rushing into marriage, how many tragedies could be averted!

When we reach communism, will there still be cases of marriage without love? Maybe, because since the world is so vast, two kindred spirits may be unable to answer each other's call. But how tragic! However, by that time, there may be ways to escape such tragedies.

Why should I split hairs?

Perhaps after all we are responsible for these tragedies. Who knows? Maybe we should take the responsibility for the old ideas handed down from the past. Because if someone never marries, that is a challenge to these ideas. You will be called neurotic, accused of having guilty secrets or having made political mistakes. You may be regarded as an eccentric who looks down on ordinary people, not respecting age-old customs – a heretic. In short they will trump up endless vulgar and futile charges to ruin your reputation. Then you have to knuckle under to those ideas and marry willy-nilly. But once you put the chains of a loveless marriage around your neck, you will suffer for it for the rest of your life.

I long to shout: 'Mind your own business! Let us wait patiently for our counterparts. Even waiting in vain is better than willy-nilly marriage. To live single is not such a fearful disaster. I believe it may be a sign of a step forward in culture, education and the quality of life.'

Notes on the Authors

AMA ATA AIDOO (1942–). Born Christina Ama Aidoo, in the Central Region of Ghana, her first play, *Dilemma of a Ghost*, was staged at the University of Ghana in 1964. Her second play, *Anowa (1969)*, was based on a story-song learnt from her mother, and her collection of short stories, *No Sweetness Here* (1970), also bears the hallmark of the oral tradition in which all her work is rooted. Her first novel, *Our Sister Killjoy: Reflections from a Black-eyed Squint*, was published in 1977 and she is currently working on her second, provisionally entitled, *Teacher Grace*.

MARGARET ATWOOD (1939–). One of Canada's foremost novelists and poets, Margaret Atwood is also mistress of the short story form. Born in Ottawa, she has travelled extensively but now lives in Toronto with her young daughter. She received the Governor General's Award in 1966 for the first of her nine poetry collections, *The Circle Game*. Her novels, which include *Surfacing* (1972) and *Bodily Harm* (1981), brought her continuing critical acclaim, culminating in the nomination of *The Handmaid's Tale* for the Booker Prize in 1986.

JUDITH CHERNAIK (1934–). Originally from New York City, Judith Chernaik moved to London in 1972 with her family. A journalist, writer and lecturer, she works part time at Queen Mary College, University of London, and has contributed many talks to the BBC. She was the creator of the scheme, Poems on the Underground, whereby poems were displayed throughout the London Underground. Her novels, *Double Fault* (1975) and *The Daughter* (1979), were published in the States and she has completed a third, *Leah* (1987).